Success in

INFORMATION
PROCESSING

SECOND EDITION

Success Studybooks

Accounting and Costing: Problems and Projects
Book-keeping and Accounts
British History 1760–1914
British History since 1914
Business Calculations
Chemistry
Commerce
Commerce: West African Edition
Communication
Economic Geography
Economics
Economics: West African Edition
Electronics
Elements of Banking
European History 1815–1941
Geography: Human and Regional
Insurance
Investment
Law
Management Accounting: An Introduction
Management: Personnel
Marketing
Office Practice
Physics
Principles of Accounting
Principles of Accounting: Answer Book
Principles of Catering
Statistics
Twentieth Century World Affairs
World History since 1945

Success in

INFORMATION PROCESSING

SECOND EDITION

Stephen Flowers
Department of Business Management
University of Brighton

JOHN MURRAY

© Stephen Flowers 1988, 1993

First published 1988
by John Murray (Publishers) Ltd
50 Albemarle Street, London W1X 4BD
Reprinted 1990 (with amendments), 1991

Second edition 1993
Reprinted 1994

All rights reserved. Unauthorised duplication contravenes applicable laws.

Typeset in 9/11 pt and 8/10 pt Compugraphic English Times
by Colset Private Ltd.
Printed in England by Clays Ltd, St Ives plc

A CIP catalogue record for this book is available from the British Library

ISBN 0-7195-5158-7

Contents

Foreword

The use of the information technologies of computers and communications devices in the business world has evolved since the 1950s. At that time only a small number of computers were in use, whereas today there can be few areas of industry and commerce that do not use these technologies in one way or another.

This increase in the application of information technology within business has placed new demands upon its users: not only must we be able to operate a particular system, we must also be able to appreciate the potential power (and limitations) of the technology and be able to apply it to the solution of business problems. We need, in short, to become *intelligent* users of IT, and it is the aim of this book to encourage this by providing a thorough grounding in the ways in which computers and communications devices may be used as part of a business information-processing system.

New products are continually coming on to the market, and it is impossible for a textbook to keep abreast of them. The principles on which they operate do not change, however – or at least not at such a tremendous rate – and this text therefore concentrates on explaining basic computer concepts and system components and on relating them to the solution of business problems, without undue emphasis on particular devices or programs. In addition, the roles of specialist computer personnel are described, and there is an overview of the development and applications of computer languages and an introduction to the use of flowcharts and decision tables in analysing procedures. The final unit looks at some of the current issues and developments in computing, including telecommuting, data protection, expert systems, and the research into fifth-generation computers.

The second edition takes account of the growth in the use of local area networks, paperless document transmission (electronic data interchange), and paperless document storage (document image processing), with new or expanded sections on all three topics.

To reinforce the emphasis on the use of information technology to serve business ends, Unit 12 contains in-depth case-studies of the successful use of IT by five major real organisations: Benetton, Sainsbury's, NatWest, the University of Brighton, and the *Guardian*. In addition, most units end with assignments related to a case-study of aspects of the operations of a hypothetical organisation, and a large case-study towards the end of the book aims to test the reader's overall understanding and ability to apply the knowledge acquired to the solution of a number of business problems.

The use of information technology in business life has increased so rapidly that there is a great demand for staff who are proficient in IT – who do understand the power and limitations of IT and can apply it confidently and efficiently to the solution of business problems. Such a proficiency does not require expert knowledge but the thorough understanding of basic principles that this book aims to provide. With it, you should be well equipped to play a successful part in the 'information revolution' as it is at present and as it develops in the future.

S.F.

Acknowledgements

I owe the completion of *Success in Information Processing* to the constant support, encouragement, advice, and understanding of Claire, my wife.

I must also thank my good friends in the Department of Business Management, the Computer Centre, and Learning Resources at the University of Brighton for their advice, ideas, and patience while the second edition was being prepared. Thanks also go to Paul Blows for forging the first link in the chain of events that culminated in the book's original publication. Finally, my thanks go to Bob Davenport, who carefully crafted the finished product from the raw material I provided.

Illustrations have been reproduced by kind permission of the following organisations: International Computers Ltd (fig. 2.4), Digital Equipment Co. Ltd (fig. 2.5), NCR Ltd (fig. 2.6), Atari Corporation (fig. 2.7), Cray Research (fig. 2.8), IBM United Kingdom Ltd (figs 3.1, 3.12 (photographer Richard Turpin), and 3.17), P.C.D. Maltron Ltd (fig. 3.2), Microwriter Systems plc (fig. 3.3), Apple Computer UK Ltd (figs 3.4 and 6.7), Data Logic Ltd (fig. 3.5), Olympia Business Machines Co. Ltd (fig. 3.6), London Borough of Bromley (fig. 3.7), Wolverhampton Health Authority (fig. 3.8), National Westminster Bank PLC (figs 3.9 (top), 3.10, 12.5, and 12.6), Thomas de la Rue & Co. Ltd (fig. 3.9 (bottom)), Kendata Peripherals Ltd (fig. 3.11), SB Electronic Systems Ltd (fig. 3.13), Norprint International Ltd (fig. 3.14), Fortronic Ltd (fig. 3.15), Victor Technologies (UK) Ltd (fig. 3.16), Inmac UK Ltd (figs 4.1 and 8.2), Newbury Data Recording Ltd (fig. 4.4 (bottom)), Siemens Ltd (figs 4.5 and 5.3 (bottom)), Facit Ltd (fig. 4.6 (top)), Hewlett-Packard Ltd (figs 4.8, 4.9 (bottom), and 5.3 (top)), Graphtec (UK) Ltd (fig. 4.9 (top)), Girobank plc (fig. 4.10 (top)), Bell & Howell Ltd (figs 4.10 (bottom) and 4.11), Austin Rover Group Ltd (fig. 4.12), Maxell (UK) Ltd (fig. 5.5), J. Whitaker and Sons Ltd (photographer Richard Hunt) (fig. 5.9), Emulex Ltd (fig. 5.10), GEC Card Technology Ltd (fig. 5.11), Apple Computer UK Ltd and Coca-Cola Great Britain Ltd (fig. 6.6), Apricot Computers plc (fig. 6.8), Sony (UK) Ltd (fig. 10.5), Vodaphone Group Services Ltd (fig. 10.8), Benetton

Spa (figs 12.1 and 12.2), J Sainsbury plc (figs 12.3 and 12.4), the *Guardian* (fig. 12.10).

The cartoons are reproduced by kind permission of *Private Eye* (page xii), *Accountancy* (pages 12, 57, 114, 194, 206, 244, and 284), and Roger Penwill (page 50 – this cartoon won *The Times*' Computer Humour Competition in 1987).

Questions from past examination papers are reproduced by courtesy of The Association of Accounting Technicians (AAT), The Chartered Association of Certified Accountants (ACCA), The Chartered Building Societies Institute (CBSI), The Chartered Institute of Management Accountants (CIMA), The Institute of Data Processing Management (IDPM), and The London Chamber of Commerce and Industry Examinations Board (LCCI). The solutions given to the exercises in Unit 14 are the author's own and are not the responsibility of the examining bodies concerned.

S.F.

'I suppose one day I'll get round to replacing the whole thing by a silicon chip.'

The role of information in business

1.1 Information and decision-making

Information can be defined as *organised facts and figures*. The 'raw' facts and figures are known as *data*. Data about sales, for example, can be used to produce information about the performance of individual members of staff, changes in customer demand, total value of sales in a given period, and a large number of other things. The same facts and figures can be used to produce information that provides several different views of the same events, so they can be used for many different purposes.

To make a decision on the manufacture of a new range of products, a company will need information on what will sell. To choose which products should be manufactured, information is also needed about the profitability of each of the items. This will be obtained by collecting information on the production costs and investment needed for the manufacture of each product. Information on projected market price, sales volume, existing products from other competitors, supply of raw materials, sales outlets, and the best location for the factory to produce the goods is all needed before a final decision is made.

Accurate information is a vital ingredient not only in the process of deciding which goods to manufacture but also in making decisions about any aspect of the operation of a business. A one-person business will have to collect and deal with all the information needed to make a decision without any help, whereas a larger firm will be able to set up departments which specialise in collecting, recording, and processing a single type of information.

This unit examines how the information a business needs for its operation is collected, recorded, processed, and used as a basis for decision-making. The term *information processing* describes the use of computers in this handling of data and information.

1.2 Information and outside organisations

To help understand why so much information is stored by all businesses, it is useful to examine the contacts that they will have with other organisations

Fig. 1.1 Organisations with whom a business will exchange information

and individuals. Figure 1.1 indicates the many organisations with whom information must be exchanged in order for a business to operate both efficiently and within the law.

Perhaps the most important information for a business is that relating to the market for its goods or services. Sales levels, profits made, ease of supply, and potential competitors must all be recorded and analysed to see if any additional competitive advantage is possible. Information concerning the financial state of the business, and the availability of additional funds for new investment, if required, is necessary so that current profitability may be monitored and possible future expansion may be planned. Information about profits must be passed on to the shareholders of the company, if any, and to the government for tax and statistical purposes. In addition to this, there are the routine contacts with the suppliers of electricity, gas, and water, as well as a number of local-government bodies like waste-disposal and the environmental-health department.

The above is just a brief summary of the many contacts that a business has with a wide variety of outside agencies, each of which involves an exchange of information. For these exchanges to take place efficiently, a business must organise the way in which it handles its information into a number of separate but connected information-handling systems. These systems, and the impact of the computer upon them, are discussed in the remainder of this unit.

1.3 Information-handling within a business

To enable information to be processed more efficiently, as a business grows, employees will specialise so that they deal with only one particular aspect of the business. This is why in a large organisation employees will be involved in only one small part of its operation, like Stores or Finance, whereas in a smaller business employees are often involved in all or most aspects of the running of the firm. In this section we are going to look at the main parts of a firm large enough to specialise and set up areas devoted to one particular function of the business.

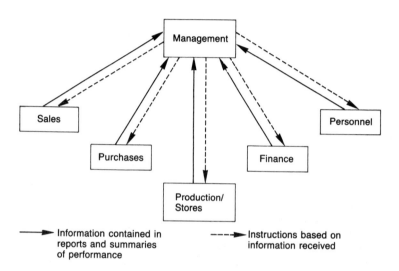

Fig. 1.2 Some specialist areas within a business

Figure 1.2 shows the major functions that a business may be divided into. Each of these 'functional areas' is concerned with information relating to its own specialised part of the operation of the business. Their activities are co-ordinated and controlled by the management, which makes decisions based on the information received from all of these areas. The next four subsections will examine the information that is received from outside or passed between each other by the Sales, Purchases, Production/Stores, and Finance functional areas.

1.3.1 The Sales area
The primary concern of the Sales area is to deal with a business's customers and to sell its products. Figure 1.3 shows the main information flows that occur between a firm's customers and its own Sales area.

Before an order can be accepted from a customer, the Sales area must check with Production/Stores that the goods requested are in stock. If the order can be satisfied from the stocks held, then the order is taken and a confirmation is sent to the customer. If the order cannot be filled immediately, a date is offered

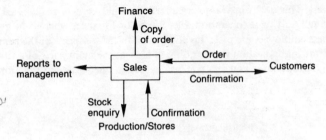

Fig. 1.3 The main information flows to and from the Sales area

to the customer by which the goods will be delivered. Once a firm order has been placed, a copy of the order is then sent to the Finance area, whose responsibility it is to send out the invoice requesting payment. Reports containing information about the performance of the Sales area are also sent to management, so that its work can be monitored and any problems can be ·dealt with.

1.3.2 The Purchases area
The other side of the system above is shown in fig. 1.4. The Purchases area is the first point of contact for a firm's suppliers and, as with the Sales area, information collected must be passed on to the other parts of the business that need it.

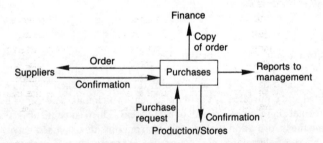

Fig. 1.4 The main information flows to and from the Purchases area

There is a distinct similarity to the system described in section 1.3.1, since the Purchases system is a mirror image of the Sales system. The starting point is the request from Production/Stores for materials that need to be replenished. This request is sent to Purchases, which will then place the order with a supplier. When the order is accepted by the supplier, a copy of the order is sent to the Finance area which then knows to expect an invoice from the supplier for the goods ordered. Periodically reports are sent to management so that the performance of the Purchases area can be monitored.

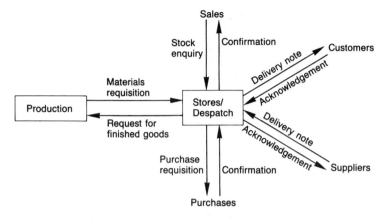

Fig. 1.5 The main information flows to and from the Production/Stores area

1.3.3 The Production and Stores area

A more complete picture of the links that exist between the customers, suppliers, and the various areas within a business can be seen in fig. 1.5.

The Production and Stores area is the second point of contact for both the suppliers and the customers. Information on stock levels is given to the Sales and Purchases areas, and in reports sent to management.

1.3.4 The Finance area

This may also be known as the Accounts area, although it is concerned with much more than just book-keeping. It is in fact the financial heart of a business, and all money matters will be dealt with here – including all payments to suppliers and employees, and monies received from customers. In addition, a number of reports and summaries on the financial performance of the company are sent to management to assist it in the running of the business. Figure 1.6 illustrates the main information flows into and out of the Finance area.

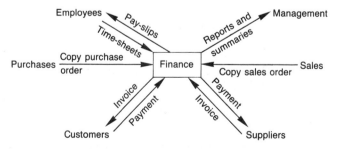

Fig. 1.6 The main information flows to and from the Finance area

As well as the information flows that are shown in fig. 1.6, the Finance area will also be concerned with information from a number of other outside organisations including the government (Inland Revenue, Customs and Excise), other businesses (competitors, alternative suppliers), employers associations (the Confederation of British Industry), trade unions (ASTMS, NALGO, NGA), and financial institutions (banks, finance companies), to name but a few.

1.3.5 *The overall view*

Figure 1.7 shows how the information that is necessary for the operation of the business is shared between the several specialist functional areas.

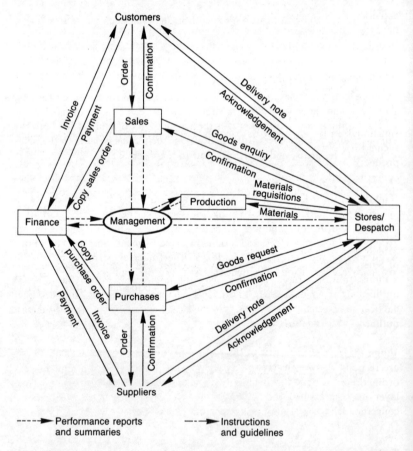

Fig. 1.7 An overall view of the information flows between the major areas of a business and its suppliers and customers

Figure 1.7 emphasises the central role that the management of a business plays in controlling the activities of the specialist functional areas. Each area will send the management reports on progress and performance, and will receive instructions and guidelines on how to proceed in the future. The aim of the information system is to provide management with a continual flow of information so that the decisions necessary to run the business efficiently can be made. Information is collected by the areas of a business and processed by them into reports and summaries to enable management decisions to be made with the benefit of the fullest and most accurate information available at the time.

1.3.6 Levels of information

As we have seen above, management plays a central role in co-ordinating the activities of the functional areas within an organisation. So far in this unit we have regarded management as a single entity, but this is not in reality the case. In order to understand better how information is used within an organisation, it is useful to divide management into the three layers of top, middle, and junior (or supervisory). Each of these layers of management has a part to play in the administration of an organisation.

Top management may include the board of directors and the heads of the functional areas. They will be concerned with the long-term strategic issues facing their organisation and will discuss issues like the development of new products or services, market trends, and similar matters. They will be concerned with the formulation of the policies that will determine the direction the organisation is to take in the future. This layer of management is sometimes called 'strategic' management, since it concerns itself with long-term issues facing the firm.

Middle management will include the senior staff in each of the functional areas of Sales, Purchases, etc. They will be concerned with running their areas on a month-to-month basis, and also with the implementation of the policies outlined by top management. This layer of management is also called the 'tactical' management layer, since it is concerned with achieving the objectives outlined by the strategic layer.

Junior management consists of the supervisors and managerial assistants that are responsible for the day-to-day running of the organisation and the co-ordination of the staff who actually provide services or make products. This layer may be termed the 'operational' layer of management, since it is concerned with performing tasks on a day-to-day basis.

To be able to operate efficiently, each layer of management must be provided with the necessary information upon which to base its decisions. The systems that we have looked at so far in this unit will have been set up to provide this information.

In order for top management to make policies and determine the direction the organisation is to take, it will need to know about market trends, its competitors, and similar information. Middle management requires information about future orders, targets to be met, and the policies that it must implement. Junior management operates on a much shorter time-scale, and will be concerned with such things as staffing and making sure that orders are filled.

The policies that are decided at the top level will be couched in broad terms like 'We need to increase production to meet market demand'. This in turn will be translated by the middle management into more specific action like 'We need to produce so many thousand more items', which will in turn be translated by junior management into the offer of overtime working to the labour force. The lower the level of management, the more detailed the information needs to be. At the same time, summaries of performance will be provided by the junior to the middle management, which in turn will provide overall summaries to top management. Information on performance will thus be successively summarised as it is passed up through the levels of management. In an efficient organisation the information necessary for each layer of management to do its job is provided by the internal information system. Such a system is often termed a *management information system* (MIS).

The relationship between each of the layers of management is illustrated in fig. 1.8. The ship represents the organisation whose direction and speed is controlled from the bridge by the top management. Middle management

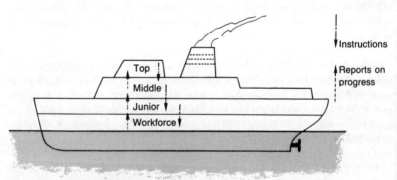

Top – objectives determined from the bridge.

Middle – objectives translated into specific goals,
and reports on progress made to top management.

Junior – specific goals implemented on a day-to-day basis,
and reports on progress made to middle management.

Workforce – tasks performed, and reports on progress
made to junior management.

Fig. 1.8 The relationship between the layers of management in an organisation

translates the general instructions coming from the bridge into more specific orders to the junior management, which in turn gives more precise instructions to the workforce.

1.4 How a computer can speed the flow of information

So far we have ignored the effect of using computer technology to assist the processing and distribution of information. To demonstrate the effects upon the system as a whole, let us look at one small part of the overall picture: sales-order processing.

1.4.1 A manual sales-order processing system

The purpose of sales-order processing is to take sales orders from customers and to inform the Finance, Stores, and Despatch areas of the details of the orders. An outline of the system was examined in section 1.3.1. To demonstrate in detail how a manual system would operate, consider fig. 1.9.

The main feature of this system is the delay that occurs as information about the order is passed to each area within the business. Once the order has been accepted, a seven-part sales-order form will be made out by the Finance area with the top cover being sent to the customer as an invoice, copy 2 being sent to the Sales area as a record of the transaction, and copy 3 being used to update the customer account records. The remaining copies are sent to other areas. Copies 4, 5, 6, and 7 will be passed to the Stores area which will update its records and pass the goods and copies 5, 6, and 7 to Despatch. Copy 4 will be used as the Stores-area file copy. Despatch will make up the delivery-van loading lists and use copy 5 as its delivery authority, and copy 7 as proof that the delivery was made. Copy 6 will be retained by the customer as the delivery note.

In a manual system there is a delay of anything up to half a working day between the order being taken and the information being passed on. Once the information has been passed on, there may then be a second delay before it is entered into the sales records, the stock level is adjusted to take account of the goods sold, or the goods are issued from Production/Stores. Once the goods have been issued, it is then up to the Despatch area to arrange for the goods to be delivered. This too will involve a delay. Finally, the goods will be delivered and the invoice will be paid.

The manual system then, has several drawbacks:

(a) The way that information has to be physically moved to each area of the business means that delays are inevitable.
(b) The management of the business cannot be certain of the state of sales at any one time, because some orders will not have been entered into the books.
(c) As everything depends upon information held on pieces of paper, loss of documents can cause serious delays in the system.

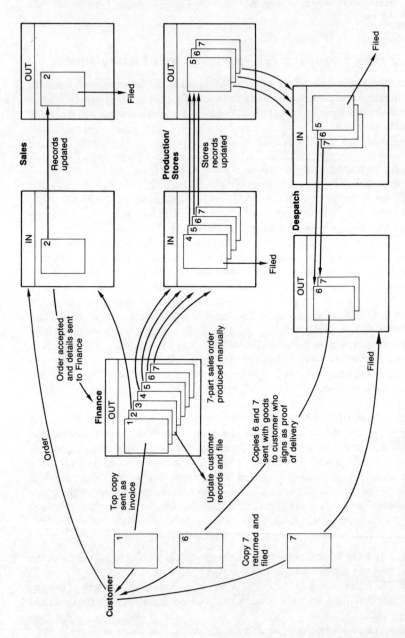

Fig. 1.9 A typical manual sales-order processing system

(d) The business will find it hard to react quickly to emergencies and unforeseen events, since the manual system has built-in delays.

This is not to say that *all* manual systems are bad, rather that there are inherent weaknesses in the manual way of processing information.

1.4.2 A computerised sales-order processing system

In a computerised sales-order processing system, the transmission of information between the areas of a business is handled by the computer system. In a centralised system the computer stores all the information that would be held separately by each area in a manual system. This means that the delays that occur in a manual system disappear, since information will be distributed to each area within a business as each transaction takes place. This is illustrated in fig. 1.10.

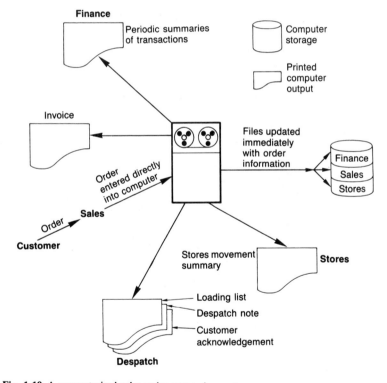

Fig. 1.10 A computerised sales-order processing system

In this system each order is entered directly into the computer, thus eliminating delays caused by the need for copies of the order to be sent between the areas of the business in the manual system. The sales-order information that might take perhaps half a working day to be distributed to each area that requires it in a manual system is, in the integrated computerised system shown in fig. 1.10, distributed virtually instantaneously. The records of all transactions are also stored centrally, increasing the efficiency of the system by largely eliminating the manual recording of the same transactions in every area.

The benefits of this system are as follows:

(a) Sales orders are entered into the system immediately with no time delay, with the effect that orders are processed more rapidly.

(b) Sales records in the Finance area are updated automatically, so that the true position of the business is always shown.

(c) The stock file is automatically changed to take account of the goods sold, and stock control can be automated with the computer signalling when the goods need to be reordered.

(d) Stock-movement summaries are automatically produced as a by-product of the changes in the stock file made in (c) above.

(e) Despatch is made more efficient, since the computer is able to calculate the loading lists and delivery schedule for each vehicle far faster than in a manual system.

(f) Management is able to obtain up-to-date information on the sales and stock levels of each product, enabling decisions to be made using accurate information.

(g) Since there is less paperwork to go astray, the opportunity for errors caused by lost or mislaid documents is reduced.

'Really, your invoice still hasn't been paid? I'm afraid our computer must be on the blink again.'

1.5 The effect of computerising an entire business

In the comparison given in section 1.4 above, the advantages of a computerised over a manual sales-order processing system come from the speed of its operation, the ability to share information between areas rapidly, and the way in which up-to-the-minute information is available to management. It is these same three benefits, only spread over an entire business operation, that come from computerising information-handling within any organisation. This means that a business may move from working on information that is at best a few days old to working on information that is at worst a few minutes old. It becomes possible to fine-tune the operation of each area within a business, with the overall result being a more efficient and effective organisation.

1.6 Glossary of terms

Data   Facts and figures.

Information   Organised facts and figures relating to a specific area.

MIS   Management information system – the internal system by means of which an organisation provides each layer of management with the information necessary to make decisions.

1.7 Exercises

1 'Information is the lifeblood of any organisation.' Using an example from your own experience, explain why this is so.

2 Today computers are in common use by businesses for the production of *operational* information. However until recently only large organisations experienced in computer use have applied them to the production of *management* information.

(a) Define the terms *operational* and *management* information.
(b) Explain why the situation has changed recently giving reasons in support of your argument.   (AAT, Elements of information systems)

3 The most important piece of information in many trading organisations is who owes them money.

(a) Why should this be so?
(b) Which area in the business will keep track of this information?

4 It is conventionally assumed that there are three levels in the organisations at which decision-making takes place. You are required to:

(a) define briefly the three levels;
(b) describe the characteristics of decision-making at the different levels;

(c) give an example, for each level, of the type of assistance or information a computer-based management information system could supply to aid decision-making.

(ICMA, Management information systems and data processing)

5 The information that is used by organisations is either received from outside or generated internally. Using examples from your own experience and the material in this unit, list five examples of each of the following types of information, stating what they will be used for:

(a) information that is received from outside the organisation,
(b) information that will be generated from within the organisation.

Task

We all have some first-hand experience of an information system, even if it is not referred to as such. Choose one of the following tasks according to whether you are in full-time or part-time employment or in education.

Full/part-time workers The work that you do will be in response to instructions received from your superior, and you will in turn provide information about what you have done. Find out where the information you provide goes and what is done with it. Draw a chart showing these information flows and link it into the information system of which your job is a part.

Education Each time you go to (or absent yourself from) a class, your attendance (or absence) will be noted on a class register. Ask your teacher or lecturer what happens to this information and what it is used for. Draw a chart that shows the overall information system of which the register is a part.

Introduction to information-technology concepts

2.1 What is information technology?

Information technology (IT) may be defined as 'a combination of computer and telecommunications techniques which makes possible new systems and products to help people at work, in education, and at home.' Information technology is thus all about the application of a wide variety of electronic technologies to the information-handling activities that are central to the operation of any organisation.

At the heart of IT is the *computer* – an electronic device that can store, retrieve, and process data in accordance with given instructions.

In any organisation the office is the place from which the activities of the organisation are controlled and co-ordinated, as we have seen in Unit 1. For management to be able to act efficiently, it is vital that up-to-date information is collected, processed, stored, and distributed as quickly as possible, to be used as a basis for decision-making. The many aspects of information technology will be examined in far more detail in later units of this book; this unit is intended only to introduce you to some of the basic terminology of the subject.

2.1.1 Hardware

The physical components that make up a computer system are referred to as *hardware*. For a typical personal computer the hardware might consist of a screen (or visual display unit, VDU), a keyboard, a printer, and the box containing the computer itself (also called the processor). Most computer systems will include these same basic components, although the detail will vary depending on how big the systems are and what they are used for.

2.1.2 Software

The instructions that determine what a computer will do are referred to as *software*. Software is also called a 'computer program', or 'program' for short.

There are two types of software: *systems software* (also called the *operating system*) and *applications software*. Systems software looks after the detailed operation of the hardware on behalf of the applications software, which consists of the programs (like payroll, accounts, or a game) designed to help the user perform a particular task.

2.1.3 Communications

The component parts of a computer system must be linked together, and it may also be necessary to link computers that are some distance apart, whether within an individual building, a group of buildings, a country, or even a continent. Communications – or 'comms' for short – is the term used to refer to the ways in which information is passed between computers. As we shall see in Unit 8, this may involve telephone lines, fibre-optic cables, or satellite links. The system of links is known as a *network*.

Communications is an important part of IT since it not only allows the sharing of information but also provides the basis for technologies that we shall be discussing in later units, such as electronic mail (a type of electronic postal service), electronic data interchange (a system for sending business documents like invoices and statements electronically), the transmission of images (using facsimile or 'fax' machines), and videoconferencing (a type of telephone system with pictures).

2.2 The structure of the computer

All computer systems have the same basic structure and are built using very similar sets of components. In this section we are going to look at the components of a typical computer system.

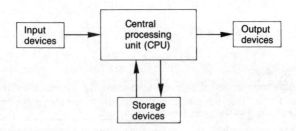

Fig. 2.1 The main parts of a computer system

Figure 2.1 is a plan of the main parts of a computer system. You will see that there are four basic parts: input devices, output devices, storage devices, and the central processing unit (CPU). (All the input, output, storage, and other devices that are connected to the CPU may also be called 'peripherals'.) We will now look at each of these four parts in turn.

2.2.1 The central processing unit (CPU)

This can be thought of as being the brain of the computer, since it is this part that controls and co-ordinates the operation of the rest of the computer system. The CPU is often referred to simply as the 'chip', the 'processor', or else as a 'microprocessor', due to the fact that advances in technology have enabled it to be reduced in size over the years. Small computer systems are likely to be designed around a single processor, although larger computers may have several processors that are able to co-operate and share the work-load.

The CPU consists of three parts, as shown in fig. 2.2.

(a) The *central memory* (CM) is used to store the software and data that the computer is to process.
(b) The *arithmetic and logic unit* (ALU) performs all the calculations and logical operations.
(c) The *control unit* (CU) acts like the conductor of an orchestra, co-ordinating the activities of all the various parts of the computer system.

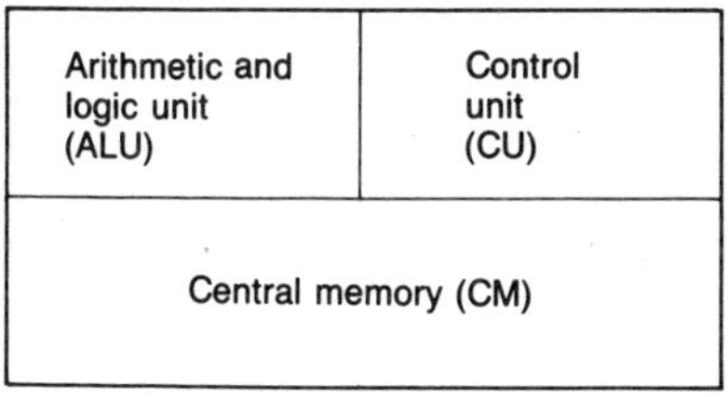

Arithmetic and logic unit (ALU)	Control unit (CU)
Central memory (CM)	

Fig. 2.2 Divisions within a CPU

There are many types of CPU chip available, and each computer is usually built around one particular type of chip. For example, the IBM PS/90 has an Intel 80486 chip, and the Apple Quadra is based on a Motorola 68040 chip. Both of these chips have the same basic structure, but they differ in their speed of operation, the amount of data that they can handle at a time, the amount of memory that each is able to use, and the number of tasks that they can perform at one time. If you own a home computer or use a personal computer at work, do you know which processor chip it uses?

2.2.2 Input devices

'Input devices' is the name given to the class of computer machinery that is designed specifically to allow data to be input (fed in) to a computer. In Unit 3 we will be looking in more detail at the very many types of input devices that have been developed, but this section will serve as a short introduction.

Each type of input device has been developed in response to a particular need – for example, the banks use a device that allows the data from large numbers of cheques to be input quickly, while architects and designers use a device that allows drawings and designs to be input easily. The most widely used input device is, however, the keyboard.

Once information has been input to the computer, it is said to have been 'captured', and 'data capture' is another term for data input.

2.2.3 Output devices

The output device is the means by which the computer is able to present the results of its processing, whether as text, graphics (illustrations), or some other form. Output which is produced in permanent form, like the familiar computer print-out, is known as *hard-copy* output. Output which is not permanent, such as that shown on some form of screen or visual display unit, is known as *soft-copy* output.

In Unit 4 we will be looking in more detail at the various types of output device that are available and the context in which each is used.

2.2.4 Storage devices

Only a small part of the information that the average computer system holds is 'live' at any one time: the rest is stored until needed. Computer storage thus provides the same facility as does the office filing cabinet, although the speed of information retrieval is considerably greater.

Computer storage – also known as *secondary memory* or *backing storage* – comes in two basic forms: disk-based and tape-based storage. If you have a home computer the chances are that you will use either an audio cassette to store your programs or else a floppy disk. These are two examples of the many types of computer storage that are available today, and in Unit 5 we will be looking in more detail at the various forms of storage available.

All computers have devices that are used to input, process, output, and store information. Whether powerful mainframe computers or small personal computers, they all have the basic structure shown in fig. 2.1, and the differences that exist between them are only in detail rather than basic principle.

2.3 Computer memory

Computer memory can be divided into two distinct types: temporary and permanent memory. Temporary memory uses electricity in order to hold programs or data. If the electricity supply is turned off, the information held is lost. This type of memory is called *random access memory* (RAM) or *primary memory* and, because the information is lost when the electricity is turned off, it is said to be *volatile*. A more permanent, non-volatile, type of memory that holds information without electricity is called *read only memory*, or ROM. Each of these types of memory has a particular role to play in the operation of microprocessor-controlled devices.

The software, or instructions, that tell these microprocessor-controlled devices how to work may well be stored in permanent memory or ROM. ROM is also referred to as *firmware*, since it is a combination of hardware and software. ROM acts as a form of knowledge, and giving a microprocessor-controlled device more ROM is similar to education: the more you have, the more things you should be able to do. So, in general terms, the more ROM a device has, the more built-in software it contains, and the more functions it is able to perform without the need for additional software. Just as we do not have to refer to a maths book when we want to add up some numbers, the computer stores in its permanent memory or ROM such essential information as how to add up numbers or how to input or output data.

The software contained in ROM cannot be altered by the user of a computer and is usually set up by the manufacturer. However, the instructions contained in ROM can be erased and reprogrammed if a special type of ROM called *erasable programmable ROM* (or EPROM for short) is used.

RAM, on the other hand, is the memory that is available for the programs or data that a computer user may wish to use in addition to those in ROM which tell the computer how to work. RAM can be thought of as the memory that is available to the user of the computer, since it is into RAM that the user will load computer programs, or software, and the data that is to be used.

Figure 2.3 illustrates the roles that RAM and ROM play in the operation of a computer. As can be seen from fig. 2.3, the control unit and the arithmetic and logic unit are both essentially ROM devices. This is because they both contain information that is necessary for the computer to operate efficiently. Between them the CU and ALU run the computer system, and to enable them to do this they both contain a large number of instructions that are more conveniently stored permanently in the computer.

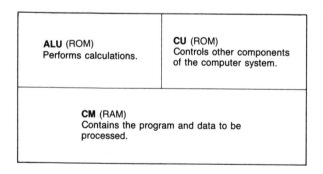

Fig. 2.3 Roles of RAM and ROM within a CPU

The central memory is an example of RAM, and all computers will have this. Generally, the more RAM a computer has, the larger the programs it can handle and the more data it can contain.

To recapitulate then, computer memory is divided into temporary and permanent storage, or RAM and ROM. RAM is the user-accessible memory that is used to store the software and data that are currently being used, whereas ROM contains the permanent instructions that control the operation of the computer.

2.4 Categories of computer

There are four main categories of computer: mainframe computers, minicomputers, microcomputers, and supercomputers.

2.4.1 Mainframe computers
Mainframes are used where there is a need for a machine that can cope with a very high volume of transactions. Typical users would be banks, insurance companies, large manufacturers, local authorities, public utilities such as the gas and electricity boards, and the government. Mainframes can be used to hold a large database of information, such as bank balances or holiday bookings, that can be updated and accessed quickly by large numbers of users. Another use would be in the processing of large numbers of similar transactions like gas bills or cheques – so-called 'batch processing'. The mainframe will be able to deal with large numbers of users and tasks at any one time, and will be able to run large numbers of input, output, storage, and communication devices.

Unlike a microcomputer, a mainframe (and sometimes a minicomputer too) will have to be housed in a special room in which temperature, humidity, and dust are controlled. Figure 2.4 shows a typical example of a mainframe computer.

2.4.2 Minicomputers
The typical minicomputer will be able to handle a number of users (anything up to 60 or more at a time) doing a number of tasks. It may be built around a number of processors, and will be able to handle several input, output, or storage devices at a time.

Minicomputers are used for a wide range of business applications, such as accounts, payroll, stock control, and those areas that require a computer to deal with a relatively high volume of transactions to be processed. Some minicomputers will be used to free a large mainframe computer from the job of handling communications links with users, thus allowing more efficient use to be made of the mainframe. Minicomputers used in this way are referred to as *front-end devices*.

Figure 2.5 shows an example of a minicomputer.

2.4.3 Microcomputers
Typically, a microcomputer is a single-user single-tasking machine, which means that only one person doing one thing is able to use it at a time. The machine will be built around a single microprocessor and will be relatively

Fig. 2.4 A typical ICL series 39 SX mainframe computer installation. The processor node is shown on the centre right.

Fig. 2.5 A DEC VAX minicomputer in use. (The processor is under the desk.)

Fig. 2.6 An NCR PC710 16-bit microcomputer

Fig. 2.7 An Atari Portfolio portable microcomputer. This weights 495 grams and can exchange data with all industry-standard PCs.

limited in terms of both speed and storage capacity. Another name for these machines is 'personal computers', or 'PCs', and this emphasises their status as individual single-user computers.

The main uses of PCs are as desk-top business computers used for word-processing, small business accounts, and financial planning, and as home computers being mainly used for games. It is possible to link PCs together to form a network that can share storage facilities, printers, or files of information. In many situations it is now possible to replace minicomputer-based systems with a network of personal computers.

A typical desk-top microcomputer is shown in fig. 2.6. Figure 2.7 shows a portable microcomputer.

2.4.4 Supercomputers
The supercomputer bears the same relation to the average mainframe that a formula-1 racing car does to a family saloon. Supercomputers are designed to operate at extremely high speeds and to be able to perform vast numbers of calculations very quickly (they are sometimes called 'number crunchers' because of this).

Users of these machines are such institutions as NASA, Boeing, General Motors, Shell, the UK Meteorological Office at Bracknell, and research and

Fig. 2.8 A Cray X-MP supercomputer. Its segmented shape is designed to reduce the distance between its component parts and so increase its operating speed.

defence establishments. One of the advantages of the supercomputer is that its speed of operation allows the early stages of design and testing, of a car or a nuclear weapon for example, to be done by the computer, without having to build and test a full-scale prototype. Weather forecasting could not be done at all without the supercomputer, since by the time all the calculations had been done by a mainframe the weather would already have arrived!

A supercomputer will contain large numbers of high-speed chips that are packed closely together and need to be specially cooled. Worldwide there are only a few hundred supercomputers installed and operational, as compared with several million microcomputers, but the trend is such that by the late 1990s there could well be thousands. Figure 2.8 shows an example.

Table 2.1 outlines the main features of all the categories of computers described above.

It is a fact of life in the computer world that change and progress are constant. This means that the features which were available on minicomputers only a few years ago are now found in some 'supermicros', and the power of mainframes a few years old is now available in a 'supermini'. The precise definitions of supercomputers, mainframes, minicomputers, and micros are thus subject to constant change, and the microcomputer of tomorrow will be as powerful as the minicomputer of today.

2.5 The size and speed of computers

In this section we are going to look at the measurement of computer memory and the speed of computer operation.

2.5.1 The measurement of computer storage and memory

The information to be processed by computers is made up of individual characters like the letters 'b' and 't', the numerals '1' and '9', and the symbols '£' and '.'. It follows, therefore, that the basic unit of storage is the amount of space which is needed to store an individual character. In computer jargon this unit of storage is called a *byte*. Just as the watt is used in measuring power and the litre is used in measuring capacity, the byte is the basic unit of measurement that is used when referring to computer memory.

All units of measurement are based upon the byte, and the terms kilobyte, megabyte, and gigabyte are all used when referring to computer memory. They are related as follows:

$$1 \text{ byte} = \text{space enough for a single character}$$

$$1 \text{ kilobyte} = 1024 \text{ bytes} \qquad \text{(about 1 thousand)}$$

$$1 \text{ megabyte} = 1\,048\,576 \text{ bytes} \qquad \text{(about 1 million)}$$

$$1 \text{ gigabyte} = 1\,073\,741\,824 \text{ bytes} \qquad \text{(about 1 billion)}$$

Table 2.1 Categories of computer

Feature	Supercomputer	Mainframe	Minicomputer	Microcomputer
Size and environment	Large. Specially controlled environment.	Very large (several rooms). Special environment.	Medium-sized. Normal office environment.	Small (desk-top). Home/office/education – car or train if portable.
Cost	Very expensive – £15 000 000 or more.	Expensive – from £200 000 to several million pounds.	Medium – from £15 000 up to several hundred thousand pounds.	Cheap – £100+ (home) £1000+ (business).
Operation	Specialist personnel needed to operate and maintain installation.	Specialist personnel needed to operate and maintain installation.	Some specialist staff may be needed, but non-specialists can operate.	Anyone can operate, given training.
Capabilities	Very fast operation – 1 billion operations per second. Able to perform multiple tasks simultaneously.	Can perform many tasks for many different users simultaneously. Able to receive information from a network of terminals and is usually remote from the user. Fast in operation. Very large storage capacity.	Able to deal with many tasks at a time, but not as many as a mainframe, for up to 50 users. Smaller storage capacity than a mainframe.	Able to perform a wide variety of tasks, usually one at a time. Only one user at a time.
Uses	Research – by Shell, Ford, ICI, NASA, and the government, for example.	Where a high volume of data must be processed – by DVLC, British Telecom, and banks, for example.	General business data processing and word-processing, stock control, payroll, and accounts.	Versatile – can be used in home, education, or business.

To make these figures a little more real, this printed page contains about 3000 characters, or else 3 kilobytes (or 3 kbyte, or 3 Kb, or 3 KB, or simply 3 K). Thus, 1 megabyte (1 Mb) of computer storage can hold the characters on something like 330 of these pages, while 1 gigabyte (1 Gb) can hold the information on an amazing 330 000 of these pages.

ROM and RAM, as types of computer storage, are measured in terms of the numbers of characters or bytes that they can contain. Thus, a typical personal computer may have 640 Kb of RAM and 48 Kb of ROM. This means that the user is provided with space for around 600 000 characters in RAM, while the manufacturer has provided about 48 000 characters of permanent instructions in ROM. Small desk-top computers may have several megabytes of user-accessible RAM, with the larger mini and mainframe computers having considerably more than that.

These units of measurement are also used in referring to backing storage, the various types of which are discussed in Unit 5.

2.5.2 The speed of computer operation

As we already know, the control unit in the CPU acts like the conductor of an orchestra, co-ordinating and controlling the activities of the computer system as a whole. The rate at which the computer operates, however, is determined by the speed of its internal metronome or clock. Modern processors may well have a clock that runs at anything up to 70 megahertz (MHz), which means that the clock is ticking some 70 million times a second. Generally, the faster its clock speed, the faster the computer is able to perform operations on data. This is only part of the story, however, since the speed at which the computer is able to process data is determined not only by the clock but also by how much data it can handle at a time.

The byte is itself made up of eight elements called *bits*. The early processors could only handle data one byte at a time, and so were called '8-bit' processors. The more modern processors are able to handle two or even four bytes at a time, and are thus called '16-bit' or '32-bit' processors.

The speed at which a computer can process data is thus determined partly by the clock speed and partly by how much data it can handle at a time – and also partly by the efficiency of the set of instructions, or program, that it is following.

2.6 How data is represented in a computer

When you press a button on a computer, a wordprocessor, a video recorder, or a modern washing-machine, a signal is sent to the processor which in turn sends a signal instructing the device to do something. All the communication inside a computer is in the form of electrical signals, and for that reason the data that is used by the computer is also stored using electrical signals.

You may well recognise the following signal:

. . . – – . . .

It is the international distress signal, SOS. The code that it uses is the Morse code, a code that is made up of dots and dashes. Inside a computer a code is used that is not unlike the Morse code in that it too has only two states, only the computer code uses an electronic dot and dash. The two states of 'dot' and 'dash' are represented in the computer electronics as an 'on' or 'off', so that · · · – – – · · · becomes: off off off on on on off off off. The two states 'off' and 'on' are in turn represented by the digits 0 and 1 of the binary number system, so that our message would now look like this: 000 111 000. (Whereas the conventional decimal number system is based on the digits 0 to 9, the binary system represents numbers by using only two digits, 0 and 1, which can be very conveniently represented by the 'off' and 'on' states of a switch of some kind.)

The major difference between Morse and the code forms used in computers is that a greater number of combinations of 0 and 1 are needed for computers, as the computer needs to be able to represent a far wider character range than is necessary with Morse. Generally, eight elements – each either 0 or 1 – are needed to represent a character using a computer code. Those eight elements are the 'bits' referred to in section 2.5.2, and each character that is stored in a computer's memory is stored as an 8-bit code.

One computer code form that is widely used is ASCII – short for American Standard Code for Information Interchange. This code has been in use since the early 1960s and is one of several that use the 8-bit code form. Table 2.2 gives some examples of the binary representation (or combinations of 'offs' and 'ons') for various characters using ASCII code.

Table 2.2 Binary representation of some characters using ASCII code

Character	Binary code
A	01000001
B	01000010
C	01000011
1	00110001
2	00110010
3	00110011

Each byte of computer storage is designed to hold the eight bits of the code as shown in Table 2.2 and, although a character may be stored as 01000001 for example, it will still come up on the screen as an A.

Other code forms that are widely used are EBCDIC (short for Extended Binary Coded Decimal Interchange Code) and ANSI (short for American National Standards Institute).

2.7 Glossary of terms

Computer   An electronic device that can store, retrieve, and process data in accordance with given instructions.

Software   The instructions, or computer programs, that tell a computer what it must do.

Hardware   The physical components of a computer system, such as the screen, printer, processor, etc.

Firmware   Software that has been permanently stored on a hardware device (usually a ROM-type chip).

CPU   Central processing unit – the microchip that controls the operation of a computer.

ALU   Arithmetic and logic unit – the section of the CPU that performs arithmetic calculations and logical operations.

Input devices   Hardware designed to enable data to be captured and changed into a form that can be handled by a computer.

Output devices   Hardware designed to output the results of processing, either in printed form (hard copy) or aurally or visually (soft copy).

Storage devices   Hardware that stores information in a form that can be readily accessed by a computer system, using magnetic (disk and tape) or optical (disk) media.

RAM   Random access memory – a form of computer memory that is used to hold programs and data.

ROM   Read only memory – a form of computer memory that is used to store programs that will be constantly used to run the computer (usually installed by the manufacturer).

EPROM   Erasable programmable ROM – a special type of ROM that can be reprogrammed.

Mainframe computer   A computer that can support a very large number of users using a number of different programs. It usually needs to be installed in a special air-conditioned room.

Minicomputer   A computer that is designed to support fewer users than a mainframe computer but which may still be able to support a large number of users using different programs. It may not need to be installed in a special room.

Microcomputer   A small, single-user computer.

Supercomputer   A very powerful computer that has been designed to process data at very high speed and which is used for calculation-intensive applications like weather forecasting.

Byte   The unit of computer storage, made up of eight bits, which may be used to store a single character.

Bit   Binary digit, 1 or 0.

Kilobyte 1024 bytes. May be shortened to Kbyte, Kb, KB, or K.

Megabyte 1 048 576 bytes. May be shortened to Mbyte, Mb, MB, or M.

Gigabyte 1 073 741 824 bytes. May be shortened to Gbyte, Gb, GB, or G.

ASCII American Standard Code for Information Interchange – a widely used 8-bit code form.

2.8 Exercises

1 Define the following terms: hardware, software, firmware.
2 Draw a diagram of the four main parts of a computer system. Write a sentence on each of the parts to explain its role in the operation of a typical computer system.
3 Discuss the main function units of a CPU.   (IDPM, Data processing II)
4 There are two main types of memory that are used within computers. What are they, and what are they used for?
5 What are the essential differences between mainframe, mini, and micro-computers? Give examples where each would be used to the best advantage.
(IDPM, Data processing II)

Task

Pay a visit to your local computer supplier or electrical shop and see what personal computers it sells. Choose one and find out and make a note of the following information:

(a) which processor it uses;
(b) whether it has an 8-bit, 16-bit, or 32-bit processor;
(c) how much RAM comes as standard, and whether this is expandable;
(d) how much ROM comes as standard, and what software it contains;
(e) the speed at which the processor runs;
(f) what input, output, and storage devices it uses;
(g) what software is supplied with it, if any;
(h) the special features that are offered by this machine – for example, good graphics, low price, reliability, expandability, etc.;
(i) how long that particular model has been available, and if it is due to be replaced soon;
(j) if a service agreement is available and, if so, how much it costs;
(k) how much the computer system, as supplied, costs.

Collecting this information will be an interesting exercise in itself, and will help to get you out into the world of IT. Make sure that you keep a note of the information that you collect – it will form the basis for tasks that will be set at the end of subsequent units.

UNIT 3

Computer input

3.1 Introduction

Since the electronic computer was developed in the 1940s, the number of ways of transferring data into a computer has increased as computers have been put to more and more uses. At one time the keyboard, punched cards, and paper tape were the mainstays of computer input, but new methods were developed to meet the demands of new computer users. This unit examines the main methods of data input that are available, describing the operation and application of each one.

3.2 Direct user input

'Direct user input' refers to the use of devices that enable the user to personally input data to a computer, using a keyboard or similar device. These devices complement the range of machines that input data contained on special documents or forms which are designed for high-volume data input.

This section will look at the variety of ways in which the user is able to input data directly to the computer.

3.2.1 The keyboard

The keyboard is at present the most widely used input device, but it is also the most inefficient in terms of its speed of input.

A typical computer keyboard is shown in fig. 3.1. It has five specialist sections: the numeric keypad, the function keys, the cursor control keys, the editing keys, and the qwerty keyboard itself (so called because the letters QWERTY appear on the top line of alphabetical keys). The numeric keypad is designed to allow the efficient input of a large volume of numbers, while the function keys allow commonly used operations to be performed at the touch of a single key. The cursor keys move the cursor – the movable marker that is used to show the place where the next character entered is to be displayed – around the screen of a visual display unit (VDU). The editing keys provide

Fig. 3.1 A computer keyboard. The top row of keys are function keys. The lower left-hand block is the qwerty keyboard and the lower right-hand block is a numeric keypad. Between these are the editing keys (*top*) and the cursor control keys (*bottom*).

facilities for inserting, deleting, and moving through the text. The qwerty keyboard is used to enter text and commands to the computer.

The keyboard is also an important part of a *teletype* – an earlier form of display that uses a paper print-out instead of a screen as a visual display. Because they produce a paper print-out, teletypes are often used when a permanent record of events is required, as in monitoring the performance of a large computer system.

The layout of the qwerty keyboard was devised at the end of the last century to slow down typists to the speed of the manual typewriters of the day, to prevent the keys clashing and becoming jammed. Despite this, a skilled typist is able to type at around 5 characters per second (c.p.s.), or 18 000 characters per hour. Data-entry personnel who use a smaller numeric keypad alone are able to enter data at around 24 000 key depressions per hour. Although in terms of human operators these speeds of data input are very fast, in terms of the speeds at which the computer is able to work (see section 2.5.2) they are still very slow.

Different keyboard layouts that improve upon the speeds above have been developed but have failed to replace the qwerty keyboard standard. Figure 3.2 shows an example of one of these alternative layouts, the Maltron keyboard. This adopts a radically different approach to the keyboard by laying out the keys ergonomically, so that hand movement is minimised and full use is made

Fig. 3.2 The Maltron ergonomically designed keyboard

of the thumbs. The keyboard itself is dished and can increase speeds by over 70%, as well as reducing the fatigue often associated with the use of the qwerty keyboard.

Other uses of keyboards or keypads (cut-down versions of a full qwerty keyboard) are in stock control in shops and warehouses and in cash registers. Figure 3.3 shows an electronic portable organiser called the Agenda, which is designed for one-handed operation. In addition to alphabetic and numeric keypads, there are also five large unmarked keys that can be used to enter text – each character requires a different combination of these keys to be pressed. Organisers like this are often designed to be compatible with PCs so that information may be transferred between them.

3.2.2 *The mouse*

The mouse is a hand-held device which, with its associated software, enables the user to move the cursor around a VDU screen without using the cursor control keys. The mouse was developed in order to get over the problem that non-typists had with using a keyboard to communicate with the computer. The mouse is also used by the Apple Macintosh and in Microsoft Windows to promote a way of using computers that relies upon the use of visual prompts rather than forcing the user to memorise large numbers of commands.

The mouse is a desk-top device in which movements of the mouse on the desk are linked to movements of a cursor on a VDU screen. The cursor travels around the screen in response to the action of the user moving the mouse around the desk. A mouse-driven computer enables a user to select a desired

Fig. 3.3 The Microwriter Agenda, an electronic portable organiser designed for one-handed operation

option by 'pointing' the cursor at an *icon* or visual prompt of the desired option and pressing a button on the mouse to select it, rather than having to type a complex command. Once an icon has been selected by using the mouse, a 'window' opens up to display the facilities offered by the option which the chosen icon represents. If one of the facilities is selected by using the same point-and-press approach, a menu of further options appears. To select an option from the menu the user will once more point the cursor at the required item and press a button on the mouse. If, for example, the user wants to perform some calculations, the calculator facility may be selected, causing a picture of a calculator to appear on the screen. To perform a calculation the user can then point the cursor at the relevant keys on the calculator by using the mouse, the result appearing in the normal way. By using the mouse, it is thus possible to perform quite complex tasks on a computer without ever touching the keyboard.

Figure 3.4 shows the Apple Macintosh, a mouse-driven personal computer.

Even using a mouse-driven system like the Apple Macintosh, it is necessary to use the keyboard sometimes – if you wish to enter some text, for example. The mouse is therefore not designed to replace the keyboard but is rather intended as a supplement to it, enabling common tasks to be performed without using the keyboard.

Other uses of the mouse have been found in graphics and desk-top

Fig. 3.4 The Apple Macintosh II microcomputer. The mouse is to the right of the keyboard.

publishing (see section 6.3.3), where its ability to move the cursor around the screen is of great use in design and layout. It is also used to provide a user-friendly face to the program that runs the computer – the systems software or operating system (see section 6.2). Several mouse-driven programs have been written which allow users to copy, delete, and generally tidy their disks and files without the need to learn the complex commands that would otherwise be necessary. Such programs also provide a number of other functions that are intended to replicate the facilities available on the typical desk, such as a calculator, a diary, a notepad, and sometimes even an executive game.

3.2.3 Touchscreens
Touchscreens, like the mouse, are designed to avoid the use of a computer keyboard when using menu-driven software. In order to select from a menu of choices displayed on a touchscreen, the user will simply touch the appropriate icon or other reference on the screen. This action will be sensed by the computer, and the option chosen will be acted upon.

This system is used in some computer systems as an alternative to the mouse, and may be found in applications in which the user may not be able to use a keyboard. Touchscreen systems have been installed in many of the currency- and share-dealing rooms in the City of London, with the on-screen options providing direct telephone links to other dealing rooms around the world without the need to dial a number. Figure 3.5 shows touchscreens installed in a dealing room.

Fig. 3.5 Two touchscreens forming part of a typical dealing-room workstation. Note the images indicating the options available.

3.2.4 Voice input

Voice input is still in its early stages of development and, although it is possible to program a computer to respond to voice commands, voice input has not as yet found a wide application.

The voice-recognition systems at present being developed are of two types: discrete-word recognition and continuous-speech recognition. The simpler discrete-word recognition systems are available now but can only cope with one- or two-word commands. Most of the present voice-recognition systems need to be 'trained' to cope with a particular voice, and they must be retrained if the user gets a cold or has a sore throat. Another problem is with homophones – words that have the same sound but different meanings ('there' and 'their' for example).

Continuous-speech recognition systems are still at the development stage and, although prototype systems exist, commercial systems are still some way off. Continuous-speech recognition is discussed in more depth in Unit 15.

3.3 Document readers

Document-based data input satisfies the needs of both the user and the computer, since these documents can be read by humans as well as by machines. This form of data input is used where there is a need to be able to process large volumes of similar documents, like cheques or gas bills, quickly. Examples of use are in the automated processing of cheques, the computer marking of multiple-choice answer sheets, and the reading of large volumes of credit-card payment slips.

3.3.1 Optical character recognition

Optical character recognition (OCR) is a system that enables information to be automatically 'read' from a printed document. There are two typefaces or fonts that have been specially designed for OCR, called OCR-A and OCR-B, although modern OCR scanners can recognise typed and neatly handwritten (printed) material. The specialist OCR typefaces are illustrated in fig. 3.6.

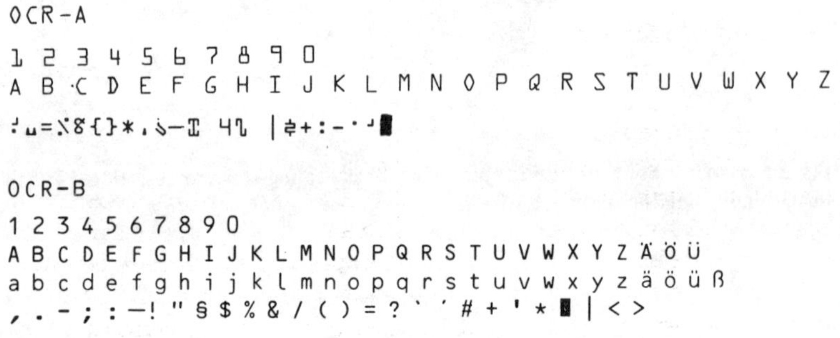

Fig. 3.6 Specialist OCR typefaces for optical character recognition. Modern OCR systems can recognise ordinary typing and neat hand printing.

OCR-A was originally developed in the United States and has a total of 66 characters. OCR-B was developed in Europe and provides 113 characters. Both typefaces are available in four sizes. OCR is used by organisations like the gas, electricity, and credit-card companies and the UK's Driver and Vehicle Licensing Centre (DVLC), all of whom need to process large numbers of similar documents in a short space of time.

OCR scanners that can recognise the common typewriter character sets (Pica, Letter Gothic, Courier, etc.) can be used in offices to input typed documents to a wordprocessor and avoid the need for retyping. The use of neatly handwritten documents makes it possible to use OCR for a far wider range of applications than was previously possible, such as reading handwritten time-sheets and order forms.

Figure 3.7 shows an OCR document designed for use in processing payments through the Girobank system. High-speed OCR systems can handle over 2000 documents per minute.

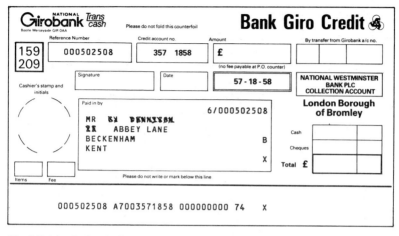

Fig. 3.7 A bank giro credit payment slip (using OCR-B characters) that will be read using an OCR system

3.3.2 Optical mark recognition

This is a simpler optical system that is designed to detect the presence of pencil marks made on a pre-printed document. Optical mark recognition (OMR) is used in areas where the data to be collected has a set number of options – applications include multiple-choice examinations, market research, stock control, and employees' time-sheets. The Electoral Reform Society (an organisation that conducts secret ballots on behalf of other organisations) uses OMR to read ballot papers. This enables the result of a ballot to be obtained far faster than by a conventional manual count of the ballot papers. Speed of input of OMR systems can be anything up to 200 documents a minute.

Figure 3.8 shows an example of an OMR document.

3.3.3 Magnetic-ink character recognition

The system of magnetic-ink character recognition (MICR) was originally developed in the United States for the American Banks Association, to enable the fast and efficient clearing of cheques. As with OCR there are two magnetic-ink character typefaces: E13B and CMC7. Developed in the USA, E13B has the numbers 0 to 9 and four special symbols; whereas the European CMC7 has 0 to 9, 26 alphabetic characters, and five special symbols. Examples of the two MICR typefaces are shown in fig. 3.9.

For MICR the characters are printed in a special ink that can be magnetised to give off a unique magnetic field that enables each character to be read. The characters of the E13B font each have a characteristic shape, while the CMC7 typeface is made up of seven vertical bars with the variable distances between the bars differentiating each character.

MICR is used by the banks as a way of speeding up the cheque-clearing system – input speeds are at anything up to 2000 cheques a minute – and magnetic-ink characters may also be seen on postal orders and credit-card payment slips. Figure 3.10 shows an MICR system in operation.

W⊞ Wolverhampton Health Authority

LUNCH   Tuesday 2   **SUPPER**   Tuesday 2

DIAB.   RED.   LIGHT   LOW FAT   DIAB.   RED.   LIGHT   LOW FAT
LOW PROT.   H. FIBRE   GL. FREE   LOW PROT.   H. FIBRE   GL. FREE

Ward   Name   Ward   Name

How to complete your menu:

Please use pencil, or a dark blue or black pen to mark each item in your choice by a mark in the solid box next to it, like this:

☐▆ Soup

If you make a mistake put a mark in the feint box as well.

For lunch and supper please select one starter, one main course, any two vegetables, and one sweet. If you do not want a main course you may choose two starters or sweets.

For breakfast choose one starter and no more than two main course items.

All items subject to availability

LUNCH		SUPPER	
1	Natural Orange Juice	1	Natural Orange Juice
2	Natural Grapefruit Juice	2	Natural Grapefruit Juice
3	Tomato Soup	3	Oxtail Soup
4	Lancashire Hot Pot	4	Poached Chicken, Sce. Supreme
5	Fried Cod's Roe	5	Welsh Rarebit
6	Egg Salad	6	Corned Beef Sand. (Wholemeal)
7	Minced Beef & Gravy	7	Corned Beef Sand. (White)
8	Curried Pork & Rice	8	Minced Pork & Gravy
9		9	Curried Lamb & Rice
10	Peas	10	Mashed Swede
11	Cabbage	11	French Beans
12	Pureed Vegetables	12	Pureed Vegetables
13	Mashed Potatoes	13	Creamed Potatoes
14	Fried Potatoes	14	Parsley Potatoes
15	Jam Tart & Custard	15	Cream Caramel
16	Reducing Stewed Apple	16	Reducing Apricots
17	Diabetic Apple Crumble & Cust.	17	Diabetic Apricots
18	Baked Rice Pudding	18	Ice Cream
19	Diabetic Milk Pudding	19	
20	Egg Custard	20	Egg Custard
21	Cheese & Crackers	21	Cheese & Wheatmeal Biscuits
22	Jelly	22	Jelly
23	Fresh Fruit	23	Fresh Fruit
24		24	
25		25	
26		26	

Portion Size: Large ☐ Small ☐   Portion Size: Large ☐ Small ☐

Fig. 3.8 An OMR menu-selection form used in a hospital catering system – options are indicated by making marks in the relevant boxes and are then read automatically.

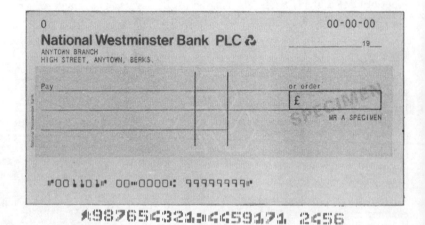

Fig. 3.9 Examples of MICR typefaces – the cheque (*top*) has account details printed in the E13B typeface; the bottom figures are from the CMC7 typeface.

Fig. 3.10 An IBM 3890 MICR system processing cheques at the National Westminster Bank

3.4 Bar-code readers

Bar codes are an arrangement of vertical bars and spaces that can be read by an optical scanner and used as a means of identifying products or stock items. Bar codes can be seen on most products purchased in supermarkets, inside library books, and on such items as freezers and computers. There are several bar-code standards, two of which are the Universal Product Code (UPC) and the European Article Numbering (EAN) systems. Examples of bar codes are shown in fig. 3.11.

In supermarkets, each product carries a unique EAN bar code that can be used both to calculate the size of the bill at the point-of-sale (POS) terminals (or check-outs) and for stock control. The system operates from a central computer which controls the POS terminals whose scanners (low-intensity lasers) read the bar code on each item. When a shopper goes through a check-out, each item is passed over the scanner (fig. 3.12) which reads the bar code and refers to the central computer for the description and price. This information is relayed to the check-out, where it is displayed on a customer panel and printed on the receipt. At the same time, the stock level for the item purchased will be reduced, providing management with up-to-date stock information and enabling more efficient stock control and ordering. (This is covered in more detail in the Sainsbury's case-study in section 12.3.)

Applications of the same technology are to be found in industrial, pharmaceutical, and photographic stock control, and bar codes are also widely

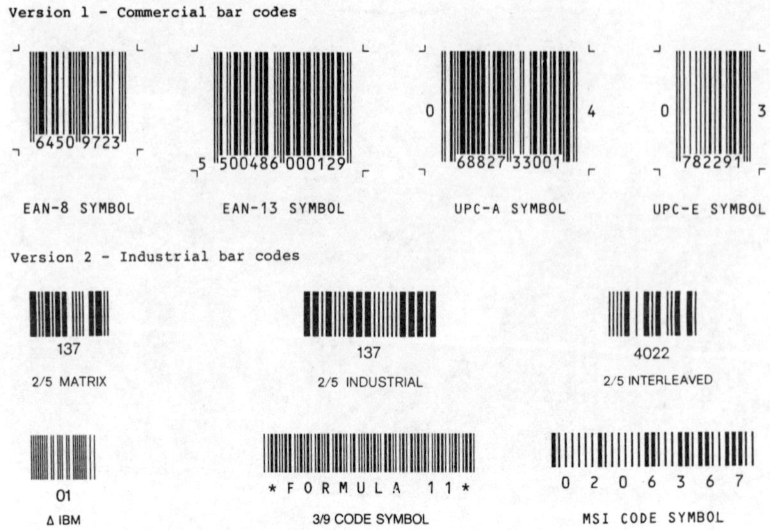

Version 1 - Commercial bar codes
6450 9723
EAN-8 SYMBOL
5 500486 000129
EAN-13 SYMBOL
0 68827 33001 4
UPC-A SYMBOL
0 782291 3
UPC-E SYMBOL
Version 2 - Industrial bar codes
137
2/5 MATRIX
137
2/5 INDUSTRIAL
4022
2/5 INTERLEAVED
01
Δ IBM
* F O R M U L A 1 1 *
3/9 CODE SYMBOL
0 2 0 6 3 6 7
MSI CODE SYMBOL

Fig. 3.11 Examples of bar codes

Fig. 3.12 A bar code being read by a scanner at a supermarket check-out

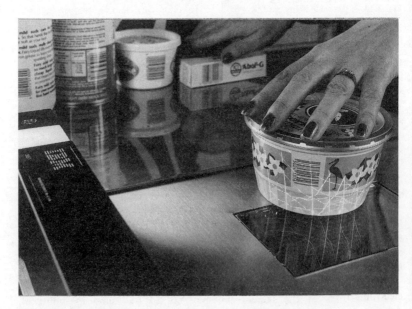

Fig. 3.13 A bar code being read by a light-pen to collect data for a stock-control system

used in libraries to control book issues. In some systems, especially in libraries, the bar codes are read by using a light-pen or wand, as shown in fig. 3.13. Input speeds are limited by the user, but data can be read in from a bar code at around 1.4 cm per second. An application of bar codes in controlling goods in a warehouse is illustrated in the Benetton case-study in section 12.2.

3.5 Card readers

A card reader is a device that reads information held in the form of a magnetic stripe on a plastic card. Applications include cheque guarantee cards, credit cards, ATM (cash-dispenser) cards, magnetic keys, and identity cards – fig. 3.14 shows examples. The magnetic stripe on the back of the card may hold the personal details of the owner and, with the necessary secret number, will allow access to restricted computing facilities, secure locations, credit facilities, or a bank account.

Card readers are becoming more common as retail outlets install them to electronically capture sales information on goods purchased with credit and debit cards. One type of transaction terminal is shown in fig. 3.15. A typical

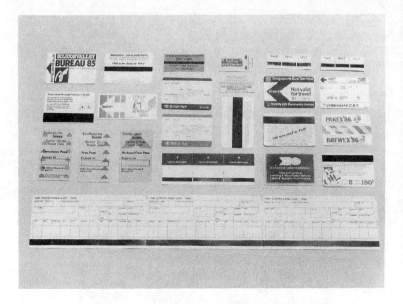

Fig. 3.14 Some cards or tickets holding information on a magnetic stripe

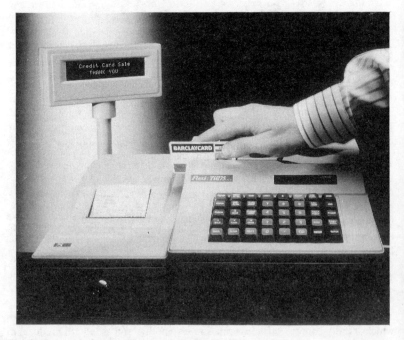

Fig. 3.15 A typical transaction terminal that is widely used in shops

transaction would start with a suitable card being offered to a sales assistant, who will enter the amount payable on the keyboard and then wipe the card through the terminal. The information on the amount and the card account number are routed automatically to the appropriate card company's computer via a data communications network to check that the transaction will not take the customer above his or her credit limit and, indeed, that the card used has not been reported as being stolen. If everything is in order, the terminal will print out a receipt which the cardholder must then sign so that the sales assistant can complete the normal signature check. Once satisfied, the assistant confirms the sale by pressing a key and the process is completed when the card company's computer allocates an authorisation-code number which is printed on the receipt.

The use of transaction terminals in retailing is advantageous to the retailer since it avoids filling in and imprinting a sales voucher and it provides an automatic card check.

3.6 Pen-based data input

The most commonly used input device – the QWERTY keyboard – represents a major barrier for many people who wish to use a computer, especially at the beginning. While many people overcome this and develop keyboard skills, a large market exists for an effective pen-based input system, and the last few years have seen the introduction of the first practical pen-based systems. Such systems (fig. 3.16) will usually contain the following components:

(a) a specially designed stylus or pen that is used to write the data;
(b) a touch-sensitive screen, usually in the form of an A4-sized notepad;
(c) powerful character-recognition software;
(d) a high-speed processor (needed to run the complex character-recognition software in something like real time);
(e) an interface to a PC.

Pen-based systems are currently intended for people who do not use desk-top PCs, such as meter-readers and travelling salespeople. The next generation of pen-based systems will be aimed at desk-based users and will have a full range of applications. The current generation of pen-based wordprocessing systems requires the user to learn a set of editing commands (for such applications as cutting/pasting text, deleting, inserting, etc.) and to be very precise in entering text, although some systems can be trained to recognise a particular user's handwriting.

3.7 Graphics input

There are several ways of inputting a graphical image to a computer, three of which – the graphics pad, the image scanner, and the video scanner – are outlined below.

Fig. 3.16 Victor Technologies' GRiDPAD pen-based PC

3.7.1 Graphics pads

A graphics pad (or graphics tablet) can be used to input a graphic image to a computer in two ways: with a stylus or with a cursor. Freehand images may be input by drawing with the stylus on the 'bed' of the pad, below which a complex grid of wires is able to sense the position of the stylus and feed this into the computer. Existing drawings may be traced by the stylus on to the bed; alternatively, they may be input by using a cursor similar to a mouse. The cursor is positioned in turn over the key points on the drawing and one of the buttons on it is pressed. The computer records these points and joins them together as necessary to define the complete image.

When used to input existing drawings, graphics pads may also be called *digitisers*.

Graphics pads can either be used to input an existing drawing to the computer for modification using a CAD (computer-aided design) package, or else they can be used to create new drawings or designs. They are used by architects to design buildings, by map makers in cartography, and as part of complex CAD systems in mechanical and electrical engineering. Figure 3.17 shows a graphics pad in use.

3.7.2 Image scanners

The image scanner is used as a means of capturing an existing two-dimensional image – a drawing or a photograph – that could not be input using a graphics pad. Image scanners divide a picture into a matrix of millions of tiny dots each of which is stored in a file in the computer. It is then possible to use this file with an existing text file in order to combine pictures with text as in a

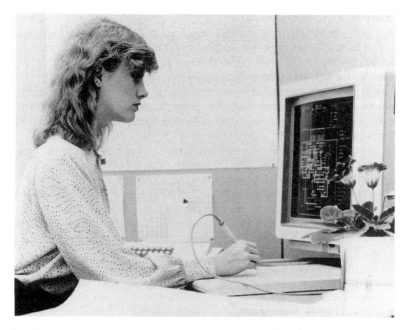

Fig. 3.17 An IBM graphics pad in use. Note the use of a stylus.

newspaper. The definition or resolution of the image will depend on the number of dots into which the picture is divided, a high-resolution image being obtained at 300 × 300 dots per square inch.

3.7.3 Video scanners
The video scanner uses a video camera to capture an image either of an existing two-dimensional picture or of a three-dimensional object whose image is to be processed. Video scanners will generally offer a higher resolution than image scanners, with 500 × 500 dots per square inch being possible.

Scanning can handle both colour and monochrome, and applications for this technology have been found in business – for producing technical manuals and letterheads – and in publishing. Microcomputer systems that are able to combine text with the pictures captured by image scanners to produce print-ready output are called desk-top publishing systems (see section 6.3.3).

3.8 Magnetic disk and tape input
A magnetic disk is a computer storage device that looks rather like an LP record that has the same magnetic coating as an audio cassette tape.

Information is recorded on to and read from the surface of the disk in much the same way as a domestic cassette tape-recorder is used to record and play back music. Magnetic tape is the computer equivalent of the reel-to-reel tapes found on professional tape recorders. Magnetic disks and tape are both widely used for the storage of computerised information.

In applications where large volumes of data have to be processed, it is usually a more efficient use of central-computer time if data is input on to a magnetic tape or disk before processing. This is because data can be transferred from a magnetic disk or tape far faster than it can be input from any other device. In applications where the data has to be entered using a keyboard, the terms 'key to disk' and 'key to tape' describe the first stage before the data is read into the computer for processing from disk or tape.

Speeds of input from magnetic tape or disk are termed *data transfer rates*, and are considerably higher than those for any other method discussed so far. The transfer rate for a magnetic disk would be around 5 Mb per second, or about 5 million c.p.s., with magnetic tape operating at something like 3 Mb per second.

When data is entered, a number of checks must be made to ensure that it is correct before it can be stored on disk for processing later. These are discussed further in Unit 9.

Figure 3.18 shows the layout of a typical key-to-disk data-entry system.

3.9 Summary

A summary of the input methods discussed in this unit is shown in Table 3.1 and fig. 3.19. Although input from magnetic disk is by far the fastest, it is still sometimes necessary to use the slowest method, the keyboard, to get the data on to the disk in the first place. Speed is not the sole criterion in selecting the input method to use: rather, the method should be appropriate to the organisation itself. It is for this reason that, although the keyboard is the slowest means of input, because it is familiar and relatively easy to operate it is the most widely used input device.

3.10 Glossary of terms

Data capture   The term applied to the use of input devices to convert data into a form that can be handled by a computer.

QWERTY keyboard   The standard keyboard layout that has the letters QWERTY on the top row of the alphabetical keys.

Mouse   A hand-held device which, with its associated software, enables the user to move the cursor around a VDU screen. Developed in order to get over the problem that non-typists have with using a keyboard to communicate with the computer.

Icon   A visual prompt for an option available in a menu of computer facilities.

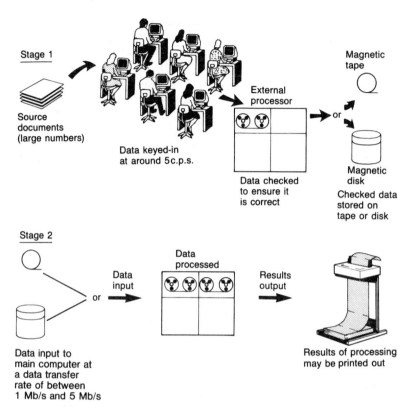

Fig. 3.18 A typical key-to-disk data-entry system

Window　A portion of a screen within which a software application may be used. Most systems are able to have more than one window on the screen at one time, but usually only one window will be 'open', i.e. active for immediate use.

Touchscreen　An input device for use with menu-driven software, the user indicating a particular choice by touching the appropriate icon or other reference displayed on the screen.

Document reader　A term applied to input devices that read information from documents, using OCR, OMR, or MICR for example.

OCR　Optical character recognition – a technique of optically reading specially printed, typed, or even handwritten information and converting it into computer-usable form.

OMR　Optical mark recognition – a system for reading marks made on specially printed documents.

Table 3.1   A summary of computer input methods

Device	Speed	Features	Applications
Keyboard	5 c.p.s.	QWERTY layout.	General text input – most widely used input device.
Mouse	–	Hand-held device that controls the movement of an on-screen cursor.	Used, with windows and menus, as a way of selecting options. Not used for text input.
Touchscreen	–	Special screen that enables user to choose options by touching images of them.	Used as a way of selecting options with a menu system. Not used for text input.
Voice	–	Can recognise single words.	Used in areas where no-hands use desired.
OCR	2000 doc/min	May read OCR-A and OCR-B, typewriter fonts, and neat handwriting.	May be used for large-scale input (gas bills), document scanning (WP input), and hand-written input (time-sheets).
OMR	200 doc/min	Reads marks in set places on special documents.	Used where there are a set number of responses – order forms; multiple-choice answer sheets.
MICR	2000 ch/min	Reads E13B and CMC7 fonts.	Used by banks to speed the clearing of cheques.
Bar-code reader	–	Reads patterns of bars which indicate a code number.	Used in grocery retailing, libraries, and stock control.
Card reader	–	Reads information on a magnetic stripe.	Used for personal security systems – ATM cards, magnetic keys.
Graphics pad	–	Enables existing or freehand drawings to be input into a computer.	Used, with CAD software, by designers.
Image scanner	–	Captures a two-dimensional image in digital form.	Used by graphic designers and as part of publishing systems.
Video scanner	–	Captures an image either of an existing picture or of a three-dimensional object in digital form.	Used by graphic designers and as part of publishing systems.
Magnetic disk/tape	5/3 million c.p.s.	Information stored magnetically on disk/tape.	Used when large volumes of data are to be input, as a way of maximising rate of input.

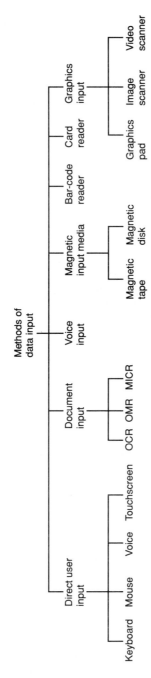

Fig. 3.19 The main methods of computer input

MICR   Magnetic-ink character recognition – a technique of magnetically reading characters printed in magnetic ink.

Bar-code reader   A device that uses a light-beam to read the information held in a bar code.

'. . .*This one's thin line, thin line, space, thick line, thin line, space, thin line, space, thin line, thin line* . . .'

Card reader   A system that can read the information held by the magnetic stripe on a plastic card.

Image scanner   A device that captures an existing picture by converting it into digital form.

Video scanner   A device that can be used to capture in digital form the image either of an existing two-dimensional picture or of a three-dimensional object.

Graphics pad   A device that enables drawings to be plotted or traced into a computer or freehand drawings to be input.

Digitiser   An alternative name for a graphics pad when used to input existing drawings.

3.11 Exercises

1 Define and describe any *four* of the following data-input devices, giving an example of the role it plays in an application system.

   (a) Teletype
   (b) Visual display unit
   (c) Bar-code reader
   (d) Optical mark reader (OMR)
   (e) Optical character reader (OCR)   (IDPM, Data processing II)

2 What are the following used for?

   (a) Magnetic-ink characters
   (b) Optical characters (OCR-A and OCR-B)
   (c) Optical-mark documents
   (d) Bar codes

3 What input device would you recommend for each of the following? Explain your reasons.

   (a) A company designing cars
   (b) A personal-identification security system
   (c) A computerised stock-control system
   (d) A manager who wishes to edit a document using a wordprocessor – he has just received the document in his post and will not have time to retype it
   (e) A college wishing to computerise the marking of its multiple-choice examination papers
   (f) A faster alternative to direct keyboard entry for a company with a high volume of data to input to its main computer

4 Rank the following in speed of input: MICR, keyboard, OCR, magnetic disk.

5 Compare and contrast the features and capabilities of the image scanner, the video scanner, and the graphics pad.

Case-study

Information Processing Services Ltd (IPS) was set up three years ago to offer a computer-based information-processing service to the local business community. At the start IPS was a success, since there was at that time a demand for a data-entry service from firms installing or changing their computer systems. The demand for data-entry services has been declining for the past year, however, and the owner – Belinda Carlisle – has decided to offer a wider range of services than is at present available.

Ms Carlisle has targeted three possible new services that IPS will offer:

   (i) *Input of pictures and designs* This service will be aimed primarily at architectural practices in the area, many of whom are computerising but have a large number of existing designs that they would like to put on to their new systems.

(ii) *A cut-price text-input service using scanning technology*   IPS has found that many small firms do not take advantage of its existing data-entry service because their budget is limited. As a way of tapping this market, it has been decided to offer a cut-price text-entry service using the new scanners that have become available.

(iii) *Multiple-choice data input*   Belinda Carlisle believes that there is a large potential market for multiple-choice data input from local educational establishments. A number of local State and private schools wish to move into attainment testing with use of multiple-choice-question examination papers across the entire age range. The sheer volume of testing means that they are looking for a fast and efficient way of marking the papers, and Ms Carlisle intends to offer a multiple-choice-questions paper-marking service.

If IPS is to be able to offer these new services, it will need to invest in a range of new computer input devices. Belinda Carlisle has contacted her bank manager to ask for a business loan to fund this expansion, and this has been agreed in principle. Before committing himself, however, the bank manager wants a lot more detail than Ms Carlisle has so far provided.

Unfortunately, Ms Carlisle has been called away on urgent business, and you, as a junior manager, have been asked to research the market for each of the input devices mentioned above and to produce a report which contains the following information:

(a) Description (in simple terms for the bank manager's benefit) of the use and operation of each of the devices required for the services mentioned above.
(b) A survey of the range of products available for each of these services.
(c) Your recommendations as to which device should be purchased for each of the above.
(d) The total cost of the devices you recommend.

Computer output

4.1 Introduction

Computer output can take the form of a display on a screen, a print-out, the control of a mechanical device, or transfer of information on to a magnetic tape or disk. Most output falls into one of two categories: hard copy or soft copy. Output in a permanent or printed form is called hard copy, whereas output displayed on a screen or in audio form is called soft copy.

In this unit the four types of computer output will be examined, with sections on soft copy, hard copy, the use of computers to control mechanical devices, and the output of data on to magnetic disks or tapes.

4.2 Soft-copy output

Information that is output as soft copy will either be displayed visually on a screen or else be in audio form, as in speech or music.

4.2.1 Visual output

The most common form of soft-copy output is information displayed on a screen or cathode-ray tube (CRT). CRTs are familiar in that one type is a component part of the domestic television receiver. They operate by converting an electrical signal into a visual display. This is achieved by converting the signal into a stream of electrons that is focused upon a phosphor coating on the inside of a screen, causing it to glow and emit light. CRTs can display information in either colour or monochrome.

A CRT is the major component in a number of devices, notably the visual display unit (VDU), and the monitor. The VDU enables the user to input information to a computer by using a keyboard, mouse, or touchscreen facilities and to view output on a CRT. A computer monitor is a high-quality CRT that is used solely for viewing output and has no other devices attached.

Images displayed on a CRT are made up of number of small dots or picture elements, called *pixels*. The more pixels a computer is able to use to generate its display, the greater the sharpness or resolution of the image. A high-resolution image is produced by using 320 000 dots, with the screen divided into 400 lines with 800 dots on each line. A low-resolution image uses only 64 000 dots divided into 200 lines of 320 dots. For specialist applications like graphics, computer-aided design (CAD), and desk-top publishing (see section 6.3.3) that require a very high-resolution image, screens capable of displaying over 1 300 000 pixels are available.

Two factors limiting the use of the CRT are its weight and the amount of power it consumes. Portable computers, which must be light and be able to operate from batteries, have thus been forced to use an alternative type of display. Liquid-crystal displays (LCDs), similar to those found on some digital watches, are both light and economical enough to be widely used for portable computers, such as that shown in fig. 2.7. The best examples of this type of display can offer high-resolution colour images that compare favourably in quality with CRTs.

4.2.2 Audio output

Audio output covers the range from the simple 'beep' to full speech synthesis. The weird noises associated with computer games are a form of computer output just as much as voice mail where spoken information is converted into a digital signal and stored in RAM or on disk to be output at a later date. Speech synthesis is the production of a sound corresponding to spoken words and it is of great use where a user is unable to look at a CRT or is occupied with another task. By combining speech synthesis with speech recognition, it is now possible to have a simple dialogue with a computer using speech alone. Applications include a voice-based telephone enquiry system that 'speaks' account information, for a major UK bank.

4.3 Hard-copy output

Hard copy can be defined as computer output that is in a permanent form. Hard copy is usually in the form of a paper print-out, although computer output on microfilm or microfiche (COM) may also be considered a form of hard copy. Paper print-out may be produced either on separate sheets or on *continuous stationery* (or 'fan-fold' stationery) taking the form of folded and perforated lengths of paper (fig. 4.1).

There are two categories of printers:

(a) matrix printers (section 4.3.1), in which the text and graphics are produced from a series of dots;

(b) fully-formed-character printers (section 4.3.2), in which text is produced by the use of elements that are a replica of the character to be printed, in the manner of print hammers on a typewriter.

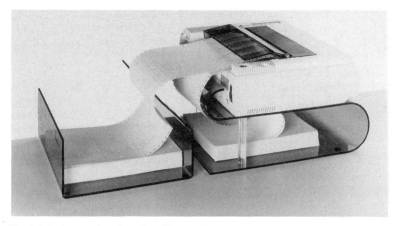

Fig. 4.1 A dot-matrix printer handling continuous stationery

It is now usual for all printers to have their own on-board RAM called *buffer storage*. Instead of the computer only sending text to a printer at the same speed that it can be printed, a buffer enables an entire document to be 'downloaded' or transferred into the printer buffer. This gets around the problem of the computer having to wait for the printer to finish before the computer can be used for something else. Printer buffers of 1 Mb and over are common in laser printers, the large memory being required to hold the location of every dot to be printed on the page – termed a 'bit map' image. Due to the large number of individual dots that make up any document or image – especially graphics – buffers in laser printers (section 4.3.1) are usually at least 1 Mb.

Graph plotters (section 4.3.3) are specialist devices designed to produce high-quality drawings and designs.

COM (section 4.3.4) provides a solution to the problem of storing large amounts of computer print-out by enabling the information to be photographically reduced on to film.

In the following sections we will look at each of the various forms of hard copy, examining the features, characteristics, and appropriate application areas of each type.

4.3.1 Matrix printers

All matrix printers produce images that are made up of a number of individual dots. To produce text of a higher quality it is necessary to use a larger number of dots in the same area, and fig. 4.2 shows the levels of quality achievable with several sizes of matrix.

The great strength of matrix printers is the flexibility with which many of them are able to produce a variety of different typefaces (also called fonts) in addition to being able to print pictures. This is possible since each of the dot-

```
This is an example of 9-pin
dot matrix output produced on
an Epson LX-80
```

```
This is an example of 18-pin
dot matrix output produced on
a NEC Pinwriter P3
```

```
This is an example of 24-pin
dot matrix output produced on
a NEC Pinwriter P7
```

Fig. 4.2 Levels of quality obtainable with different sizes of dot-matrix print head

producing elements in the print head can be commanded individually by the controlling computer to produce images outside the printer's own internal typeface.

The output from a matrix printer ranges from the lowest quality called 'draft' to the highest quality called 'letter quality' (LQ). The fastest quoted printer speeds for many matrix printers refer to draft quality, and the slowest to LQ. Terms such as high-density, correspondence, and near letter-quality (NLQ) are also used to differentiate between the standard of output available for a particular typeface. Many printers will also offer a type in a variety of pitches (number of characters to the inch), with 10, 12, 15, 17, and 20 pitch being available.

Although all matrix printers make use of the same basic principle to reproduce text, each printer has limitations on the size of matrix it can produce and thus on its quality of output. In this section we are going to look at the various types of matrix printer available and examine the characteristics and applications of each one.

(a) Dot-matrix printers   The dot-matrix printer is widely used as a microcomputer peripheral. It gets its name from the way in which a number of needles in the print head are used to print text as a series of dots using a carbon ribbon. The positions of the dots that need to be printed to create each letter are held by the printer in ROM, although it is sometimes possible to download a different set of codes from the computer into the printer to enable a new typeface to be printed. Figure 4.3 shows the principle of the dot-matrix print head.

The current generation of dot-matrix printers will have anything up a dozen standard typefaces in a variety of pitches and qualities held in ROM, in addition to the capability to produce so-called 'dot-addressable' graphics in a variety of colours using multi-coloured carbon ribbons. Figure 4.4 shows examples of the typefaces and graphics that can be produced by dot-matrix printers.

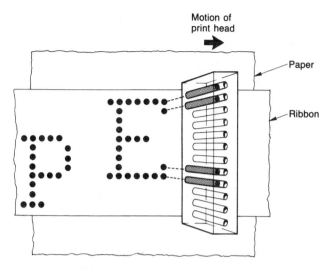

Fig. 4.3 The principle of the dot-matrix print head

The speed at which a dot-matrix printer is able to operate depends on which typeface is being printed. A low-quality draft-mode setting on one of the fastest dot-matrix printers available will produce a speed of around 500 characters per second (c.p.s.), whereas letter-quality (LQ) print may be produced at

I'm replenishing the dot matrix printer'

This is 10 pitch LQ print
This is 12 pitch LQ print
This is 15 pitch LQ print
This is proportionally-spaced LQ print
This is 10 pitch draft quality
This is 12 pitch draft quality
This is 15 pitch draft quality
This is 17 pitch draft quality
This is 20 pitch draft quality

This is underlined
This is **BOLD** output
This is BOLD and underlined
This is in italics
This is superscript output

Subscript output looks like this

A sentence that shows the use of
underlined, *italics*, bold, **bold
underlined**, superscript, and subscript
will look like this

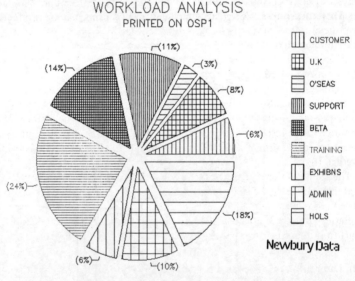

WORKLOAD ANALYSIS
PRINTED ON OSP1

CUSTOMER
U.K
O'SEAS
SUPPORT
BETA
TRAINING
EXHIBNS
ADMIN
HOLS

Newbury Data

(11%)
(3%)
(8%)
(6%)
(14%)
(24%)
(18%)
(6%)
(10%)

Fig. 4.4 Dot-matrix printer output: examples of the range of typefaces and levels of quality obtainable from a 24-pin NEC Pinwriter P7 dot-matrix printer (*top*) and a pie chart produced by a dot-matrix printer (*bottom*). 'Pitch' is the number of characters per inch.

only 100c.p.s. This large difference in speed is due to the fact that to achieve high-quality print it is usually necessary for each line to be printed twice. Typical speeds for a dot-matrix printer may range between 40 and 500c.p.s. according to the print quality.

(b) Ink-jet printers The ink-jet printer forms characters by projecting ink at high speed from a number of small ink nozzles on to paper, and for this reason it is termed a non-impact printer. Characters are produced from dots in the same way as by the dot-matrix printer, so both printers share many of the same advantages.

Ink-jet printers are flexible in usage and can reproduce many different type-styles and produce high-quality colour graphics by using a number of coloured inks. The ink-jet printer is able to produce high-quality text and graphics output due to the fact that the droplets of ink, once on the paper, will run together to form a more solid image. Colour graphics produced on an ink-jet printer can be of a very high quality, with the colours being more 'solid' than those produced by a dot-matrix printer, due to the ink flowing together.

The major advantage over a dot-matrix printer is the very low level of noise of the ink-jet printer in operation, due to the fact that printing does not involve any impact other than that of the ink upon the paper. Typical speeds for an ink-jet printer are from 200c.p.s. for draft quality to 100c.p.s. for letter-quality output.

(c) Thermal printers Thermal printers use heat to transfer the image from the print head to the paper. Text and images are made up from a series of dots, in common with other matrix printers, but with this process the print head may be either a fixed array of thermal elements that stretches across the entire width of the paper or else a moving print head. As with all matrix printers, the greater the number of dots per inch used to create an image, the higher the image resolution will be. Some thermal printers are able to print using 300 dots to the inch, producing high-resolution colour output using colour print ribbons, although lower-resolution monochrome output is more typical. Print speed is measured by the time it takes to print a single page, with 60 seconds being an average figure.

The ability of thermal printers to produce very high-resolution output means that they can be used as part of a computer-aided design (CAD) system to produce high-quality colour images.

Battery-powered portable thermal printers can be used by travelling sales staff to produce invoices, or even by traffic wardens to print parking tickets.

(d) Laser printers The laser printer – also termed a page printer, because it appears to print an entire page at a time – shares the same image-printer technology as the photocopier. It is in the use of a laser beam to create the image to be printed that the two methods of printing differ. The print image is produced by a laser beam which scans across the print drum line for line as the print

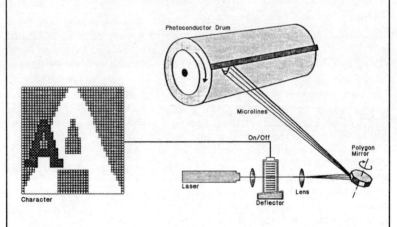

The rotating **Photoconductor Drum** has a semiconductive coating which is charged *positive* while in the dark and then, when the semiconductor is exposed by the **Laser Beam**, it is discharged to *negative* polarity.

The **Laser Beam** produces an image that is not visible to the human eye because it exists only in the form of *positive* and *negative* electrical charges.

The Photoconductor Drum is exposed by the Laser which is directed by an optical system made up of a Lens and a revolving mirror, known as a **Polygon Mirror**. The constantly revolving polygon mirror causes the laser beam to scan the photoconductor drum line for line. What cannot be seen here, is that the optical system splits the Laser Beam into several smaller beams producing very fine lines called **Microlines** thereby increasing the speed of the printer.

Fig. 4.5 The principle of the laser printer. (This illustration was produced by a high-speed Siemens laser printer.)

cylinder rotates. This is shown in fig. 4.5. The typestyles to be printed may either be held in ROM in the printer, or else be obtained by using special font cartridges (containing a ROM chip) that can be plugged into the printer as required.

The laser printer is another matrix printer in that characters may typically be produced from an inch-square 300 by 300 matrix (referred to as having a resolution of 300 dots per inch, or 300 d.p.i.), giving output that is of a higher quality than daisy-wheel print. In common with the other matrix printers, the laser printer is an extremely flexible means of printing, since it is capable of high-quality print in a large number of different typestyles in addition to being able to produce high-resolution graphics (in some cases in colour). This ability makes it the ideal output device for desk-top publishing systems (see section 6.3.3) which need to be able to output high-quality documents that combine text and graphics on the same page. In order to produce output of quality high enough to be used for professional phototypesetting purposes, laser printers with a resolution of 2540 d.p.i. may be used.

Print speeds are measured in pages per minute (p.p.m.), 1 p.p.m. being equal to approximately 100 c.p.s. Desk-top laser printers can typically print 6 to 10 p.p.m. (equivalent to 800 to 1000 c.p.s.), while the fastest machines can produce over 200 p.p.m. (equivalent to 20 000 c.p.s.).

Laser printers are finding applications in a wide number of areas, and their constantly falling price and improving performance may mean that they will eventually supplant many other types of printer.

4.3.2 Fully-formed-character printers

Fully-formed-character printers are direct descendants of a technology that started with the development of the first printing press in Germany over 500 years ago. Applications of this technology include typewriters, line printers, and daisy-wheel printers. All reproduce text by means of a permanent image of each character, and they are thus specialised machines. This specialisation means that, while they have only the most rudimentary ability to produce graphics, some fully-formed-character printers are able to produce text output of the highest quality.

(a) Daisy-wheel printers The daisy wheel from which this printer takes its name is a flat disc with a number of stalks, or 'petals', radiating from its centre, each of which has a character at its tip. Each of these characters is fully formed, like the letters on a typewriter hammer, and this produces output of a consistently high quality, termed 'letter quality'. In use, the daisy wheel rotates at high speed and the 'petals' are pushed on to a ribbon which in turn transfers the characters to the paper. A bolder image can be printed by striking each letter twice. Figure 4.6 shows a daisy wheel and a sample of output.

The daisy-wheel printer is a specialist device which, unlike some matrix printers (such as the dot-matrix printer), is designed to produce high-quality text, and it will at best be able to produce only elementary graphics. It is possible to alter the type style only by changing the daisy wheel, although a large number of alternative character styles are available, including OCR-B. The speed at which a daisy wheel can print will range from 10 c.p.s. for an inexpensive machine to more than 100 c.p.s. for a more expensive printer. An additional feature on the more expensive machines is the ability to handle individual sheets of paper by using a cut-sheet feeder.

A variation on the theme of a daisy wheel is the *thimble printer*. This machine has a print head that resembles a daisy wheel whose petals are inclined at about 110° to the central disc. The operation and characteristics of this machine are essentially the same as those of the daisy-wheel printer.

(b) Line printers The line printer gets its name from the way in which it prints a line of text at a time. There are two types of line printer – the chain printer

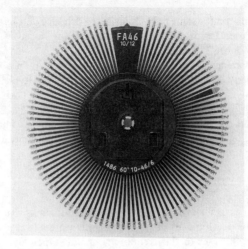

This text is produced on a Brother HR15
daisy-wheel printer using a Brougham
10 pitch daisywheel.

This is BOLD type in which each letter
is printed twice.
<u>This is UNDERLINED printing.</u>
<u>This printing is BOLD and UNDERLINED.</u>

Italic printing is not possible without
changing the daisywheel.

Fig. 4.6 A daisy wheel and a sample of its output

and the drum printer – and, although they operate slightly differently, they produce similar results.

The main feature of line printers is their speed, the fastest machines printing text at around 5000 lines per minute (l.p.m.). This is achieved by hitting the paper against the character and printer ribbon, rather than vice versa as with most other printers.

With the chain printer the character set is made up of individual print elements linked together to form a continuous chain that rotates at high speed. Opposite this chain is a set of print hammers, one for every character position on the page. The line to be printed is held in a memory buffer in the printer and analysed so that the position of each letter on the line to be printed is known. Instructions are sent to the print hammers to strike the paper against the correct character as it travels past the paper, the process continuing until

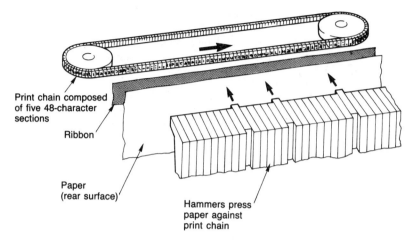

Print chain composed
of five 48-character
sections

Ribbon

Paper
(rear surface)

Hammers press
paper against
print chain

Fig. 4.7 The principle of the chain printer

the line is complete. In this way one line of text is printed at a time, with the process being repeated for each line of text.

The principle of the chain-printer mechanism is shown in fig. 4.7. The drum (or barrel) printer operates in a similar way, except that the characters are embossed on to the surface of a drum rotating about a horizontal axis.

Although the line printers are extremely fast – typical speeds are between 600 and 5000 l.p.m. – they are not able to produce high-quality print, and to achieve the highest print speed they may be limited to a restricted character set or print only in upper-case (capital) letters.

The main applications for a line printer are in those areas that need high volumes of printed output for which quality is not of prime importance. Applications include internal business reports on stock, debtors, or creditors, and such things as the printing of pay-slips and bank or credit-card statements. The speed and cost of line printers means that it is unlikely that they will be used with a microcomputer, and they are usually associated with mini and mainframe computers in organisations that need to produce high volumes of standard documents and reports.

4.3.3 Graph plotters
The graph plotter is a specialist device that is designed to produce high-quality pictures and designs. Unlike matrix printers, a graph plotter reproduces the human action of drawing by using a pen. The graphs produced using this device are thus of a higher quality than can be obtained by using a matrix printer, and for this reason graph plotters are widely used by architects and designers of all kinds.

All graphs have a horizontal *x*-axis and a vertical *y*-axis, and the graph plotter will draw an image using a pen that is moved either horizontally or vertically by two separate motors. Circles and diagonal lines are drawn by moving each motor in turn. The smaller the distance that the pen can be moved – termed the 'increment' – the higher the quality of image that a plotter is able to reproduce. High-quality plotters will have an increment as low as 0.006mm. Figure 4.8 shows typical graph-plotter output.

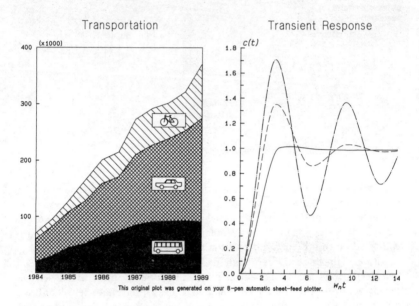

Fig. 4.8 Examples of graph-plotter output

There are two types of graph plotter – flatbed and drum. The flatbed plotter draws by moving the pen in both the x- and y-axes, while the drum plotter only moves the pen to plot in the y-axis, moving the paper itself to plot in the x-axis. These two types of plotter are shown in fig. 4.9.

Plotters are graded according to the size of paper that they can handle – A0, A1, A2, A3, or A4. The speed at which plotters are able to draw is quoted in centimetres per second (cm/s), with fast speeds being around 80cm/s. Other facilities may include electrostatic paper hold and the ability to produce drawings while automatically selecting different colour pens.

4.3.4 Computer output on microfilm or microfiche

As an alternative to printed output, another form of hard copy is computer output on microfilm or microfiche (COM). COM is the recording of what would otherwise be printed output direct in reduced form on to either rolls or sheets of photographic film. Microfilm is a roll of film that is usually in 16mm or 35mm format, whereas microfiches are individual sheets of film that are

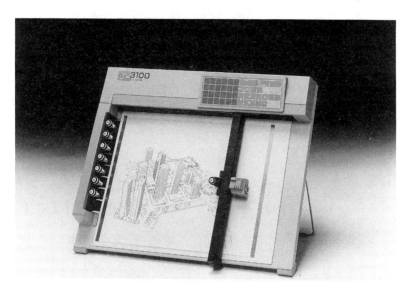

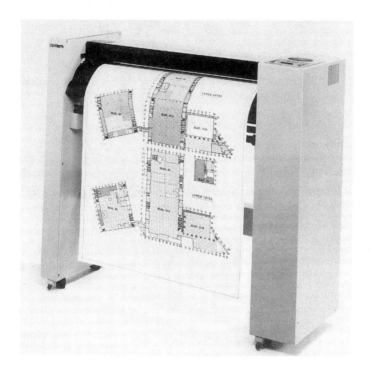

Fig. 4.9 The two types of graph plotter: flatbed (*top*) and drum (*bottom*)

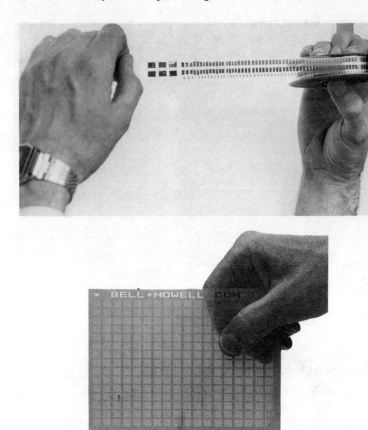

Fig. 4.10 Microfilm (*top*) and microfiche (*bottom*)

usually 105 mm × 148 mm in size. Both types of microform ('microform' is the name given to media like film and fiche that contain micro-images) are shown in fig. 4.10.

The most obvious advantage of COM is the ability to compress a large amount of information on to a single fiche or roll of film – a single fiche can hold up to 270 A4 pages of information. This compactness means that COM is widely used for archiving records of past transactions, library catalogues, car parts manuals, and stock-item lists. Reduction rates of between 20 times and 48 times are standard, and data may be output on to microform at anything up to 90 000 l.p.m.

To assist the user to locate a particular item of information on a piece of microform, indexes can be computer-generated and stored on the microform at the time of output. A special reader is necessary to be able to look at the information held on microform, similar to the one shown in fig. 4.11.

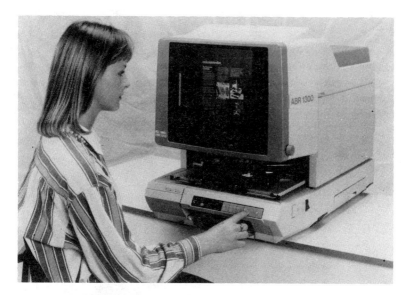

Fig. 4.11 A Bell & Howell ABR 1300 microfiche reader

4.4 Computer control of machines

Computer control of machines has been the driving force behind the automation of manufacturing industry in the past decade. Computer-aided manufacture (CAM) and computer integrated manufacturing (CIM) are both examples of the way in which the application of computers to manufacturing has revolutionised industry.

CAM is the use of computers to control manufacturing processes – the BUSCON (Build Sequence Control) system at the Austin Montego/Maestro manufacturing plant is an example. The BUSCON system controls and monitors the movement of body parts and the robots that assemble them, as well as controlling the activities of the automatic conveyors within the plant. Figure 4.12 shows part of a computer-controlled car production line.

CIM is the integration of the use of computers from the initial design stages, through prototyping and modification, to the eventual manufacturing process itself.

Both CAM and CIM are discussed further in section 15.4.1.

Another example of a computer being used to control a machine is the automated teller machine (ATM) situated on the outside wall of high-street banks and building societies to enable cash to be withdrawn from accounts.

In the home, 'intelligent' refrigerators, telephones and cookers are on the way. (In this context, 'intelligent' means that a device has a microprocessor built in that enables it to make decisions and perform simple tasks.)

Fig. 4.12 A robot arm welding a car door panel

4.5 Computer output to disk or tape

Information may be output to disk or tape as an intermediate stage before producing hard copy, using storage as a buffer between the processor and the output devices. This allows programs using the slow (compared to the CPU) printers to be completed quickly, freeing the computer for use with other programs. This technique of printing from tape or disk, rather than direct from the CPU, is called *spooling* of output.

Information may also be output to disk or tape to produce a back-up copy for security purposes.

The rate at which information can be output on to disk or tape is extremely fast, with data-transfer rates being from 1 to 5 Mb per second.

4.6 Summary

The entire range of computer output covers soft-copy and hard-copy output, computer control of external devices like robots, and even the output of information on to other computer devices like disks and tape. The uses of computers to control external devices and data storage will be dealt with in later units, so Table 4.1 is concerned only with a comparison of the major features of hard-copy and soft-copy output.

Table 4.1 A summary of hard-copy and soft-copy computer output

Device	Speed	Features	Applications
VDU	—	Soft-copy. May be colour or monochrome, high/low resolution.	Widely used. High-resolution versions used with CAD systems.
Dot-matrix printer	40–500 c.p.s.	Hard-copy. Able to produce colour graphic output.	Used for all types of output, from low to high quality.
Ink-jet printer	100–200 c.p.s.	Hard-copy, non-impact. Able to produce high-quality colour graphic output.	Quiet. Used for all types of output. Especially good at colour graphics.
Thermal printer	60 s/page	Hard-copy, non-impact. Able to produce high-quality colour graphic output.	Quiet. May be used for quality colour output. Can be portable.
Laser printer	6–100+ p.p.m.	Hard-copy, non-impact. Monochrome. Graphics.	Used to produce high-quality print and graphics.
Daisy-wheel printer	10–100+ c.p.s.	Hard-copy, impact.	High-quality output. No graphics.
Line printer	Up to 5000 l.p.m.	Hard-copy, impact.	Used for high-volume output where low quality is acceptable.
Graph plotter	Up to 80 cm/s	Draws graphs/designs in colour.	Used by designers etc.
COM	Up to 90000 l.p.m.	Output photographically reduced.	Used for output that is to be archived.
Output to disk/tape	1–5 Mb/s	Information stored on disk or tape.	Used for taking back-ups of programs or data, and spooling output.

4.7 Glossary of terms

Soft copy   Visual or audio output.

Hard copy   Output in a permanent or printed form.

CRT   Cathode-ray tube – a device which converts electrical signals into an image on a screen.

VDU   Visual display unit – a device which enables a user to input information to a computer by using a keyboard, mouse, or touchscreen facilities.

Resolution   A term relating to the clarity of the image on a CRT or a print-out.

Monitor   A high-resolution CRT used for viewing output of a computer system.

LCD   Liquid-crystal display – a device (similar to those used in some digital watches) producing an image by means of crystals sensitive to electrical signals.

Matrix printer   A printer in which the output is composed from a large number of individual dots – for example, dot-matrix, ink-jet, and laser printers.

Fully-formed-character printer   A printer in which the output is created by using a permanent image of each character printed – for example, a daisy-wheel printer.

Graph plotter   A specialist device that produces high-quality graphic images.

LQ   Letter-quality – a term applied to the highest-quality hard-copy output.

NLQ   Near letter-quality.

Draft-quality   A term applied to the lowest-quality hard-copy output.

COM   Computer output on microfilm or microfiche.

Spooling   The technique of outputting to tape or disk, rather than direct to the printer, for printing later.

4.8 Exercises

1 Describe the relative merits of producing computer output in *each* of the three following forms:

   (i) computer print-out,
   (ii) laser printed,
   (iii) COM.   (CBSI Management services)

2 Various options are available for the output of a computer system and four possibilities are as follows:

(a) mechanical impact printers;
(b) laser printers;
(c) computer output on microform (microfilm or microfiche);
(d) visual display units.

You are required to explain the characteristics of each type of output, its advantages and disadvantages, and the circumstances in which it would be most appropriately used.

(CIMA Management information systems and data processing)

3 Describe the following types of printers:

(a) Typewriter printer
(b) High-quality dot-matrix
(c) High-speed dot-matrix
(d) Plotters
(e) Line printers   (IDPM Data processing I)

4 Using the columns indicated, explain the factors which you would bear in mind when considering the purchase of three different types of printer from the list below:

Type	*Approx. cost*	*Advantages*	*Disadvantages*
Daisy-wheel			
Dot-matrix			
Laser			
Ink-jet			

5 In what situation are you likely to find the following output devices used? Explain your answers.

(a) Daisy-wheel printer
(b) Graph plotter
(c) Line printer
(d) Microfilm
(e) High-resolution VDU

6 What output device would you recommend for the following? Explain your answer.

(a) A company designing cars
(b) A company that wants to keep a hard copy of all its accounts but does not have the room to store the originals
(c) A company that wants to print out a very large number of high-quality letters to its customers
(d) A company that wants to attach a quiet letter-quality printer to each of the personal computers in its offices
(e) A company that wants a printer that is capable of producing high-quality output as well as colour graphics

7 Rank the following in order of speed of output: dot-matrix printer, laser printer, line printer, COM.

8 Compare and contrast the features of the ink-jet printer and the daisy-wheel printer. Which of these two printers would you choose for an office producing letters to be sent to other organisations? Explain your answer.

Case-study

Information Processing Services Ltd (IPS) was set up four years ago to offer a computer-based information-processing service to the local business community. IPS has been something of a success story, with the initial growth coming from the demand for a data-entry service from firms installing or changing their computer systems. As this demand declined, the owner – Belinda Carlisle – decided to offer a wider range of data-entry services (as discussed in the case-study at the end of Unit 3), and this has maintained the steady growth that IPS has enjoyed.

The ambitious Ms Carlisle has now decided that the market is ready for a specialist data-output service as well, and has once again targeted three possible new services that IPS will offer:

 (i) *A high-volume* high-quality *output service*   This is aimed at companies who wish to send out large numbers of letters to prospective clients.
(ii) *A high-volume* draft-quality *output service*   This is aimed at companies and others who wish to send out a large number of statements, bills, and other documents that do not have to be printed in the highest quality.
(iii) *A graphics output service*   This is aimed at architects and designers who wish to have their designs printed out on large-format (A1 or A0) paper using a high-quality printer.

For IPS to be able to offer these three new services, it will need to invest in a range of new computer output devices. The bank has been approached to provide a loan for the purchase of the necessary hardware, but before making a decision the manager wants a lot more background information.

As systems manager at IPS, it is your job to research the market for each of the output devices mentioned above and produce a report which contains the following information:

(a) Description and overview of the use and operation of each of the devices required for the applications mentioned above.
(b) A survey of the range of products available for each of these services.
(c) Your recommendations as to which device should be purchased for each of the above.
(d) The total cost of the devices that you recommend that IPS should purchase.

Storage and retrieval of information

5.1 Introduction

Secondary or backing storage provides a means whereby information may be accessible to a computer without being held in the central memory. The main forms of secondary storage are magnetic media (disks and tapes) and the several types of optical disk.

The development of computer storage has been driven by developments in the use of computers in business, with new applications demanding larger amounts of storage that can be accessed more rapidly. Magnetic disks and tapes are more established forms of storage and are widely used with all types of computer. The newer optical disks seem destined to eventually replace magnetic media, as the technology offers a larger storage potential.

An interesting development is the way in which computer storage technology has been used to create credit-card-sized personal storage media.

5.2 Magnetic disks

5.2.1 Introduction – features

The magnetic disk is the most widely used form of secondary storage. It is a flat disk that has both sides coated with a magnetic material that is able to store data by a magnetic recording process. The two main types of disk – hard and floppy – differ in the material of which the disk itself is made. The hard disk is made of metal and is rigid, whereas the floppy disk has a flexible plastic base. Data is both read from and recorded on a magnetic disk by means of a special read/write head that operates as the disk rotates at high speed.

In order to enable data to be retrieved easily, each surface of a magnetic disk is organised into a number of concentric tracks, with the disk as a whole being divided into sectors, as shown in fig. 5.1. The intersection of a track and a sector is called a *block*, and this is the smallest unit that can be either written to or read from on a disk. All blocks on a disk hold the same amount of data, and yet it can be seen in fig. 5.1 that the blocks at the outer edge of a magnetic disk

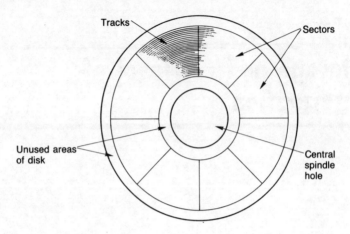

Fig. 5.1 Organisation of data storage on a magnetic disk. The section of a track contained in one sector is called a *block*.

are larger than those at the centre. In order to ensure that all tracks store the same amount of data, the data is stored more densely at the centre than at the rim of the disk. The 'packing density' of each track – that is, the amount of data stored in a given area – is thus higher the nearer the track is to the centre of a disk.

The way in which the sectors and tracks are laid out on a disk is called the disk format, and different makes of computer usually have different ways of 'formatting' disks. Floppy disks may be formatted to have 9 sectors and 48 tracks on each side, for example, while a hard disk may be formatted with 8 sectors and 500 tracks.

An item of data to be read from a disk is located by the computer after reference to a directory track which records the name, size, and location of each file of data that is held on the disk. The location of a file of data – also called its *address* – is referred to by disk surface, sector, and track, so that on a single disk a file may be read by moving the read/write head to side 2, sector 5, track 36, for example.

An item of data held on a magnetic disk may be accessed by moving the read/write head to the relevant track and waiting for the rotation of the disk to bring the block of data to the head to be read. This ability to access any part of the disk is termed 'random access' and is of great use since it enables data to be accessed at great speed. In contrast, a piece of data held on magnetic tape can be accessed only by reeling through the tape until the data is found – a far slower process called 'serial access'.

5.2.2 Hard disks

Hard-disk technology which was once associated only with mini and mainframe computer installations is now widely available and is in common use with microcomputers. Hard disks enable large amounts of data to be stored, accessed, and read at very high speeds. These features make the hard disk essential for tasks that demand the ability to access and update information rapidly, as in an airline bookings system or a stock-control system.

Hard disks rotate at speeds of around 3000 revolutions per minute, creating a draught of air that enables the read/write head to 'glide' a few micrometres above the surface of the disk. All read/write operations are performed without the head ever touching the surface of the hard disk, and the fine tolerances necessary for this mean that no contaminating particles (dirt) can be allowed to enter the hard disk environment to cause a 'head crash' (fig. 5.2).

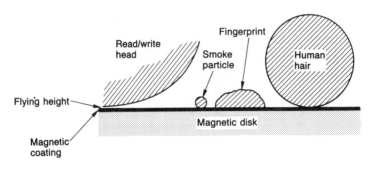

Fig. 5.2 Particles that can cause a 'head crash' with a magnetic disk

Hard disks can store data very densely, with some disks containing over 500 tracks, as compared with the floppy disk's 96 tracks. In addition to this, the high speed of rotation enables data access times to be around 30 milliseconds (30/1000 of a second) and the speed at which data can be read from disk (the data transfer rate) is over 1 Mb per second. Figure 5.3 shows various types of hard disk.

A single hard disk will have a read/write head for each side of the disk, with the head moving to the correct track in order to retrieve information when it is needed. In order to increase the amount of information stored, hard disks may be combined to form a 'stack' of up to twelve disks. A 'stack' of six disks, as shown in fig. 5.4, may have ten read/write heads that move as a single unit (one for each disk surface except the top and bottom ones – although the Winchester and fixed-head disks discussed below will use all twelve surfaces).

The delay in locating information on a disk is partly determined by the time it takes to move the read/write heads to the correct position. To reduce the number of such delays, and reduce the disk access time, large files of information can be stored on the same track on the surface of each disk, thus avoiding the need to move the read/write heads. This method of storage is called a 'cylinder of information', and a hard disk stack with 200 tracks has 200 such cylinders.

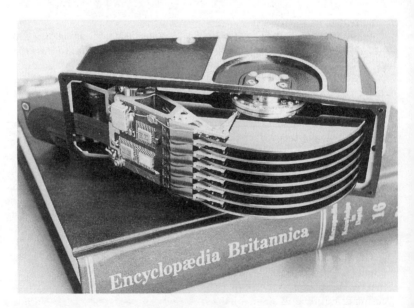

Fig. 5.3 Single and multiple hard disks

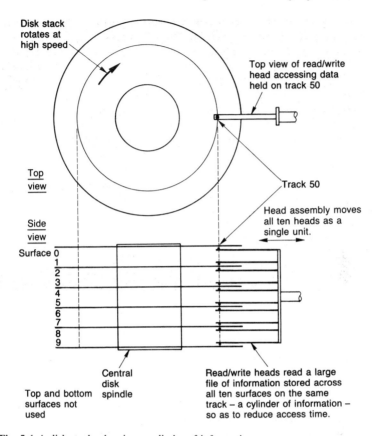

Fig. 5.4 A disk stack, showing a cylinder of information

(a) Exchangeable disks A common form of hard disk in use with mini and mainframe computers is the exchangeable hard disk. This form of disk may come individually or in 'stacks' of up to twelve disks. The term 'exchangeable' refers to the fact that, when the data they contain is required, these disks must be loaded by an operator into a special disk drive to enable them to be read by the computer. The storage capacity of exchangeable disks will depend on the number of disks in a stack, and the density with which data is stored on the disk, but 600 Mb per disk-pack is common.

This form of disk storage has the advantage that, by using a number of different disk-packs, secondary storage can be almost limitless. For applications that require a large amount of storage – as in banking, where details of every customer must be available at all times – it is not unusual for the main computer to be on-line to large numbers of exchangeable disk drives.

(b) Fixed disks   As the name suggests, fixed disks are located permanently inside a computer. This form of disk storage will generally offer better performance than a comparable exchangeable disk, since the disk assembly is often in a sealed environment that permits higher operating tolerances to be achieved. A single fixed-disk drive will often contain a number of disks, and storage capacities of several gigabytes per drive with very fast access times are possible.

One form of fixed disk is the 'Winchester disk', originally developed by IBM for use with mini and mainframe computers. Winchester disks are now widely used with microcomputers too, and systems are available that will store over 700 Mb and offer average access times as low as 25 milliseconds.

Tandon, an American company, has introduced an exchangeable Winchester disk called a Data-pac which can be used in much the same way as a floppy disk. Data-pacs can store up to 30 Mb of data and are designed for users who wish to carry their programs and data around with them from place to place.

(c) Fixed-head disks   Most hard-disk systems make use of a single set of read/write heads to access the 400 or so tracks that are on the surface of each disk. When accessing an item of data, there is an inevitable time delay while the heads are moved to the correct track, and it is this time delay that is eliminated with fixed-head disks.

A fixed-head disk system has a read/write head fixed permanently over each track on the surface of the disk, so a disk with 400 tracks will have 400 heads for each surface. This makes for very high access speeds, since the delay caused by moving the head is eliminated. Fixed-head disks can store several gigabytes of data and have access times of a few milliseconds.

5.2.3 Floppy disks

Floppy disks are thin, flexible, magnetically coated disks that are not unlike the flexible records that are sometimes given away with music magazines. In order to protect such a fragile item from damage, a floppy disk is protected by a semi-rigid jacket from which it is never removed.

There are four main sizes of floppy disks – 8 inch, 5¼ inch, 3.5 inch, and 3 inch – and these are shown in fig. 5.5. The 3.5 inch and 3 inch disks are a development of the other two in that they have a rigid jacket that provides far more protection than is afforded by the standard sleeve.

Figure 5.6 is an illustration of a 3.5 inch floppy disk with the metal cover pulled back to expose the read/write slot. This would only normally occur when the disk is inserted into a drive. Opening the write-protect tab prevents data on the disk from being altered.

Floppy disks are inferior to hard disks in all respects, with slower data access times and data transfer rates, and lower levels of storage. Typical values for data access are up to 800 milliseconds, with data transfer at around 60 Kb per second. Storage on a floppy disk can vary between 90 Kb and 4 Mb unformatted, depending on the disk format. Despite these drawbacks, floppy disks are extremely popular since they offer a degree of portability and security that is not always possible with hard disks. For many business applications, however,

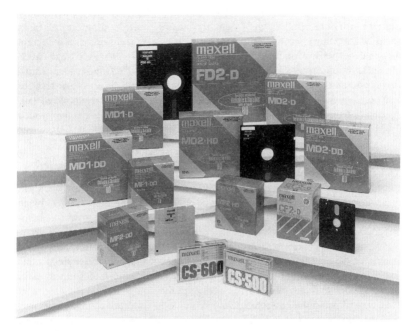

Fig. 5.5 Floppy disks – 8, 5¼, 3.5, and 3 inch

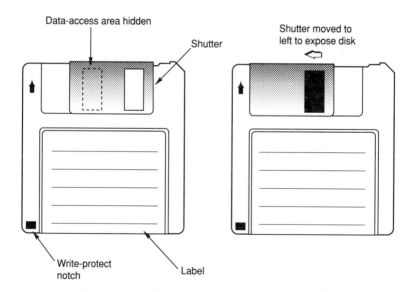

Fig. 5.6 Features of a 3.5 inch floppy disk

floppy disks are unable to offer the speed and storage capacity demanded by modern software applications. In many business microcomputers the main form of secondary storage will be a hard disk, with the floppy disk being a means of either loading new programs or copying data from the hard disk.

One form of floppy disk – the Floptical – is a hybrid of a floppy drive, a hard drive, and an optical disk. Based on the 3.5 inch format, it uses laser technology to place the tracks far closer together – 1245 tracks per inch compared with 45 to 135 t.p.i. for other floppy disks. This gives the Floptical a capacity of 20 Mb.

5.2.4 Uses and applications of magnetic disks

The various forms of magnetic disk have been developed to satisfy what seems to be a never-ending demand by computer users for more storage. As computers are applied to more and more areas of business and commerce, and existing installations are expanded, there is a continual movement towards high-capacity storage devices.

The main difference in secondary storage between micro, mini, and mainframe computers is in the amount of storage needed to meet the demands made upon the system. Mainframe computers are often found at the hub of large organisations and will be used for a large number of activities ranging from finance and personnel to research and production. In order to make information on all these activities rapidly available to users, on-line storage needs to be able to access and update vast amounts of data. The choice of storage device in this situation is thus limited to exchangeable, fixed, or fixed-head disks, according to what percentage of the data held needs to be on-line at any one time and how fast it needs to be accessed.

With the microcomputer, the choice of storage device will be similarly determined by the uses to which it is put. A business micro that is used to run the accounts of a small firm may not be able to contain all the data used on a single floppy disk, and so a 100 Mb Winchester disk may be needed. On the other hand, a micro destined for home use will probably be able to operate quite efficiently with only floppy disks for storage.

The choice of storage devices is thus determined by the applications for which the computer is to be used.

5.3 Magnetic tape

5.3.1 Introduction – features

Magnetic tape as used with computers is a plastic tape coated with a thin film of magnetic material. It can be supplied on an open reel or in a cassette or cartridge. As a means of storage, tape suffers from the big disadvantage that it is a 'serial access' medium since to access an item of data at the end of a tape it is necessary to reel past the rest of the tape first. For this reason, tape is not an efficient means of storage if the data it contains is to be accessed at random.

5.3.2 Reel tape

Magnetic tape held on reels is most often used with mini and mainframe computers either as a means of storing data that is to be input for processing or else for the 'backing-up' (taking a copy for security purposes) of information held on hard disks. The tape itself is 0.5 inch wide and is supplied in reels of 2400 feet in length which can store up to 100 Mb. The density with which data can be stored on tape is measured in bits per inch (b.p.i.), a typical tape storing 6250 b.p.i.

Data is stored as a series of bits across the width of the tape one character at a time, as shown in fig. 5.7. The 6250 b.p.i. figure given above will thus translate into 6250 characters of storage per inch of tape.

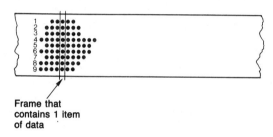

Fig. 5.7 How data is stored on 9-track tape

Each reel of tape will have a structure similar to that shown in fig. 5.8, with beginning-of-tape and end-of-tape markers, a header label, and a trailer label, with the data stored as a series of blocks. The header label contains information about the tape itself, including the file name, the creation date, and the date after which it can be overwritten. When a tape is loaded, the details on the header label are checked before processing begins, ensuring that the correct tape is loaded. After processing, the trailer label provides a cross-check that processing is complete.

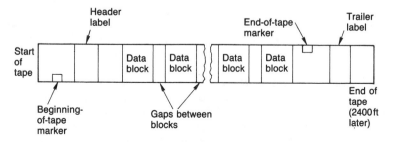

Fig. 5.8 Structure of data storage on a reel of tape

Data is read from and written to a tape one block at a time, and transfer rates in excess of 1 Mb per second are achievable.

5.3.3 Cassette and cartridge tape
Tape in cassettes or cartridges is often used to take copies or back-ups of files held on hard disks. The widespread use of Winchester disks on microcomputers has led to the rise of a number of devices that copy the data held on a disk on to a special tape cartridge. These devices are often referred to as 'tape streamers'. Audio cassettes are often used to store data and programs from home computers.

5.3.4 Uses and applications of magnetic tape
The way in which magnetic tape is used has changed as computer technology has improved to enable more data to be processed when it becomes available – termed *on-line* processing – rather than when it can be fitted into the processing schedule. This development towards on-line processing has meant that the role of magnetic tape has become more that of backing-up disk storage, storage of intermediate processing results, or storing results before printing, rather than that of storing master files of data. This is because magnetic tape is a compact form of storage, but being a serial-access medium it is unable to offer the low access times necessary for on-line processing.

5.4 Optical disks

5.4.1 Introduction – features
Optical disks store information in the form of a series of microscopic pits in the surface of a plastic disk. The information can be read from these pits with the use of a finely focused laser beam. The major advantage that optical storage has over magnetic storage is that it is possible to store data at a far higher density than is possible with magnetic media. By way of comparison, a high-density 5¼ inch floppy disk is able to store 1.2 Mb, whereas an optical disk of the same size can store around 500 Mb of data. It is this enormous storage potential that makes optical storage an attractive replacement for existing magnetic means of storing data.

In addition to its massive storage capacity, optical storage has other advantages over magnetic media. Since optical media are read by a laser beam, disks do not suffer from wear. Also, the disk surface is protected from damage by a clear plastic coating that enables disks to be handled, unlike magnetic media.

5.4.2 Read-only optical disks
The use of read-only disks, or CD–ROM (compact disk – read only memory), is based on the same technology as domestic audio compact-disk players. Data is recorded sequentially on a spiral track – unlike conventional magnetic disks, which have several hundred separate tracks – and typical storage values for a single disk are around 550 Mb.

The main feature of CD–ROM is that it is a permanent form of storage, and the data recorded cannot be altered. This permanence has meant that CD–ROM is being used as a means of distributing large amounts of information in a compact form. An early application of CD–ROM was by the Post Office, which compressed 23.5 million private and business addresses on to a single compact disk to assist with enquiries and address validation. Other applications include disks containing reference material on a wide range of subjects including financial trends, engineering, chemistry, books in print, and advertising, all of which are accessible with the use of a microcomputer.

Fig. 5.9 A CD–ROM disk

5.4.3 Write-once optical disks

Write-once disks were originally developed as a means of storing large volumes of information in a permanent form for use with mainframe or minicomputers. The write-once drives are able to both record and read data from an optical disk, with the disks varying in size between 5¼ and 12 inches. Since write-once technology offers a permanent record once the data is written, these disks are often called 'write-once read-many', or WORM (see fig. 5.10).

Write-once technology is not as standardised as CD–ROM, and disks are available in a number of sizes, with data being recorded on to the disks in a similar format to magnetic disks. The larger disks are able to store up to 4 Gb and can be combined into multiple-disk units to offer vast permanent storage potential, while the 5¼ inch disks are able to store up to 600 megabytes of information.

WORM technology is an alternative to keeping large volumes of printed output, and is a far more compact form of storage than COM (computer output on microfilm).

Fig. 5.10 A WORM disk and subsystem

5.4.4 Reusable optical disks
Reusable optical disks based on magnetic–optical technology can hold up to
128 Mb of data in the 3.5 inch format and offer access times of 40 milliseconds
and a data transfer rate of 625 Kb/s – figures that compare favourably with
magnetic-disk technology. To record data, a laser heats an alloy recording layer
so that it can be magnetised, storing data in much the same way as any conventional hard disk. Apart from cost, the main barrier to the widespread adoption
of magneto-optical (MO) disks as the main form of data storage is incompatibility between different manufacturers' drives.

5.4.5 Uses and applications of optical disks
The main benefit of optical-disk technology is the tremendous increase in
storage capability that it offers over any form of storage medium.

CD–ROM is able to store large amounts of written, graphic, or audio data,
making it an ideal means of distributing databases, catalogues, software, or
journals. Once the master has been produced, it is possible to mass-produce
CD–ROMs in the same way that audio CDs are manufactured. In the long term
this may make available a CD–ROM-based encyclopaedia, that can be read
using the home CD player, at audio-CD price levels.

WORM drives offer the possibility of making a permanent record that
cannot be erased. This is very attractive to organisations like banks and
building societies which need to keep permanent records of all the transactions
that affect their investor's accounts.

The most important long-term application of optical storage is the eventual
replacement of the existing magnetic storage media with reusable optical-disk
storage.

5.5 Personal storage media

The storage media that we have looked at so far are intended to provide computers with additional memory and, apart from the floppy disk, are generally not designed to be portable. The technology that has gone into magnetic storage has, however, been developed to provide forms of storage that can be easily transported. This transportable storage is designed to enable people to carry around large amounts of important personal information in the widely accepted credit-card format.

5.5.1 The smart card

The smart card, originally developed in France, is the same size and thickness as a credit card but contains a microprocessor and a memory capable of holding at least 8 Kb of data. The smart card may be used for financial transactions and could replace cheque guarantee cards and travellers cheques, as well as being used to pay for air and train tickets. The smart card holds details of the holder's account, credit limit, and previous buys on a chip whose contents are updated with each new transaction. Figure 5.11 shows the organisation and uses of one form of smart card.

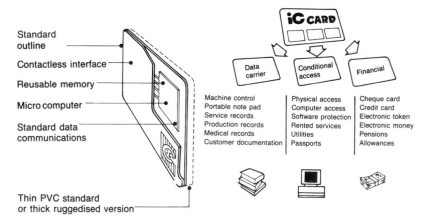

Fig. 5.11 The GEC intelligent contactless (iC) card – a form of smart card that can be accessed at up to 20mm from a read/write coupler

Other applications for smart cards include holding an individual's recent medical history, with details of current treatment and even images of X-rays.

5.6 Conclusion

As computer technology has developed, the capacity and speed of secondary storage has assumed a greater importance as information is increasingly processed as soon as it becomes available. To satisfy this demand for high-capacity fast-access storage, computer users have relied upon magnetic disk storage, with magnetic tape playing a supporting role. However, the development of optical storage technology, using lasers to read the data, seems likely to make this the major form of data storage in the long term.

The storage devices and media described above fall into three categories: reusable storage, write-once storage, and personal storage. The choice of storage medium is largely determined by the job it is being asked to do. Suppose you have been asked to recommend which medium should be used to store a set of stock records that will be accessed and updated continually by a large number of users. It is relatively easy to rule out personal and write-once storage for insufficient storage potential, and magnetic tape for being too slow because of its serial access. The choice can thus be narrowed down to some form of disk storage. Exactly which type of disk storage will depend on how much data is to be stored, and how fast it needs to be accessed. If several gigabytes of stock data need to be accessed continually (so that very low access times are necessary to avoid undue delays) then fixed-head magnetic storage may be the answer. If details of a few hundred items of stock are to be accessed by a single microcomputer, a 40 Mb hard disk may be adequate.

Table 5.1 shows the comparative characteristics of the storage media discussed in this unit.

Table 5.1 Characteristics of storage devices

Medium	Type of access	Capacity	Access time	Transfer rate
Exchangeable disk stack	Random	600 Mb	30 ms	>1 Mb/s
Fixed-head disks	Random	3 Gb	5 ms	>1 Mb/s
Floppy disks	Random	1.4 Mb	800 ms	60 Kb/s
Reel tape	Serial	100 Mb	Up to 60 s	1 Mb/s
CD-ROM	Random	550 Mb	1 s	170 Kb/s
WORM	Random	4 Gb	50 ms	1 Mb/s
MO disk	Random	128 Mb	40 ms	625 Kb/s

Since this information is intended to provide easy comparison between storage media, performance figures quoted are only approximate. Performance of all storage media is constantly being improved.

5.7 Glossary of terms

Floppy disk A flexible magnetic disk contained within a protective jacket.

Hard disk A rigid magnetic disk.

Fixed-head disk A hard disk that has a read/write head for every track, giving very fast access times.

EDS Exchangeable disk stack – an assembly of up to twelve hard magnetic disks that must be loaded into a special disk drive before the data it contains can be accessed.

Winchester disk A hard-disk assembly contained in a sealed environment.

Reel tape 0.5 inch magnetic tape that may be in reels containing up to 2400 feet.

Tape streamer A tape cartridge that is used to take back-up copies of the data held on hard disk.

CD–ROM Compact disk – read only memory. A reference storage medium based upon the domestic compact disk.

WORM Write-once read-many memory. A write-once optical disk.

Magneto-optical disk A reusable optical disk – sometimes referred to as an 'MO disk'.

Smart card A credit-card-sized system that contains a microprocessor and a memory.

Format The term used to refer to the combination of tracks and sectors, packing density, etc. used to store data on a magnetic disk.

Serial access A method of access in which it is necessary to work from the start of the file when searching for a particular record. Usually associated with magnetic tape. Also called *sequential access*.

Random access A method of access in which it is possible to access each record directly. Associated with magnetic disk storage.

Cylinder of information Information stored on the same track on each surface of a stack of disks.

Header label Information located at the start of a reel tape that includes the file name, the creation date, etc.

Trailer label Information located at the end of a reel tape that is used as a cross-check once processing is complete.

Access time The amount of time taken to locate a particular record on a tape or disk.

Data transfer rate The rate at which data can be read from the storage medium, usually expressed in bits per second (b.p.s.).

5.8 Exercises

1 With what type of computer system are the following storage devices likely to be found?

(a) Cassette tape
(b) WORM optical disk

(c) 10Mb Winchester disk
(d) 5¼ inch floppy disk
(e) EDS

2 What storage device would you recommend for the following?

(a) A company that uses its PC only for wordprocessing, producing at most 20 documents a week

(b) A company that wants to keep a permanent unerasable copy of all the documents it creates on its wordprocessing system, to be available on-line when needed

(c) A company that needs to store several gigabytes of customer account information that must be available in an on-line form in the shortest possible time

(d) A company that wants each of the stand-alone personal computers in its offices to be able to store more than is possible by using floppy disks

(e) A company that wants to take back-up copies of all its disk-based on-line data storage

3 Rank the following in order of storage capacity: EDS, WORM optical disk, 3.5 inch floppy disk, CD–ROM.

4 Compare and contrast the Winchester disk and the CD–ROM. Give three examples (for each one) of likely application areas.

5 (a) Describe the way in which records are organised, accessed, and updated on:

(i) Magnetic tape files,
(ii) Magnetic disk files.

(b) Give an illustration where each of the above media would be used for file storage, and provide a brief justification of your choice.

(AAT, Elements of information systems)

6 Define the functions of:

(a) Input devices
(b) Buffering
(c) On-line backing storage
(d) Off-line storage   (IDPM, Data processing I)

7 You are engaged in a discussion with your financial director concerning the merits of using magnetic tape as storage for your computerised stock-control system. You are against its inclusion.
Required:
Give three reasons why it may be advantageous to purchase a system using magnetic disks and three reasons why it may be disadvantageous to purchase a system using magnetic tape.

(ACCA, Numerical analysis and data processing (part))

8 Required:

    (i) Distinguish the main differences between floppy disks (sometimes known as diskettes) and Winchester (or fixed) disks.

    (ii) Describe with suitable illustrations what is meant by the cylinder concept as applied to magnetic disks.

(ACCA, Numerical analysis and data processing (part))

Case-study

Information Processing Services Ltd (IPS) was set up nearly five years ago to offer a computer-based information-processing service to the local business community. IPS has been something of a local success story, moving from offering data-input services to offering a range of sophisticated data-input and data-output services (see the case-studies at the end of Units 3 and 4).

The ambitious owner – Ms Belinda Carlisle – has once again decided that the market is ready for a new service, and she intends to offer a consultancy service for the local small business user. This service will advise on all aspects of choosing and using a microcomputer, and she has decided that, with your experience in the field of hardware research and selection, you are the ideal person to run this service.

The first project that IPS Consultancy Services has been asked to undertake is advising a local publisher on setting up its office information-processing system. Before this contract is finally agreed, however, the publisher wishes to see a sample of IPS's work, and it has been agreed that an analysis of computer storage needs will be completed.

An investigation has revealed that the publisher has the following information storage and retrieval needs:

(a) *Letters and correspondence* This information will need to be held individually by each of the office staff, who will each have anything up to 300 separate documents to store.

(b) *Contracts* More than 350 separate contracts, each of which are over five pages long, will be held by the managing director's personal secretary.

(c) *Records of all business transactions* Details of books sold, prices, and discounts to over 1000 bookshops in the UK and overseas; records of books sent out on inspection to 8000 educational establishments in the UK and of whether the books were paid for, returned, or recommended for class use and retained free of charge; records of royalty terms and payments for 300 authors.

Produce a report which analyses the overall storage needs of the publisher and makes a specific recommendation for each of the needs outlined above. In making your recommendations, be sure to include an explanation which justifies your choice.

UNIT 6

Software

6.1 Introduction

Software is the name given to the sets of instructions, or programs, that control the operation of computer hardware. There are two types of software: *systems software* and *applications software*. Systems software is primarily concerned with controlling the operation of computer hardware, whereas the term 'applications software' is applied to any program that has been written to do a particular job, such as the calculation of a company payroll.

In order to use applications software, it is necessary for some part of the systems software to be present in the computer's memory. The systems software translates the commands received from the applications software into instructions specific to the hardware concerned. Without the presence of systems software it would be impossible to run an applications program, since the applications software would be unable to communicate with the computer hardware.

A computer user wishing to run a payroll package may enter data that will be received by the applications software. If some calculations are required, say, the applications software will then react to this data by sending instructions to the systems software, which in turn relays them to the processor, to perform the calculations. Once the hardware has completed the calculations, a signal will be sent back, via the systems software, to the applications software indicating that the hardware is free to perform the next task. In this way, messages are sent back and forth between the hardware and the applications software, with the systems software acting like an interpreter.

The rest of this unit will look in more detail at systems and applications software.

6.2 Systems software

The set of programs that controls the operation of computer hardware is collectively termed 'systems software'. While applications software determines what work a computer will do, the systems software (sometimes also termed the *operating system*) controls how this work is carried out. It may be helpful to imagine the hardware of the computer as a hotel, with the applications software being the guests and the systems software being the hotel staff. The hotel is there for the benefit of the guests, whose wishes are carried out by the hotel staff who know how to make best use of the resources of the hotel to satisfy the guests. Hardware is similarly a host to applications software that sends out commands to systems software that has been specially written to make the best use of that particular computer. Systems software is thus a set of programs written for a particular processor that relieves the applications software of many routine tasks, just as the staff of a hotel look after the routine needs of their guests.

In the early days of computing, information processing was very labour-intensive, with computer operators being required to perform many tasks to enable a program to be run. At that time, computers were able to run one only program at a time, with data relating to each area of use (like the sales made that day, for example) being processed in batches of, say, a day's transactions. Systems software was developed in order to reduce the number of jobs the operators had to do, and to enable the jobs previously done by the operators to be done at the speed of the computer, rather than that of the operators. Since those early days, the developments made in systems software have increased processing capabilities while at the same time enabling computer operation to become increasingly automated. The facilities offered by modern systems software are examined below.

6.2.1 Systems-software features
The capabilities of many computer are partly determined by the power of the systems software. As the capabilities of systems software have increased, so has the terminology that describes it. The terms below all describe the various features of systems software.

DOS Disk operating system – describes a disk-based operating system in which relevant programs are loaded from disk as they are needed.

Single-user Describes a system which is able to deal with only one user at a time.

Single-tasking Describes a system which is able to run only one program at a time.

Multi-user Describes a system which is able to share resources among a number of different users.

Multi-tasking Describes a system which is able to execute a number of tasks simultaneously.

Multiprocessing The technique of running programs by using a number of processors.

Multiprogramming   The technique of appearing to run a number of programs simultaneously in a single-processor machine.

Time-sharing   The technique by which a computer is able to handle a number of users and peripherals by allocating processor time to each user or peripheral in turn.

Virtual memory   The partitioning of a computer's memory into separate sections for each of the programs to be run, with only the active parts of each program being in the memory at any one time.

As was mentioned above, the facilities that a computer system is able to offer to the user are determined partly by the systems software (or operating system) and partly by the hardware. The computers of the 1940s and early 1950s were limited in what they could do as much by the hardware as by their systems software. These computers tended to be only capable of dealing with one task at a time, and such machines came to be called *single-tasking* because of this.

As the hardware became more powerful, and the systems software more sophisticated, computers that were able to handle several tasks at a time were developed – the *multi-tasking* machines. *Multi-tasking* and *multiprogramming* systems rely on the time of a single processor being shared between competing tasks. This *time-sharing* operates by allocating a few microseconds of processor time to each user's task in rotation, executing a small portion of each program at every step. Since the machine can perform operations in a few millionths of a second, all users have the illusion that they have the computer's undivided attention. A more sophisticated system, called *multiprocessing*, is able to run a number of tasks simultaneously by sharing them among several processors within the computer.

In order to accommodate the increasing number of programs with their data within the central memory of a computer, the technique of *virtual memory* was developed. This involves the memory being partitioned into separate sections for each of the programs to be run, with only the active parts of each program being in the memory at any one time. Using this system the computer will load into memory only the parts of a program that it needs, leaving the rest of the program in the secondary storage. When another part of the program is needed, it is loaded from disk storage automatically by the operating system, replacing the program that is not needed. (Each part of such a program is called an 'overlay'.) The size of the central memory is thus no longer such a limiting factor on the number of users, because the operating system is able to provide a 'virtual memory' that includes the secondary storage.

The main features of the systems software that is typical for micro, mini, and mainframe computers are shown below:

(a) *Microcomputers*   Generally, single-user, single-tasking, disk-based operating system (DOS) – although single-user, multi-tasking systems software is available.

Limited to such single-user applications as wordprocessing, small business accounts, and financial planning.

(b) *Minicomputers* Able to support a number of users running a number of different programs, and thus will be multi-user and multi-tasking.

Larger applications, like multi-user accounts and stock control, may be run on the computer at the same time. May be used in larger organisations that have a need for multi-user, multi-tasking processing.

(c) *Mainframes* Able to support large numbers of users and programs, sharing the tasks out between a number of processors and employing virtual-memory techniques. Such machines may be called multi-user, multi-tasking, multiprocessing systems.

May be used in a large-scale-processing environment, with a large number of users running different programs, or for processing high volumes of transactions.

It should be noted that the above refers to 'typical' computers in each class, but there will in fact be some overlap in the facilities offered by each type of system.

6.2.2 Systems-software functions

Systems software controls the way in which the tasks associated with the operation of application programs take place. It is designed to be largely invisible to the user, performing the tasks needed to manage the computer system while remaining in the background.

The number of tasks that systems software will have to do will depend very much on the size of the hardware configuration that it has to manage. The systems software, or operating system, of a mainframe computer may have to look after the operation of the programs and the allocation of the data of several hundred users, a large number of disk storage units, several printers, and a large number of communication links. A microcomputer operating system, on the other hand, will need to deal with only a single program and its data, a couple of disk storage units, a VDU, a printer, and a single communication link. Since the typical microcomputer has single-tasking systems software, it will be able to handle only a single device at a time. It is obvious, then, that a mainframe computer's operating system will be a far larger and more complex piece of software than that needed to run a microcomputer. All such operating systems will, however, need to perform broadly similar tasks in order to manage their computer system efficiently.

Typically, systems software may include control of the following items:

(a) start-up of the computer;
(b) loading and unloading of programs;
(c) input and output operations, including the temporary storage of material to be printed – spooling (see section 4.5);
(d) allocation of central memory between users – if needed;
(e) sequencing of user programs – if needed;
(f) communications from remote terminals;
(g) time-sharing and on-line operations – if needed;

(h) user access and system security – if needed;
(i) logging of hardware errors.

It is usual for only a part of the systems software – called the *executive program* – to be present in the central memory at any one time. This program is able to handle the most heavily used tasks of program loading, data loading, and device control, and it can call on programs held in secondary storage to deal with the less commonly used tasks. In this way, efficient use is made of the central memory by keeping the least-used parts of systems software immediately accessible but on disk.

6.2.3 Graphical user interfaces
Traditionally the interface between the user and the computer was a blank screen containing only a command prompt like

    C:>

at the bottom left of the screen. In order to do anything useful, the user had to memorise a large number of commands. While this is fine for experienced users, occasional or novice users find it very unfriendly.

An alternative to this 'command-line' approach is a graphical user interface, or GUI. As the name suggests, this approach relies upon the use of graphical images or 'icons' on the screen, to depict programs, data, or commands. This type of interface is also sometimes termed a 'WIMPS' system (windows, icons, mouse, and pointer), and it is typified in the Apple Macintosh GUI, as shown in fig. 6.1.

An integral part of the GUI approach is the use of a mouse to point to and select icon or menu options, the mouse largely replacing the keyboard except for entering numbers or text (see section 3.2.2).

The Apple Macintosh family of microcomputers was designed from the outset to have a GUI, and the interface was based on research work undertaken by Xerox and Hewlett-Packard. The Macintosh GUI is actually an integrated component of the operating system, and this means that applications software like wordprocessors, spreadsheets, and databases all have a very consistent interface. This reinforces the user-friendliness of the Macintosh environment and is of great benefit to the user when moving between applications.

The IBM PC-compatible environment was originally built around the use of MS-DOS, a command-line operating system. Microsoft, which also created MS-DOS, has produced a PC-based GUI called 'Windows' which has many features similar to the Apple Macintosh Interface. Designed to operate on the Intel processor family (80286, 80386, 80486, etc.), some versions of Windows are multi-tasking and can run different applications in separate windows simultaneously.

While it is probable that most interfaces will move towards the use of a GUI, their slow speed (both to use and in operation) compared to command-line interfaces means that GUIs are unlikely to be adopted by all types of user.

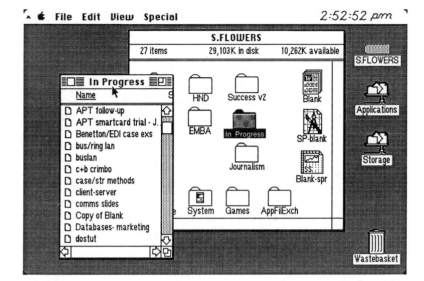

Fig. 6.1 A good example of the kinds of icons used in a GUI; in this case from an Apple Macintosh

6.2.4 Systems-software utilities

Utilities are programs that are designed to assist with the routine tasks of running a computer system. Examples of common utilities are programs to copy or delete files, rename files, and format new disks. Utilities like text editors (used to write and amend programs) and debuggers (used for finding errors in programs) may also be available to assist in the writing and debugging of computer programs.

6.3 Applications software

Applications software is any program that is designed to enable a computer to do a particular job. The range of application software is as wide and varied as the uses to which computers are put and includes accounts, financial planning, record-keeping, wordprocessing, and games. Applications software is sometimes also called 'applications packages', 'packaged software', or simply 'packages'. The terms come from the package of resources – including the program itself, training files, the user manual, and various utilities – that is supplied when the software is purchased.

Applications software cannot be used without first loading the systems software which will control the computer hardware. Applications software tends to be designed to run with one particular operating system. The difference in systems software between the Apple Macintosh and the IBM PS range is one reason why it is not generally possible to run Apple Macintosh applications software on the IBM PS range and vice versa.

Early business applications, and thus early applications software, tended to be in those areas that could justify the great expense of installing computer systems. Financial record-keeping and stock control were usually among the first applications to be cost-effective to computerise. As the cost of hardware fell and powerful mini and microcomputers were developed, however, it became economic to use computers in more and more business applications. The introduction of the first practical business microcomputer, the Apple II, in 1977 created a whole new market of computer users. This market was to some extent standardised by the introduction of the IBM PC in 1981, which created for the first time a mass market into which could be sold comparatively cheap standard software. This market was expanded dramatically by the introduction of cheap 'clones' of the IBM PC, manufactured in the Far East, which brought business computers within the reach of virtually every organisation.

The creation of the cheap microcomputer has led to a massive growth in the application of computers to a wide range of business problems. The software that has been written to help solve the most common of these problems is examined in more detail below.

6.3.1 Accounting software

Accounting software is designed to record financial transactions and to enable reports and summaries to be produced as required. The central importance of the accounting system to business operations meant that accounts was one of the first business applications of computers.

An accounting system is basically made up of the two main areas of sales and purchases, with each area being made up of a number of sections. The information relating to each area used to be stored in a special book called a 'ledger', so transactions are still said to be recorded in either the 'sales ledger' or the 'purchases ledger', even though these 'ledgers' may now take the form of computer files. Reports and summaries of transactions can be produced from both the sales and purchases ledgers, with the results being combined in a 'nominal ledger'. The nominal ledger contains information taken from the other ledgers and combines it to produce a statement of the profit or loss made. The nominal ledger is thus at the centre of the entire system of accounts. This basic system is illustrated in fig. 6.2.

Accounting software is usually produced in specialist modules that deal with one particular area like the sales ledger. This approach enables a business to add further modules as required, so that the accounting system can grow with the business. A list of typical modules and their functions is shown below.

(a) *Nominal ledger*   This is the core of the system. Information is extracted from each of the associated modules to produce profit-and-loss statements and balance sheets (showing assets and liabilities).

(b) *Sales ledger*   This records information on all sales made, keeping customer accounts up-to-date by entering invoices, credit notes, and payments made. It should also be able to produce reports such as an 'aged debtor'

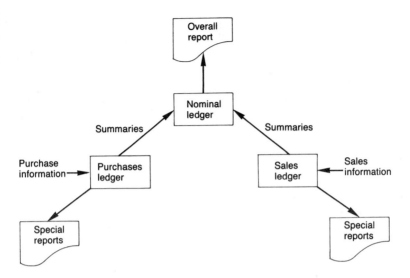

Fig. 6.2 A basic accounting information system

list showing the duration and size of amounts owed. It may also take care of invoice production and sales-order processing.

(c) *Purchases ledger* This performs the same functions as the sales ledger only for purchases and outstanding creditors. It will keep a record of all payments, and may print cheques and calculate discounts and VAT. It should also be able to take care of the progress of all purchase orders made – termed purchase-order processing.

(d) *Stock control* This records stock movements, noting purchase and selling prices and discounts received. It should keep a check on stock levels and produce information on the value and turnover of stocks. It may be linked to the sales ledger via invoicing, and to the purchases ledger via purchase-order processing.

(e) *Payroll* This will allow the calculation of pay on an hourly, weekly, or monthly basis, keeping a record of all paid staff. Calculations of PAYE, National Insurance payments, and all other deductions should be made automatically. Pay-slips should also be printed. It may be linked to the nominal ledger.

An *integrated* accounting system will be able to share information between modules, enabling overall reports and summaries of transactions to be produced. Such a system is shown in fig. 6.3.

All accounting systems will incorporate a method of tracing individual transactions from their original entry to their final destination – termed an *audit trail*. This facility is needed to enable the records to be checked and to ensure that all transactions have been processed correctly.

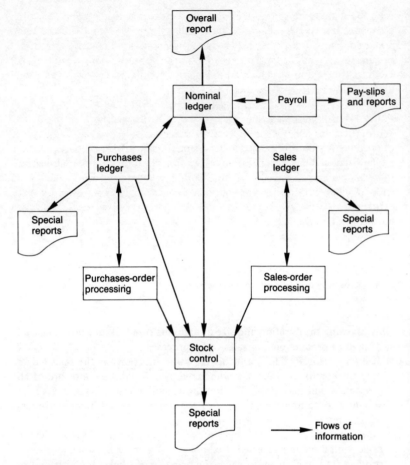

Fig. 6.3 An integrated accounting information system

The size and complexity of an accounting system should reflect the size and complexity of the business whose information it contains.

A small business will probably be able to operate efficiently using a few standard accounting modules that will run on a single-user microcomputer (if, indeed, it needs a computer at all).

A medium-sized company will need to process a far higher volume of transactions and may use a minicomputer to run a standard accounting system that has been customised to fit the business's operations. Such a system may allow a number of users to use the program at the same time, making it a multi-user program.

A large corporation may divide its accounting system to enable each part of the company to operate independently, but also feed information back to the centralised accounting system. Each division may run its operation on a mini-computer that is able to communicate and share information with the main-frame computer at head office. The multi-user software for such a system will be capable of handling large numbers of transactions, provide extensive report facilities, be able to consolidate information from each division, and would almost certainly have to be specially written.

6.3.2 Wordprocessing

Wordprocessing (WP) is the application of computer technology to the typing of documents. Wordprocessing differs from traditional text-preparation using a typewriter in that wordprocessed text can be stored and reused. This means that changes can be made to the text without it being necessary to retype an entire document, as with a typewriter. Documents created on a wordprocessor exist only in the computer's memory until they are either saved to disk or printed out, as illustrated in fig. 6.4.

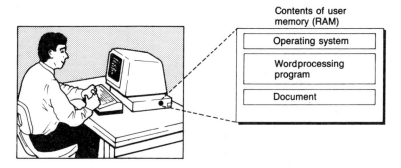

Fig. 6.4 Contents of memory in a wordprocessing system

The creation of text in the computer's memory, rather than directly on to paper, enables wordprocessing to offer a number of facilities that are not available with a typewriter. In addition to the ability to store and retrieve text, it is possible to move blocks of text to different positions in the same document, insert and delete lines, alter the layout, and check for errors before printing.

The use of the wordprocessor has had a great effect upon the way in which documents are produced in business. The need to retype documents has now largely disappeared, and it has become possible to assemble letters from a number of standard paragraphs stored on disk. This facility is particularly useful in the preparation of long documents like contracts and other legal documents, which are often a combination of standard paragraphs.

The ability to merge a list of names and addresses with a standard letter – termed a 'mail merge' – enables a circular letter to be personalised and has led to a growth in direct-mail advertising. The way in which a mail merge works is shown in fig. 6.5. The standard letter is to be sent to a number of people, and so the name, address, and salutation are left blank. The list of names and

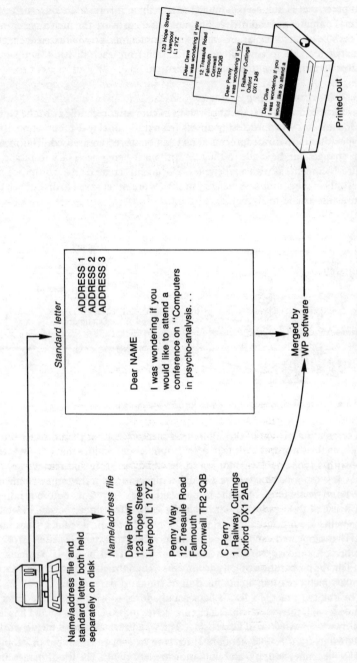

Fig. 6.5 Producing a mail-merge letter by combining a list of names and addresses with a standard letter format

addresses of those who will receive the letter (sometimes called a database file) has been created separately and will be used to personalise the standard letter. This is done by the mail-merge program which extracts the name and address of each person on the list, placing them into the spaces provided as each letter is printed.

By reducing the amount of repetitive work involved in document preparation, use of a wordprocessor has enabled increases in typing productivity of over 200%. It has been estimated that the text in some 70% of all word-processed documents sent out from sales offices had been used previously, with only 30% of documents being newly created.

The following are a number of facilities that are offered by wordprocessors:

Store text   Store text for later retrieval, enabling it to be recalled, amended, and reused.

Move text   Blocks of text can be moved to different positions in the same document, or else moved to another document.

Search and replace   Locates a word or phrase and exchanges it with an alternative word or phrase.

Spelling checker   Automatically checks text for misspellings.

Thesaurus   Enables the user to access an on-line thesaurus which provides a list of alternative words with similar meanings.

Communications   Enables documents to be sent to one or more locations simultaneously, using an electronic-mail facility.

The areas of work in which a wordprocessor can be used may be divided into five main categories:

(a) The preparation of documents like newspaper articles and minutes of meetings that may need many alterations before printing, thus avoiding retyping. (This book was typed on a wordprocessor that has many of the features mentioned above.)
(b) The production of standard letters – like circulars, bills, and final demands – that can be 'merged' with a list of names to produce personalised correspondence.
(c) Assembling documents like contracts and job quotes from a number of standard paragraphs.
(d) The regular updating and sorting of internal telephone directories, product catalogues, and procedures manuals.
(e) The use of electronic-mail facilities like Telecom Gold to send documents over the telephone network (see Unit 8).

6.3.3 Desk-top publishing

Desk-top publishing (DTP) refers to the use of a personal computer to produce documents that combine text with pictures and look as if they have been professionally typeset and made-up (like the pages of this book).

DTP is one aspect of what is known as 'electronic publishing' – that is, the use of computer systems to produce typeset and laid-out pages ready for printing. Electronic publishing ranges from systems such as those used by the national newspapers, with their customised hardware and software, to the ready-made systems that will run on a standard microcomputer. DTP is at the ready-made end of the market, and it attempts to offer some of the facilities of the professional electronic publishing systems within a program that will run on a desk-top microcomputer – hence its name.

Many organisations spend a lot of time and money creating and publishing documents like management reports, product manuals, forms, and newsletters. Wordprocessing enables the text contained in these documents to be produced quickly and easily without the need for retyping, but with only limited page-design features. A DTP system enables the user to be more creative and to integrate text, data, graphics, and pictures within the same document. This is not to say that a DTP system will give you the skill of the professional typesetter: rather it provides the user with far more control over the layout of a document than was previously possible.

Among other facilities, these programs enable the user to:

(a) import text produced on a wordprocessor and rearrange it in one or more columns (as in a newspaper);
(b) select the font (typeface) or fonts in which the text will be printed, and alter the size of text to produce headings or headlines (once again, as in a newspaper);
(c) import and combine pictures with the text – altering their size or cropping them if necessary;
(d) introduce style features like tinting and format lines for emphasis;
(e) move text and pictures to a desired position;
(f) edit the text;
(g) display one or more finished pages – complete with pictures – exactly as they will be printed out (a full WYSIWYG – or 'what you see is what you get' – display).

A document produced by a DTP system is shown in fig. 6.6.

A DTP system is more than just a program, however, and to be successful it requires a powerful microcomputer linked to a number of additional devices to handle input, output, and storage. To give an idea of what is needed we will now look at the peripherals that may be used as part of a DTP system.

Input devices　An *image scanner* (section 3.7.2) converts the text and graphic images into a digital form that can be understood and handled by a computer. A scanner can be used to capture an image that is to be incorporated into a DTP document. In addition to capturing images, some scanners are able to act as optical character readers (OCR) by recognising each letter in a piece of text and converting it into ASCII code. The scanner may then be used to convert either pictures or text into a digital form that can be handled by a DTP system.

A *video scanner* (section 3.7.3) uses the picture from a video camera to

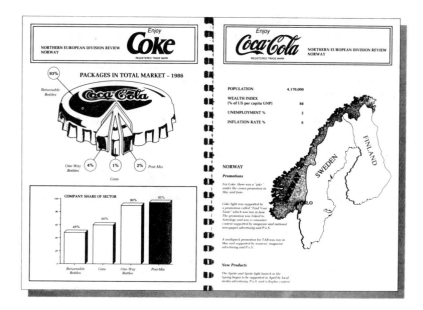

Fig. 6.6 Part of a Coca-Cola marketing newsletter produced on an Apple DTP system, including a digitised version of the company's tightly specified trade mark. ('Coca-Cola' and 'Coke' are registered trade marks of the Coca-Cola company.)

capture colour images, offering a higher resolution than is available with an image scanner. Once the picture has been captured, it can be manipulated in the same way as graphs, diagrams, and text, and incorporated into a DTP document.

A *graphics pad* or graphics tablet (section 3.7.1) is another type of device that converts an image into digital form, but in this case it enables the image to be input freehand using a stylus or by 'tracing' with a stylus or cursor. Once a free-hand drawing has been input to a computer, it is possible to use a graphics package to modify the image before it is incorporated into a DTP document.

Output devices A *large high-resolution visual display unit* (section 4.2.1) is an essential part of a good DTP system since it enables the user to see a full 8.5 × 11 inch page on a single screen. This makes editing and layout far easier because it becomes possible to see the whole page at once. Some large 19 inch screens enable two full-size pages to be displayed at the same time, allowing a two-page spread to be viewed as it will appear in the finished document. The resolution of a display will depend upon the number of pixels that are used, with a resolution of 1024 × 1024 pixels providing a very sharp image.

A *laser printer* (section 4.3.1(d)) is the essential output for any DTP system, since no other form of printer is able to offer the resolution necessary to produce output of text and pictures of the required clarity. The majority of laser printers that are used with small computer systems can print with a resolution of 300d.p.i. (in a 300 × 300 matrix) and this will produce a result that is good enough for some kinds of publicity material. This resolution is, however, a long way from the professional typesetting quality (ranging from 1270d.p.i. to 2540d.p.i.) needed to produce high-quality brochures and advertisements.

Many laser printers will contain their own powerful microprocessor, to control the layout of the finished result, and a large amount of RAM that acts as a buffer when a DTP document comes to be printed.

A typical DTP system is shown in fig6.7.

Fig. 6.7 An Apple DTP system in which two Macintosh microcomputers share a laser printer

Using a DTP system   The creation of a DTP document might proceed along the following lines:

1 The typeface in which the text is to be printed is selected and the text is keyed in. Left and right margins are specified, and the text is set into one or more columns (as in a newspaper). Mistakes are edited and the text is stored.
2 The final appearance of the document is determined, with the relative positions of the headings, text, and pictures being adjusted to give the best result. Features like boxes around the text, and lines or shading to break up the page, might be added at this point. The page layout can now be stored.
3 Each picture to be included in the document will now be read into the computer's memory using a scanner.
4 The picture is combined with the page layout and text and its size and position are adjusted until the best result is obtained. It is now possible to proof read the document and make any final alterations.
5 The document can now be printed out on a laser printer.

Steps from this process are illustrated in fig.6.8.

Case-study – *Legal and General Investment Management*
Legal and General Investment Management (LGIM) is one of the largest investment management companies in the UK. As a substantially autonomous

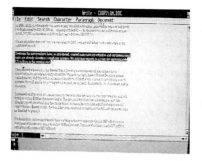

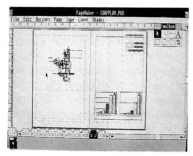

1. The text is typed in and saved to disk.

2. Pictures that have been captured using an image scanner are arranged on the page layout.

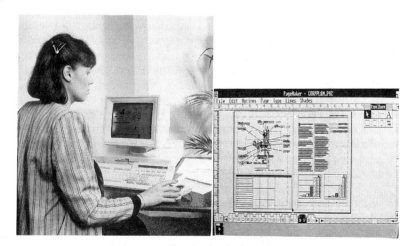

3. The text is now included into the document and final adjustments are made before the document is saved to disk.

4. The finished document may now be printed using a high-quality laser printer.

Fig. 6.8 Stages in producing a document using a DTP system

member of the Legal and General Group plc, it manages investments of over £12000 million for a variety of clients including pension funds, charities, private investors, and other group subsidiaries.

The variety of documents to be produced within the company is extensive, ranging from unit price information sheets for investors to quarterly and annual reports for major clients, frequently with very short print runs. Before it introduced a desk-top publishing system, LGIM produced most of its documents using wordprocessors and photocopiers, with the more complex jobs being sent out for typesetting. The document production cycle was around three weeks, and material could only be practically updated on a monthly basis. With the use of the DTP system, amendments can now be made immediately and the up-to-date document can be produced within a matter of minutes.

The introduction of an in-house DTP system has established a consistently high quality of presentation, with content, layout, fonts, and graphics created and merged by the system. This combination of numbers, text, and graphics enables the information held on the document to be understood rapidly, aiding communication between company and client.

The DTP system used by LGIM is a networked departmental publishing system based on Rank Xerox office systems technology running Viewpoint software. The hardware consists of four Xerox multi-function workstations, six wordprocessors, a shared hard disk (file server), a shared communications link (comms server), and a laser printer, all of which are linked by an XNS (Xerox Network Systems) local area network. The system is also linked to the LGIM mainframe computer in Surrey from which data can be transferred, displayed and formatted at the workstations, and incorporated in relevant documents. The heart of this system is the integrated multi-tasking Xerox Viewpoint electronic publishing software. This incorporates extensive features for the creation, design, and formatting of both text and graphics into documents.

6.3.4 The spreadsheet

The spreadsheet is a general-purpose calculation program. The name 'spreadsheet' is taken from the term applied to the large sheet of paper used by accountants in preparing accounts. The spreadsheet package has been called a software 'tool' since the calculation facilities offered can be applied to virtually any problem.

All spreadsheets operate on the same principles and are made up of rows (1,2,3,...) and columns (A,B,C,...), like the one illustrated in fig. 6.9. Each location or 'cell' within a spreadsheet is given an address based on its co-ordinates. Thus A4 is the co-ordinate of row 4 in column A, and Z99 is the co-ordinate of row 99 in column Z.

Most spreadsheets will have far more than 26 columns (A to Z) and 100 rows (1 to 100) – Lotus 123, a widely used spreadsheet, offers 8192 rows and 256 columns, giving over 2 million cells! Of course, with so many cells it is only possible to see a screenful of data at a time, the screen acting as a 'window' through which you can view only a portion of your spreadsheet.

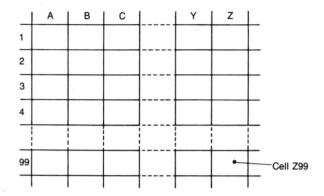

Fig. 6.9 Spreadsheet structure, showing rows and columns

It is usual to refer to the contents of a spreadsheet by the cell locations – for example, on the spreadsheet in fig. 6.10, Qtr 1 Sales is in cell B9, and Qtr 4 Shrinkage is in cell E12. All calculations are performed on the cell addresses, so that if you want to alter the figures in the cells the actual arithmetic process is not affected, although the answer is of course different. This feature of automatically recalculating results as the figures are changed makes the spreadsheet very useful for forward planning. In the example in fig. 6.10, the question 'What would happen to gross profit if we increased discounts by 20%?' could be answered by amending the Discounts amount and then letting the spreadsheet program recalculate the Gross Profit amount.

For example, the Gross Profit in B13 would be calculated as follows:

B13 = B9 − SUM (B10 ... B12)

This can be read as follows:

> The contents of cell B13 are equal to the contents of cell B9 minus the sum of the contents of cells B10, B11, and B12.

To perform the same calculation for columns C, D, and E the spreadsheet allows you to copy the formula to these columns, automatically changing all the column B references to column C, D, and E references.

Just as a wordprocessed document exists only in the computer's memory until it is either printed out or saved to disk, so too does a spreadsheet. The facilities of inserting and deleting, moving, copying, and merging text are paralleled in the spreadsheet's ability to do similar things with numbers. A list of the main facilities offered by most spreadsheets is given below:

Store formulae Stores spreadsheet formulae, numbers, and text headings, enabling them to be recalled, amended, and reused.

Copy formulae Formulae expressing the relationships between a set of numbers can be copied with updated cell references.

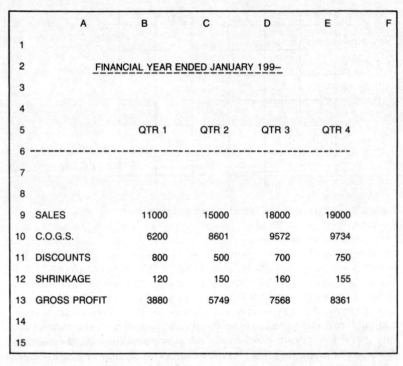

	A	B	C	D	E	F
1						
2		FINANCIAL YEAR ENDED JANUARY 199–				
3						
4						
5		QTR 1	QTR 2	QTR 3	QTR 4	
6	---					
7						
8						
9	SALES	11000	15000	18000	19000	
10	C.O.G.S.	6200	8601	9572	9734	
11	DISCOUNTS	800	500	700	750	
12	SHRINKAGE	120	150	160	155	
13	GROSS PROFIT	3880	5749	7568	8361	
14						
15						

Fig. 6.10 A sample spreadsheet. (Note: C.O.G.S. = cost of goods sold; shrinkage = loss of stock through breakages and theft.)

Format numbers The way in which numbers are shown can be altered to the required precision (number of decimal places) or format (currency, percentage, etc.).

Graphs Most spreadsheets enable the user to produce a wide range of graphs and diagrams from the data held in the spreadsheet.

Store information Some spreadsheets enable lists of names and addresses and other data (sometimes called a *database*) to be stored, using the rows and columns to hold the data.

Special functions These are some of the functions available:
mathematical – logs, pi, square roots, rounding
statistical – average, standard deviation, sum of values, variance
financial functions – IRR (internal rate of return), NPV (net present value)

A spreadsheet can be used for a wide variety of applications, such as

(a) forecasting likely return on investments,
(b) comparison of buying versus leasing,

(c) cash-flow analysis,
(d) break-even analysis,
(e) depreciation schedules,
(f) conversion tables,
(g) customer database,
(h) performance analysis,
(i) costing and presentation of tenders.

6.3.5 The database

A database is a collection of records that have been organised to enable them to be easily retrieved. A telephone directory is an example of a database that contains information about telephone subscribers organised alphabetically to enable a particular number to be found easily. If a telephone directory is not available, it is possible to ask the Directory Enquiry service to find a particular number for you. The Directory Enquiry service has access to a telephone directory, or database, that is stored on a disk and is managed by a program called a *database management system* (DBMS). The DBMS acts as a sort of filing clerk that not only systematically organises information but also answers enquiries and will help find the number you are looking for.

A telephone directory, like any other database, is a *file* containing *records* of each telephone subscriber, with a number of items of information (name, address, and telephone number) being held in *fields*. This is illustrated in fig. 6.11. The file contains many records, each of which is made up of a number of fields. Although the files, records, and fields are stored differently in a computer system, the structure is the same. The database of telephone subscribers will be the same whether it printed as a directory for general use or else stored on a disk and searched with the help of a DBMS.

Databases are so much a part of our everyday life that we tend to take their existence for granted. Ceefax, Oracle, 4-Tel, and Prestel are all highly visible examples of databases, as is your local public reference library. Many organisations maintain a database on their employees, called a personnel file, and another database containing information about their customers, while many

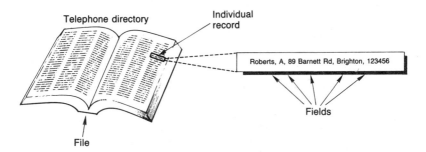

Fig. 6.11 The parts of a typical non-computerised database – a telephone directory

of us will maintain a database of the addresses and telephone numbers of our friends.

The main strength of a computerised database is the ease with which information can be obtained from it. To illustrate this, assume that you have lost your address book and have asked Directory Enquiries to find the telephone number of your friend Andrew Roberts who lives in Barnett Road in Brighton. The operator knows that each record in the database of subscribers is made up of the following fields:

Surname / Initials / Street / Town / Telephone number

The operator might ask the DBMS to show the records of all the Roberts in the database, with the instruction:

Surname = Roberts

The DBMS searches the database and tells the operator that there are 243 people who have this name on file. The operator decides to narrow this down by entering another search criterion:

Surname = Roberts   AND   Town = Brighton

(This means 'Show all subscribers who have the surname Roberts and who also live in Brighton'.)

This still produces 54 subscribers, and so another criterion is added:

Surname = Roberts   AND   Town = Brighton   AND   Initials = A

(This means 'Show all subscribers who have the surname Roberts, and who also live in Brighton, and who also have the initial A'.)

This produces six subscribers, few enough to be displayed on the screen so that the correct record can be found by a brief visual search.

This process of searching a database by entering one criterion after another illustrates the way in which the DBMS can reduce the hard work of searching a file of information. In reality, an experienced database user will often enter several search criteria at the start to speed up the searching process. A list of the facilities offered by database software is shown below.

Record search   Records may be located and displayed by referring to the contents of one or more fields, as in the above example.

Indexes   As you add records to a database, it automatically adds the record to one or more indexes. Just as in the Yellow Pages there is an alphabetical list of companies by type, a DBMS may set up a separate index sorting each field alphabetically.

Report generation   In a simple package this will mean the ability to merge the names and addresses held in the database with a standard letter. More complex programs will enable reports to be printed based on the information held in the database.

Maths functions Some databases allow the production of invoices or purchase-order forms.

Single-/multi-file A single-file database allows you to work on only one file at a time, whereas a multi-file DBMS means that more than one file can be accessed at once and that links may be set up between records in different files (for example, a personnel file and a payroll file).

Programmable The most sophisticated database is one that can be programmed to perform certain regular operations, like the printing of weekly reports.

Applications of databases include:

(a) estate agents – matching houses and clients,
(b) travel agents – holiday availability,
(c) general – suppliers/purchasers listing,
(d) computer dating – matching couples,
(e) clubs and societies – membership lists,
(f) general – personnel records,
(g) mail-order companies – customer listings,
(h) Prestel – general business,
(i) Ceefax/Oracle – general,
(j) police – criminal records,
(k) Inland Revenue – tax records,
(l) legal database containing recent decisions.

Public databases The public database of yesteryear was epitomised by the local reference library, Companies House, or the Public Record Office, each of which would provide certain types of information – eventually. The public databases of today are held on mainframe computers and are often called 'on-line information services' or 'value-added network systems' (VANS). There are a large number of such services, providing information on a wide range of subjects including company details, stock-market prices, foreign exchange and commodity markets, and economic and financial matters. The list below covers only a few of the many on-line information services available.

(a) *Pergamon Infoline* A British service that offers around 55 databases on a wide range of subjects, including all British registered companies, worldwide patents, business news, and industrial market location. All the databases can be searched using a standard set of commands.
(b) *Nexis* An American database that contains the full text of 175 newspapers, magazines, and newsletters from around the world. Searched by typing in a key word or words, it is possible to locate references in any part of the database.
(c) *Dunsprint* A British service which contains information on the ownership, accounts, and financial standing of all UK companies.

(d) *Quotron*   An American service that offers up-to-date prices and quotations for equities, bonds, options, and commodities markets on stock exchanges in North America, Europe, and Asia.

6.3.6 Other types of applications software

All applications software can be categorised as either general-purpose or specialist. General-purpose software is designed to be used by a wide variety of businesses, whereas specialist software is intended to be of use to only one particular type of business.

The range of applications to which computers are put is constantly increasing as the costs of computer power continue to fall, leading to a continual growth in the range of applications software. General-purpose applications software like wordprocessing, spreadsheets, and databases has been sold in millions, whereas the more specialist software is more likely to be sold in hundreds. The result of this is that the price of specialist software tends to be high relative to the price of general-purpose software, especially if it has to be custom-written for a large-scale application.

The most popular general-purpose applications software tends to be the wordprocessor, spreadsheet, and database. The 'integrated package' is a single program that contains all three of these applications – this has the advantage of enabling data to be shared easily between each of the areas and of being relatively easy to learn by using a set of commands that operate in a standard way.

Accounts, wordprocessing, spreadsheet, and database packages can be used by any type of business. Other types of general-purpose software and examples of specialist software are examined below.

(a) *General purpose*   Examples include:

   (i) *Graphics*   Software designed to enable graphic images to be created using spreadsheet data, or else a graphics pad.
   (ii) *CAD*   Computer-aided-design software that enables on-screen design.
   (iii) *Communications*   Designed to assist in the setting up of computer communication links over the telephone system.

(b) *Specialist*   Examples include:

   (i) *Estate agent*   Modular software designed to take care of the many specialist aspects of an estate agent's business operation, such as property management and document preparation.
   (ii) *Building*   A system to assist in the production of estimates, invoices, and accounts using building-trade procedures.
   (iii) *Solicitor*   Software that will produce standard letters and contracts and keep track of monies involved in property conveyancing.

These are only a few examples from the constantly increasing number of applications to which computers are being applied. To find more examples, look through the advertisements in any business computing magazine.

6.4 Glossary of terms

Systems software Programs that control the operation of computer hardware. Systems software is usually made up of programs written for a particular processor to relieve the applications software of routine hardware-control tasks and to provide operators with a number of system-management utilities.

Operating system Another name for systems software.

Time-sharing A systems-software feature enabling the processor to handle a number of users and peripherals by allocating time to each task or peripheral in turn – a prerequisite of most large business information-processing systems.

Single-user Systems software designed to enable the processor to handle only one user.

Multi-user Systems software which enables the processor to be able to deal with a number of users – commonly associated with time-sharing.

Utility programs Software designed to assist the operator to perform routine tasks like copying files and making back-up copies of disks.

Executive program That part of systems software that controls the operation of the computer and is resident in the central memory.

GUI Graphical user interface – a mouse-driven method of using software that involves screen-based windows and icons to operate the software.

Applications software Programs that are designed to enable the computer to do a particular job. They are sometimes also called 'applications packages', 'packaged software', or simply 'packages'.

Accounting software Accounting software is designed to record financial transactions. An accounting system is basically made up of the two main areas of sales and purchases, with each area being made up of a number of sections. Reports and summaries of transactions can be produced from both the sales and purchases ledgers, with the results being combined in a 'nominal ledger'.

Wordprocessing Wordprocessing is the application of computer technology to the typing of documents. Wordprocessing allows text to be stored and reused, enabling changes to be made to the text without it being necessary to retype an entire document.

Mail merge The ability to merge a list of names and addresses with a standard letter, enabling standard letters to be personalised.

Desk-top publishing The use of specialist software on personal computers to produce documents that combine text with pictures and look as though they have been professionally typeset and pasted-up.

Spreadsheet A general-purpose calculation program in which data and labels are entered in cells, with all operations being performed on the contents of the cells. May be applied to virtually any calculation problem.

Cell An individual location in a spreadsheet. Each cell is referred to by its row and column co-ordinates.

Database A collection of records that have been organised to enable information in them to be easily retrieved.

Database management system (DBMS) A program that not only systematically organises information but also answers enquiries and will help find particular records in a database.

File A collection of individual records, as in a personnel file.

Record A component of a file, containing a number of fields.

Field An area within a record that may contain a single item of information, like a name, address, or phone number.

Search criterion A requirement that enables a DBMS to retrieve desired records from the database.

Integrated package Applications software that is made up of several general-purpose programs, usually wordprocessing, database, and spreadsheet. It provides for easy data transfer between areas.

'I just worry and ply the computer with "what if" enquiries'

6.5 Exercises

1 (a) Define and explain the difference between the terms 'application package' and 'general-purpose package' assuming that dBase II and Visicalc are examples of the latter.

(b) Give an example of the use of an 'application package' and an example of the use of a 'general-purpose package'. In each case list three benefits of using package software for the purpose.

(AAT, Elements of information systems (pilot paper))
[Note: dBase II is a database package, and Visicalc is a spreadsheet.]

2 Explain the function and principal features of the spreadsheet application package. (AAT, Analysis and design of information systems)

3 Your personnel department has recently purchased a microcomputer and a data management package (such as Cardbox) for use in records management.

(a) Identify the typical features offered by such a package.
(b) Explain the steps that would need to be taken when implementing a personnel records system using such a package.
(c) What information could the department expect from such a system?

(AAT, Elements of information systems)

4 Describe the components of a typical microcomputer as used by a small business under the following headings:

(a) Central processing unit
(b) Data storage
(c) Input/output
(d) Operating system (AAT, Elements of information systems)

5 Your manager is keen to introduce a departmental wordprocessor for use in document preparation.

(a) Identify the factors which should be considered when selecting a suitable wordprocessor.
(b) Give five examples which illustrate the potential uses of a wordprocessor.
(AAT, Elements of information systems)

6 (a) List and briefly describe the advantages of:

(i) an 'applications package'
(ii) a 'tailored or purpose-written' system

(b) Identify eight factors which should be considered in the selection of an applications package. (ACCA, Systems analysis and design)

7 (a) Databases and spreadsheets are associated with many microcomputer applications in the world of business and commerce.
Required:

(i) Explain the purpose of a database and give an example of its use.
(ii) Explain the purpose of a spreadsheet and give an example of its use.

(ACCA, Numerical analysis and data processing (part))

8 Discuss the relationships between operating system, application program, and data.   (IDPM, Data processing I)

9 Prepare a checklist of questions to be asked when considering the purchase of a stand-alone wordprocessor for a company manufacturing ladies' fashion wear.   (LCCI, Information processing)

10 Define *four* types of software you associate with computer systems.
                                              (IDPM, Data processing I)

11 The managing director of your company has just attended a seminar on computers and data processing during which he heard a brief reference to 'spreadsheets' and 'spreadsheet packages'. On his return he has asked you, as an accountant attached to the DP department, to explain these terms.
    You are required to describe:

   (a) spreadsheets and spreadsheet packages;
   (b) the typical facilities provided by a spreadsheet package;
   (c) an accounting application of such a package.

        (CIMA, Management information systems and data processing)

12 (a) Distinguish between *software* and *hardware* and indicate the categories of software in common use.
   (b) Describe the functions of a typical *operating system*.

                              (CBSI, Management services (part))

Case-study 1

You work for Brightmouth Computer Consultants as an assistant computer consultant. BCC has been approached by Pelham Fashions, a rapidly-growing local fashion company, to assist in the selection of a range of computer equipment. You have been placed in charge of the contract, as the senior consultant originally in charge of the project has left your company. Before she left, however, she visited Pelham Fashions and made the following notes on what is required:

General Pelham Fashions want to buy one personal computer with a colour monitor that will initially be used for the preparation of letters and reports, but which will also be used for designing garments in the near future.

Software Pelham Fashions will require a wordprocessing package, and also a copy of the latest version of the disk operating system (DOS).

Input In addition to general document preparation. Pelham Fashions will also need a device to enable the freehand input of designs. There is also a large volume of existing typewritten documents that need to be put on to the system – Pelham Fashions wish to do this without having to rekey it all in.

Output A large amount of high-quality documents, like letters to clients, will need to be produced on the new system. They also need to be able to produce documents for internal use (stock summaries etc.) which only need to be of low quality. Once the CAD system is operational, there will be a need to produce the A1-size drawings it generates.

Storage Pelham Fashions wish to be able to store all of their programs and data on the same disk. They also need to be advised on the security procedures to be taken to protect their data in the event of the computer system breaking down.

You should prepare a report to be sent to Pelham Fashions which should contain your recommendations for the personal computer and other devices needed to satisfy the company's needs. (Make sure that you include the cost of each device you recommend.)

Notes

(a) Your report should be headed as follows:

REPORT ON COMPUTER SYSTEM FOR PELHAM FASHIONS

(b) The report may be laid out using the above headings.
(c) At the end of the report, type the date and your name.
(d) Current prices may be obtained from local computer dealers, electrical shops, or magazines.

Case-study 2

IPS Consultancy Services is a division of Information Processing Services Ltd, a company that offers a range of specialist data input and output services to the local business community.

IPS has been approached by a local financial-services company that has heard about DTP and feels that it could make use of it. Before buying, however, it has approached IPS Consultancy Services for answers to the following questions:

(a) We have heard a lot about DTP, but much of what we have heard has been very 'woolly'. Would you be so kind as to provide us with a paragraph that explains *exactly* what DTP is, please?
(b) We currently produce a lot of documents using either typewriters or word-processors. From the following list of written communication needs, please identify which would be best done on a typewriter, a wordprocessor, or a DTP system:

   (i) short letters to clients (that may be on a variety of subjects);
  (ii) the company newsletter (usually a mixture of pictures and news);
 (iii) customer presentations (long lists of figures that would be better if they were shown in graphical form);

(iv) large-scale personalised mailings to prospective and existing customers;

(v) production of contracts from a number of standard paragraphs;

(vi) creation of short memoranda on a variety of subjects.

(c) If we wished to be able to use a DTP system to create documents with text and graphics in them, could you produce a list (with guide prices) of the hardware and software that we would need to buy?

Practical exercise 1 - accounts

From advertising literature or specialist magazines, gather information on two contrasting accounting packages. Make sure that you choose programs from opposite ends of the price scale. Using the list of features below, draw up a table which compares the features offered by each package.

Features of accounts software: single-/multi-user, maximum number of accounts, audit trail, sales ledger, purchases ledger, invoicing, stock control, sales-order processing, purchases-order processing, job costing, payroll.

(a) Which of the above features would be required by:

(i) a corner shop selling cigarettes and newspapers,

(ii) an electrical wholesaler that carries 1200 stock lines and employs twelve staff,

(iii) a medium-sized building firm with 24 employees?

(b) Which package would you recommend to each of the organisations mentioned above? (If you have selected a modular package, list the modules recommended.)

Practical exercise 2 - spreadsheet

You work for a wholesale electrical company in the finance department.

It is Friday morning and there is panic in the office because the main computer has gone down and the payroll calculations must be done to enable the cashier to make up the pay packets by lunchtime.

Your boss has heard that you are able to use the spreadsheet on the office micro and has asked you to calculate the payroll figures:

You have been provided with the following information:

Employee	Rate per hour (£)	Basic hours	O/T hours
Anderson, G.	3.80	40	–
Atlee, C.	4.80	40	6
Dawson, T.	3.80	40	8
Sharma, A.	3.80	40	–
Green, T.	5.00	40	12
Harris, W.	3.80	40	10
Roberts, A.	3.80	40	4
Stevens, P.	4.40	40	2

Notes

(a) Basic pay = Basic hours × Rate
(b) O/T pay = O/T hours × O/T rate (O/T rate = Rate × 1.5)
(c) Gross pay = Basic pay + O/T pay
(d) Use the current tax rate
(e) Use the current National Insurance rate
(f) Trade Union sub is £2
(g) Tot deds = Tax + Nat Ins + TU sub
(h) The structure of your spreadsheet should include the following headings:

Name	Rate	Basic hours	Basic pay	O/T hours	O/T rate	O/T pay	Gross pay	Tax	Nat Ins	TU sub	Tot deds	Net pay
•												
•												
•												
•												
Totals												

Practical exercise 3 – database

This exercise is intended to introduce you to the process of creating and searching your own database. You are to create a personnel database of the type that would be of use to a company in storing information about its employees. You must decide what information will be needed by the company, other than the obvious things like name and address.

The stages that you should work through in this exercise are as follows:

(i) Decide exactly what information will be needed by a company about its employees, and the size and name of the fields you will need to store it.
(ii) Plan how the fields will be laid out on the screen.
(iii) Create the database using a database program.
(iv) Save the database on your own disk.
(v) Enter six records to your database.
(vi) Use the search facilities to practise interrogating your database; for example

Name = Smith

Name = Smith AND Dept = Hardware

Name = Smith OR Languages = French

Notes

(a) Make sure that you have planned what you are going to do before you start – it will save a lot of time once you start to create the database.
(b) Once you have searched your database, find out if you can print reports from it.

Practical exercise 4 – integrated package

You have worked in the retail electrical business for several years and have been offered the chance to start your own business.

A friend of the family has found a small shop that you would be able to rent for £100 a month which will be ideal since it has a room at the back in which you will be able to do a few repairs.

Your friend Pauline, a business consultant, has done some careful research and believes that you can expect the following income from the business:

	Sept	Oct	Nov	Dec	Jan
Sales	350	400	425	1000	800
Service	50	70	100	100	100

At the same time, Pauline has advised you to budget for the following expenses:

	Sept	Oct	Nov	Dec	Jan
Rent	100	100	100	100	100
Heat + light	20	25	30	40	40
Wages	400	400	400	400	400

Doing a few rough calculations, Pauline has realised that your income will not cover your expenses for the first few months, and she has decided that you must write to the bank to ask for a loan.

In order to provide the bank manager with all the information that he will need before giving you a loan, Pauline has recommended that you do the following:

(i) Produce a forecast of your financial state for the next five months, using the figures given above and a spreadsheet program.

Once you have completed the spreadsheet print out a copy to enclose with your letter.

(ii) When you have calculated how much you need to borrow, use a word-processor to write the letter to the bank manager. The letter is intended to explain:

(a) how much you need,
(b) for how long you wish to borrow it,
(c) when you will pay it back.

(iii) Once you have done this, print out a copy of your letter.

(iv) To give your letter some additional impact, copy your spreadsheet into your letter, rather than printing it out separately.

Programming languages

7.1 Introduction

The major problem in telling a computer to do something is that it does not understand our 'natural' language of communication – English. The instructions, or programs, that define the steps that a computer must follow in order to do something must be written in a special language if they are to be understood, but the gulf between natural English communication and computer operation codes has only been partially bridged by these languages.

As the use of computers has spread from military and scientific applications into business, education, and engineering, specially designed languages that reflect the particular needs of these new areas have been developed. Today, there are many languages that have been developed for use in specialist application areas. This unit will examine both the development of programming languages and a number of the most widely used specialist languages.

If you are only interested in an overview of computer language then you need only read section 7.2. Those who are interested in a more detailed look at languages should read the whole unit.

7.2 The development of programming languages – the story so far

The development of ways to program the computer described in the following sections can be seen as a movement from the language of the computer – electrical impulses – towards our own natural language – English.

7.2.1 Machine code

To fully understand the way in which computer programming languages have developed, we must remind ourselves of the way in which the computer operates. In section 2.6 we saw how information is stored in the computer's circuits as a series of electrical 'ons' and 'offs'. These 'ons' and 'offs' are combined, like the dots and dashes of Morse code, to form codes that can be used either to store information or to tell the computer's processor to do something. The two values, 1 and 0, of the binary number system conveniently reflect the 'ons' and 'offs' of the computer's circuits. This enables information and instructions shown in binary form to accurately mirror what is stored inside the processor. Some examples of binary code are shown below:

Value	Binary code
A	01000001
B	01000010
C	01000011
1	00000001
2	00000010
3	00000011

The base level of operation for a computer is thus at the 'on' – 'off' level that can be represented in binary code. At this base level, separate codes are needed to instruct the processor to perform each of the individual operations necessary for it to do anything useful like arithmetic or graphics. With early computers it was necessary to write all programs as a series of these individual binary operation codes, called *machine code*. Such an early machine-code program to add two numbers together and output the result written in binary might have resembled the example shown below:

```
00111110   00000011   00000101   00000100
00001100   00010001   01100110   01111110
```

Machine-code programs, in which each instruction corresponds to a specific processor operation code, came to be written using decimal (base 10: i.e. 0–9), hexadecimal (base 16: i.e. 0123456789ABCDEF), and octal (base 8: 0–7) number systems. This made it a little easier to write machine-code programs, but it was still very laborious and involved memorising large numbers of codes and keeping track of everything in the computer's memory. In addition to this, each type of processor had its own set of operation codes, so that machine-code programs written for one processor could not be used on another.

This machine-dependent method of programming using machine code is sometimes called a 'first-generation' language, or '1GL'.

7.2.2 Assembly languages

To make programming easier, each operation code was eventually given an English-like tag, such as 'ADD' or 'SUB' for the codes to add or subtract values. This was a big step forward, since it is obviously easier to remember the mnemonic (or memory-aid) 'LD' (short for LOAD) rather than the binary code 00000101. Mnemonic versions of machine-code instructions came to be called *assembly languages*. An example of part of an assembly-language program, to clear a screen and load data into memory for a Z80 processor, is shown below compared to a hexadecimal version of the same program:

	Hexadecimal		Assembly language	
01	5E00	3E16	LD	A,16H
02	5E02	CD1200	CALL	0012H
03	5E05	060A	LD	B,0AH
04	5E07	21615E	LD	HL,DATA
05	5E0A	5E	LD	E,(HL)
06	5E0B	23	INC	HL
07	5E0C	56	LD	D,(HL)
08	5E0D	23	INCH	HL
09	5E0E	EDA0	LDI	
10	5E10	CD425E	CALL	TMDLY
11	5E13	FE31	DJNZ	-9

The development of assembly languages meant that programs could be written more easily using the English-like mnemonic codes (although still a long way from 'natural' English). In order for the processor to be able to understand these codes, however, they had to be translated from assembly language into binary. Although this was done manually at first, a special type of program called an *assembler* was developed to translate assembly-language instructions into their machine-code equivalents automatically.

The term 'low-level' is often applied to assembly-language (and machine-code) programs, to emphasise the way in which each instruction corresponds to a machine-code equivalent.

Programming using assembly language was (and still is) a laborious process since it is necessary to define every individual operation a processor must do, as well as keep track of all the data and the results in the computer's memory. It is still used, however, since well-written assembly code can be used to produce operating-system routines that run faster than those produced by other programming methods.

A major problem with these 'second-generation' languages (2GLs) was that programs written for one type of computer could not be used on some other type of computer. This is due to the fact that assembly languages are closely linked to each computer's individual machine code.

The next development in programming languages was designed to overcome these problems.

7.2.3 High-level language

The next stage in the development of programming languages was to distance the programmer from the individual operation codes of the processor. This was done by devising a language in which a single English-like instruction would be equivalent to several machine-code instructions. This meant that the addition of two numbers, which would have required several machine-code instructions, could be written as a single high-level instruction like $a = b + c$. The management of the data and results was also largely left to the computer itself. This new approach enabled languages to be devised that were geared towards particular areas like science, mathematics, or business. These new languages were thus 'problem-oriented' and came to be called 'high-level' or 'third-generation' languages (3GLs) for this reason.

This emphasis on the application area rather than the computer provided a means by which programs could – in theory – be made to be 'portable' between different computers. This is achieved by using a special piece of software to translate the high-level program into a particular processor's own machine code. This special piece of software is called a *compiler* and it is one way in which a program written in a high-level language can be translated into machine code (see section 7.4). The advantages of this type of language have led to a large number of specialist high-level languages being developed in order to deal with specific areas of work. Examples are the business language COBOL (see section 7.5.1) and the educational language BASIC (see section 7.5.2).

7.2.4 Applications generators

Applications generators – sometimes also called 'program generators' – are a special class of software that will create the detailed program code given an outline of the application you wish to create. They are not a programming language in themselves: rather, they provide a means by which an applications program in a high-level language like COBOL can be created by non-programmers.

Since these types of software take the production of programs in the third-generation high-level languages one stage further, they are often called 'fourth-generation' languages (4GLs).

7.2.5 Non-procedural languages

The latest stage in the development of programming languages is to relieve the programmer of the need to specify the exact procedure involved in arriving at a solution. Using standard high-level languages, programming involves telling the computer both the precise order in which instructions are to be carried out and where to store the intermediate results of processing. With non-procedural high-level languages, programming becomes a matter of defining the rules, relationships, and variables that apply to a problem.

This type of language lends itself to use in artificial-intelligence (AI) applications which attempt to simulate the way in which humans solve problems. An example of this would be the use of such languages to write programs which simulate the deductive processes of human experts – 'expert systems'. These non-procedural languages are referred to as 'fifth-generation' languages (5GLs).

The development of the various generations of programming language, moving away from the machine code of the processor, can be represented as a series of steps in a language ladder that connects the computer with its human operators, as shown in fig. 7.1.

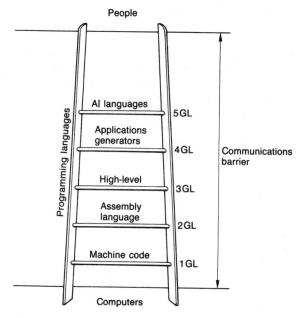

Fig. 7.1 The ladder of computer languages

7.3 Types of language

The languages that are in use today can be divided into high-level and low-level languages. Low-level languages, like assembly language, use instructions that have a single corresponding machine-code equivalent. High-level languages, on the other hand, use English-like instructions that are each equivalent to several machine-code instructions. These high-level languages differ in two ways: portability and command structure.

7.3.1 Portability

Due to its closeness to a particular processor's machine code, an assembly-language program for one processor cannot be used on a different processor. Assembly languages are said to be 'machine-orientated' because of this, and are thus not portable between machines.

In contrast, each high-level language is designed around the procedures used in a particular area, like business or engineering for example. To enable high-level language programs to operate, they have to be converted into machine code by a special translation program. As each processor has its own set of machine codes, it will also need its own translation program to convert high-level-language programs into usable form. A program written in a high-level language is thus independent of the processor and, given a translation program, may be used on a number of machines. For this reason, programs written in a high-level language are said to be 'portable' between machines.

7.3.2 Command structure

Each high-level language has been designed to deal with a particular area of use. For this reason, the commands in each language provide functions that will be especially useful in that area. The high-level language COBOL, for example, was designed for business use and has facilities designed to cope with the file-handling procedures common to such applications. FORTRAN, the first high-level language and still widely used, was designed to offer the many mathematical features needed by scientists and engineers.

In contrast, low-level languages reflect the command structure of a particular processor, and so are not designed to offer any specialist features related to an area of use.

7.4 Translation programs

Translation programs are a special class of software designed to convert programs into machine code. Translation programs were needed as soon as software began to be written in anything other than machine code. The instructions to be translated are called the *source code*, which on translation becomes *object code*, a machine-code version of the original instructions. There are two main types of translation software:

(a) programs that produce a complete machine-code version of an entire source-code program – *new-version translators*;
(b) programs that translate and execute one line of the source program at a time – *one-line translators*.

We will now look at each of these in more detail.

7.4.1 New-version translators

With this type of translator, a machine-code version of the original program is produced. The user will thus have the original source-code version of the program in addition to the object-code translation. This is equivalent to having the novel *The Three Musketeers* in both its original French edition and the translated English edition.

The new-version translation program used to convert high-level-language programs to machine code is called a *compiler*, and such programs are said to have been 'compiled'. Low-level-language programs use a translation program called an *assembler* that produces an 'assembled' version of the source code.

Compilers and assemblers will usually perform a number of checks on the source code before translation, in order to assist the programmer. Checks will be made to ensure that the program language has been correctly used, and that the program has the correct structure.

The main advantage of compilers and assemblers is that they produce efficient machine-code versions of source programs that operate much faster than one-line translation programs. Their big disadvantage is in the time it takes to correct errors (or debug) and recompile the source code if changes have to be made to the program.

The three stages in using a compiler to develop a program are:

(a) writing the source code,
(b) compilation to translate into object code,
(c) execution.

The compiler will pick up syntax errors (the incorrect use of the program-language grammar), but errors in the programmer's logic will be picked up only when the program is tested. Using a compiler to develop a program can be slow if a lot of mistakes need to be corrected and the program has to be repeatedly recompiled.

The process of compilation is illustrated in fig. 7.2. A similar process is involved when an assembler is used.

7.4.2 One-line translators
A one-line translator converts and executes each line of the original program in turn, so that no new version is produced. This is equivalent to reading the

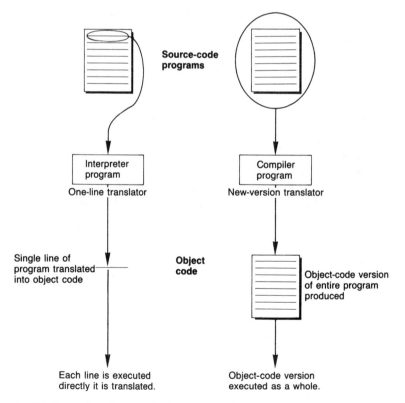

Fig. 7.2 Comparisons between the interpreter and compiler translation programs

French edition of the novel *The Three Musketeers*, translating it into English one line at a time – the novel is translated, but a new English version is not created. This type of translator – called an *interpreter* – is usually associated with high-level languages. Interpreters are useful since they enable the effect of small changes in the source program to be seen virtually immediately, since the compilation process is avoided. The disadvantage is that interpreters are not very efficient in operation, with an interpreted version of a program operating many times slower than a compiled version.

An interpreter is very useful when developing programs, since there is no need to recompile after every change, thus speeding up the development process. For this reason it is often better to develop and test a program using an interpreter but, once it is correct, compile it and then use the more efficient compiled version.

The relationship of these types of translation program is illustrated in fig. 7.2.

7.5 Survey of high-level languages

High-level computer languages tend to be designed to include terminology and facilities that relate to a particular area of use. For this reason, each high-level language is often associated with a particular application area, like business or science. The languages examined below have each been designed to include features that will make them useful in writing programs for a particular application area.

7.5.1 COBOL

COBOL (*CO*mmon *B*usiness *O*riented *L*anguage) was originally produced in 1960 as a language that would provide the facilities to enable efficient software to be produced for business applications. COBOL programs are structured into four parts or 'divisions', each of which will contain information relating to the program itself and to the procedures, data, and hardware that it needs in order to operate. A powerful language that is good at handling files of information, COBOL uses standard English words and has been subject to continual revisions so that it is still probably the most widely used language for creating business programs.

Originally designed for mainframes, versions have been produced to enable COBOL to be used on microcomputers. This is useful since it enables large-scale programs to be first developed on a micro before transferring the completed program on to the mini or mainframe computer for general use.

As it is the most widely used language for business, examples of programs that are likely to be written in COBOL include payroll, accounting, stock control, and personnel systems.

7.5.2 BASIC

BASIC (*B*eginners' *A*ll-purpose *S*ymbolic *I*nstruction *C*ode) was developed in 1964 in the USA for use as a means of introducing non-science students to the fundamentals of programming. A very easy language to learn, it has become widely used in education and home computing. An extremely flexible language using recognisable English words, it tends to be good at general presentation and calculations and weak in handling disk-based files.

A criticism of BASIC is that its flexibility encourages bad programming, since it enables programs to be written that have no real organised structure, making them hard to maintain.

Its great popularity has led to the existence of a large number of different versions or 'dialects' of the original language. This has resulted in a high degree of incompatibility between the many BASICs available, although they all share the same core of original commands. A BASIC interpreter is supplied on ROM with many microcomputers, and a large number of BASIC compilers are also available.

As BASIC has been developed, a large number of additional features have been added, and the programs that would be typically produced using it cover a wide range from games to simple calculation routines. The features added to the language have also enabled such sophisticated programs as Pegasus (an advanced accounting package) and Delta (a sophisticated database) to be written using a compiled BASIC.

7.5.3 FORTRAN

The first high-level language to be developed (in 1957 by IBM), FORTRAN (*FOR*mula *TRAN*slator) was devised to enable programs to be written using English-like commands. In reality, FORTRAN uses a semi-English/semi-mathematical language that is not very accessible to the non-programmer. Since FORTRAN is provided with a range of powerful mathematical facilities, it originally proved particularly useful to engineers and scientists, although it is also used across a range of commercial problems. Continually developed like COBOL, FORTRAN is still in widespread use.

Typical applications that would be written in FORTRAN might include a stress-analysis system for use in engineering.

7.5.4 PROLOG

Developed in the early 1970s, PROLOG (*PRO*gramming in *LOG*ic) differs from COBOL, BASIC, and FORTRAN in that it is a *non-procedural* language. The term 'non-procedural' reflects the fact that, unlike with some other high-level languages, the emphasis is placed not on the procedure involved in solving a problem but rather on specifying the relationships between the variables involved. Programming in PROLOG is thus about defining the logical relationships needed in solving a problem, rather than about defining each step of the problem-solving process.

PROLOG is used in artificial-intelligence applications, and has been chosen as the language to be used in developing the software for Japan's fifth-generation computer project (see Unit 15). PROLOG is available in both compiled and interpreted versions, and can be used for programs called 'expert systems' that mirror the decision-making processes of a human specialist.

7.5.5 *Other languages*

APL (*A Programming Language*)   A powerful, flexible, procedural high-level language.

PL/1 (*Programming Language 1*)   A general-purpose high-level language that combines many of the features found in COBOL, FORTRAN, and other languages.

FORTH   Fourth-generation general-purpose language.

PASCAL   Named after the French philosopher and mathematician Blaise Pascal, this is a highly structured language designed for use in the teaching of programming.

C   A high-level language designed for professional programmers.

ADA   A high-level structured language developed for the US Department of Defense to improve software reliability, portability, and maintainability.

In addition to the languages mentioned above, there are a very large number – possibly hundreds – of specialist high-level languages in use today.

7.6 Applications generators

These are special types of software that are designed to make the process of creating a computer-based application easier by doing the programming for you. The user must first establish a data dictionary which defines the data input and output screen displays, the data validation checks, the information to be stored, and any calculations that are to be done. The applications generator will then create the program code that will perform the tasks that have been defined.

Different types of applications generators will, like the program code they produce, generally offer facilities that make them more useful for either business or scientific applications. They are all useful, however, since they can quite considerably reduce the amount of time it takes to create a working version of a proposed application. This is an advantage since it becomes possible to produce several alternative versions of a program using an applications generator in the same time as it takes to produce a single version using standard programming techniques. This can cut down the overall time taken to produce a 'finished' application program.

Applications generators – also called 'program generators' and 'fourth-generation languages' (4GLs) – are commonly used as a 'prototyping' tool in a large-computer environment to produce a program pattern from which a final program can be written using traditional programming techniques. These programs are also used in the microcomputer environment to produce finished applications without the need to involve specialist programming personnel.

7.7 Conclusion

Since it is not possible to communicate with computers in our own 'natural' language of English, we must instruct computers using specialised programming languages. The development of these languages can be conveniently seen as a series of language generations, starting with machine-code as a 1GL and ending with 5GL artificial-intelligence languages, as shown in fig. 7.1

The continual development of new computer languages is a movement towards the use of 'natural language', although it is unlikely that the existing specialist high-level languages will ever be abandoned, for two reasons: firstly, because of the massive investment many companies have in the software that they have developed to run their organisations using such languages as COBOL and FORTRAN; secondly, due to the adoption, and continual updating, of an industry-wide standard for each of the main languages. The adherence to such standards, promoted by such bodies as the American National Standards Institute (ANSI), ensures that languages are continually updated and that language 'dialects' (created by manufacturers and software houses) do not proliferate.

The ease with which it will be possible for non-programmers to create applications programs is likely to increase as applications generators become more user-friendly. Natural-language 4GLs, which use English words rather than a complex programming language, convert instructions into program code using a data-dictionary to define each of the terms used. The demand for programmers is not likely to fall for some time to come, however, since some types of software (like operating systems) will still need to be written in low-level languages. In addition to this, the analytical skills needed to design an efficient application program will still be needed if efficient programs are to be produced.

7.8 Glossary of terms

Machine code   The lowest level of computer language, in which each instruction is a code instructing a processor to perform a specific operation. Machine code is a processor-dependent language, not portable. Also called a 'first-generation' language.

Assembly language   A development of machine code in which each instruction has been given an easy-to-remember code. Processor-dependent, not portable. Also called a 'second-generation' language.

High-level language   A language which uses English-like instructions, each of which is equivalent to a number of machine-code instructions. A problem-orientated language designed for use in a specific application area. Also called a 'third-generation' language.

Applications generator   A program which creates program code in a high-level language based on an application definition. Also called a 'fourth-generation' language.

Non-procedural language A method of programming in which it is not necessary to define the steps in a solution, the solution instead being achieved by a precise definition of the rules, relationships, and variables that apply to a problem. Also called a 'fifth-generation' language.

Natural language The language in which we ourselves communicate – English.

Source code A program written in its original programming language, before translation.

Object code A translated machine-code version of a program.

COBOL A high-level language designed for use in business applications.

BASIC A high-level general-purpose language originally designed for use in education, but which is also used in a wide range of other areas.

FORTRAN A high-level language designed for use in scientific and engineering applications.

PROLOG A non-procedural, fifth-generation language used in expert systems and artificial-intelligence applications.

Interpreter A translation program which converts a single line of a high-level program into machine code and executes it before returning for the next line.

Compiler A translation program which creates a machine-code version of a complete program written in a high-level language.

Prototyping The use of an applications generator to produce an applications program. This early working-version 'prototype' program may be used as a basis for producing a final version of the application using traditional programming techniques.

7.9 Exercises

1 Which high-level language is likely to be used in writing the software for each of the following applications?

(a) A stock-control system
(b) A home-computer game
(c) An expert system
(d) An aircraft engineer's design program

2 Explain why, when using a high-level language, it may be more efficient to use an interpreter while developing a program, but a compiler to translate the finished version for general use.

3 With the increasing use of microcomputers, one of the most widely used programming languages is BASIC (Beginners' All-purpose Symbolic

Instruction Code), which is a relatively simple example of a particular type of programming language.

(a) State what type of programming language BASIC is and the main features of this type of language.
(b) Explain why languages of this type were developed and are being increasingly used today.
(c) State what other levels of programming languages are available and the circumstances in which such languages are used.

4 (i) Distinguish between a low-level language and a high-level language.
   (ii) Distinguish between a compiler and an interpreter.

(ACCA, Numerical analysis and data processing (part))

5 (a) Describe *six* characteristics of:

   (i) low-level languages,
   (ii) high-level languages.

(b) The programs used in a company might consist of some written wholly or partly in low-level languages and some written in high-level languages. What are the reasons for this and how is it decided whether high- or low-level language is most appropriate?

(IDPM, Programming and operations)

6 A software house writing programs for small business systems makes use of interpreters and compilers in its work.

   (i) Explain what is meant by an interpreter and a compiler.
   (ii) Explain why a compiled version of a program will run more quickly than an interpreted version of the same program on the same machine.

(IDPM, Programming and operations (part))

7 In computer programming:

(a) For languages such as COBOL describe compilation and its output.
(b) Describe the interpretive method commonly used for BASIC.

(IDPM, Data processing I)

8 Briefly describe:

(a) operating-system programs,
(b) user programs,
(c) utility programs,
(d) compilers.

(IDPM, Data processing I)

Computer communications and networks

8.1 Introduction

As the number of computers continues to rise, the demand to exchange information and access data held in other distant computer systems grows. This unit deals first with terms and ideas relating to linking computers to the existing telephone communication system, then examines the reasons for which computers can be connected together to form networks, how these networks are formed, and the services that are available over the communications network.

8.2 Linking computers to the telephone system

The world of data communications (sometimes called just 'comms') is based upon the ways in which data can be transmitted between computers using the telephone system. You will recall from section 2.6 that computers hold each character of data as a 'byte' composed of eight 'bits'. These eight bits (each of which may be either a 1 or a 0) are used in the form of a code to represent the information that the computer has to deal with. Computer communication, at the lowest level, is concerned with the transmission of the bits that make up each byte or character. For such computer-to-computer communication to take place over the existing telecomms system, a special device – either a modem or an acoustic coupler – is needed.

8.2.1 Modems and acoustic couplers

Computer communication often takes place over the same telephone network that we use for voice communication. The original telephone network was built long before modern computers were conceived and so was not designed to be used for computer communication. The problem is that, as was discussed in Unit 2, computers deal with information as digital signals (a series of electrical 'ons' and 'offs', or, in binary, 1s and 0s) whereas the telephone system is designed to transmit voices as analogue signals of varying magnitude. In order to be transmitted over the present telephone system, therefore, digital computer signals have to be converted into analogue signals. This may be done by a special device called a *modem*. Another modem (the name comes from *modula-tor/dem*odulator) is required at the receiving end to convert the analogue signal back into digital form. The arrangement works as follows:

1 The user of computer A wishes to send a message to the user of computer B over the telephone system.
2 Computer A's digital transmission is converted into an analogue signal by the transmitting modem. (The signal is *mod*ulated into analogue.)
3 The converted analogue signal is transmitted down the telephone line to the receiving modem.
4 The receiving modem converts the analogue signal back into a digital signal (the signal is *dem*odulated) which can be understood by computer B.
5 The user of computer B receives the message.

This is illustrated in fig. 8.1.

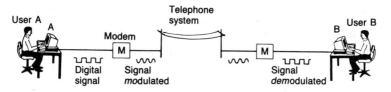

Fig. 8.1 Communication between distant computers over the telephone network, using a modem

The modem makes no use of the standard telephone handset, being wired directly into the telephone system. An alternative device, called an *acoustic coupler* (fig. 8.2), is designed to be used with a standard telephone, although it does the same job as a modem in converting signals from digital to analogue or vice versa. The acoustic coupler fits over both the earpiece and the mouth-piece of a telephone handset, and the data is sent and received in much the same way as for a normal telephone conversation. Acoustic couplers can be useful as a way of connecting a portable computer carried by a salesperson into an electronic mail service (see section 8.7.1), for example. Their only drawback is that they are unable to transmit data at the same speed as a standard modem, due to their use of the telephone handset that was designed to be used for voice rather than computer communications.

At present, either a modem or an acoustic coupler is essential if you wish to use the telephone system for computer communications. The UK telephone system is being converted to digital switching (using 'System X') and when this is complete (by the mid-1990s) it will no longer be necessary to use a modem for computer communications. The additional services that are likely to be available over this fully digital system are discussed in Unit 10.

Fig. 8.2 An acoustic coupler

8.2.2 Speed of transmission

The speed at which data is sent over a communications link is measured in bits per second (bit/s or b.p.s.), a value that is also known as the 'baud' (pronounced 'bored') rate. The speeds at which data can be transmitted can vary between 110 and 19 200 baud, depending on the volume of data being transmitted and the capabilities of the modem. Baud rates that are frequently used are 300, 1200, and 2400.

Baud rates are expressed as send/receive values, so that 300/300 baud means that data is both sent and received at 300 baud. The transmission rate chosen depends on the amount of data being sent/received, with higher rates being necessary with large amounts of data. Prestel – the British Telecom viewdata service (see section 10.2.5) – has a baud rate of 1200/75. This difference in send/receive rates is justified because the service is designed as a means of sending large amounts of information to the user (at 1200 baud) but does not require much data to be received from the user (hence 75 baud).

A rough way of converting the baud rate into the number of characters per second is to divide the rate by ten. Thus 1200/1200 baud becomes a transmission rate of around 120 characters per second sent or received, and 300/300 baud a rate of around 30 c.p.s.

8.3 Computer communications in practice

8.3.1 Type of transmission

One factor that affects the speed of at which data is transmitted is whether both the sending and receiving modems are able to synchronise their transmissions. (Such synchronisation involves transmitting each bit according to a given time sequence so that there is no need to mark the transmission of each individual byte.) If they are, there is said to be *synchronous data transmission* between the two computers. This is contrasted with a situation where the sending and receiving modems are not able to synchronise their operation but must send extra data to identify each byte being transmitted. With this method, each byte is preceded by an extra bit to signal the start of a transmission and is followed by an extra bit at the end to signal the end of a transmission. This is called *asynchronous data transmission*, and is obviously slower than synchronous transmission of data since two extra bits are needed for each character transmitted.

8.3.2 Types of communication link

A communications link is described as being *full duplex* if data can be both sent and received at the same time. If data can only be either sent or received, but not both at the same time, then the link is described as being *half duplex*. A channel which is designed either to send or to receive data in one direction only is described as *simplex*.

8.3.3 Communications protocols

All computer communications are governed by a set of protocols (agreed ways of sending and receiving data) which determine the speed and manner of data transmission. For a computer to communicate with another computer, it is important that they are both using the same protocol, otherwise the transmissions cannot be interpreted correctly. Some communications devices are able to deal with a number of different protocols by sensing the recognition signal or 'handshake' of the other computer as soon as it starts to transmit. The use of such 'intelligent' devices is becoming more common and is making the task of setting up communication links much easier.

There are a number of differing protocols being promoted by manufacturers or industries, and there has been only slow movement towards the adoption of a standard protocol for all communications. The International Standards Organisation (ISO) has proposed a seven-layer model called the Open Systems Interconnection (OSI) which defines seven protocol levels which it hopes will be adopted by manufacturers. The Comité Consultatif International Telephonique et Telegraphique (CCITT) is another body concerned with international communication standards. The CCITT has laid down standards covering data transmission over both telephone circuits and data networks, and these standards are adhered to by many manufacturers and users.

8.3.4 A single-user link

A typical microcomputer system designed for use over the telephone system will need a modem, communications software, and a telephone link. Once these items have been purchased and connected, it is then possible to set up communications with other computers.

If communication is over a standard telephone link – also called a 'dial-up' line – the cost is the same as for a standard telephone call, plus any other charges made for accessing the other computer. This is fine for occasional use, but suffers from the disadvantage that the old-fashioned UK telephone system can

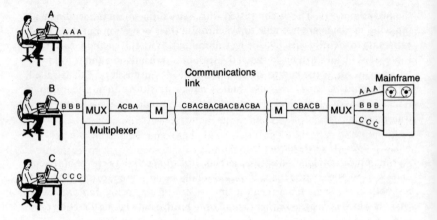

Fig. 8.3 Sharing a communications link by using a multiplexer

generate a lot of 'noise' in the form of electrical interference which reduces the speeds at which communication is possible. For this reason, it may be necessary to use some other type of connection. (For descriptions of other types of connection, see section 8.3.7.)

In order to set up communications with another computer, the user will need to configure, or set up, his or her communications software with the agreed protocol before dialling the number to make the connection. Once the connection is made, it may then be necessary to 'sign-on' (using a password) to the host computer before the service can be used. Some communications software can be set up to take care of the dialling and signing-on procedures automatically, thus making life easier for the user.

8.3.5 Sharing a single link – multiplexing
For a business with a mainframe or minicomputer which has a number of terminals located in another part of the country, it would be uneconomic for each terminal to have its own communications link (telephone line). A device called a 'multiplexer' enables a number of terminals to share a single communications link, thus cutting down on the line costs. The way in which a multiplexer operates is shown in fig. 8.3.

The type of multiplexer illustrated operates by sharing out the time for which each terminal has access to the link. The three terminals – A, B, and C – are all communicating with a remote computer at the same time, with the multiplexer sharing the single link out between them. At the receiving end, another multiplexer will sort out the different messages and route each one via a separate channel into the receiving computer. The speed at which multiplexing operates means that the four users are not aware that they are sharing one link –

the multiplexer makes it appear as if they each have their own individual line to the remote computer. The larger the number of users that share a single multiplexed communications link, the higher the baud rate needs to be, however, so as to ensure the minimum delay in sending and receiving information.

A typical example of the use of multiplexing would be in a high-street building-society office which has several terminals linked into the society's mainframe computer many miles away. It is very likely that these terminals will all share a single multiplexed line to the mainframe computer.

All multiplexers operate in a similar way, but some types share out access to the single link according to the amount of data being sent by each user (statistical-time-division multiplexing) whereas others allocate different frequencies to each of the terminals (frequency-division multiplexing).

8.3.6 A specialist telephone system for computers – the PDN system

With the growth in the number of computers using the telephone network, a special system purely for the transmission of computer data was needed. The British version of this system is called the Public Data Network (PDN) and is based on the packet-switching principle discussed below. This system is based around a number of exchanges containing specialised computers that manage the data that goes into and comes out of the PDN.

Each one of these computers (called a PAD – short for *Packet Assembly/Disassembly unit*) is designed to divide outgoing messages into a number of small standard-size 'packets', each of which is headed with the address of the receiving computer, and to reassemble similarly divided packets which it receives. A typical message might be divided into several packets which the PAD nearest the sender will feed into the system when there is a space in the traffic using the network. The packets will usually be sent by the shortest route to the local PAD nearest the destination, where they will then be reassembled into the original message before being sent on to their destination. This system, like multiplexing, is designed to make the fullest use of a communications link.

Figure 8.4 shows four of the large number of PADs that can be used for the transmission of data. If a company based in Bristol wishes to send a file of information to a branch in Brighton using the Public Data Network, it will first have to dial in to the local PAD in Bristol. Once it is accepted into the system and links have been set up with the Brighton branch, the information can be sent. The PAD will take care of the way in which the packets of information are transmitted, and will send them by the shortest route (via Southampton). A feature of this system is that, if the direct route to a destination is fully used, then the system will reroute the packets of data that go to make up the message via the available links. If the network link via Southampton is being fully used, then the system is able to redirect the information via the next best available route, which may be via London. This facility of rerouting packets of data ensures that the system is always fully utilised and that users do not need to wait for a direct line to become free before they are able to send data. It is this feature that gives rise to the name 'packet switching'.

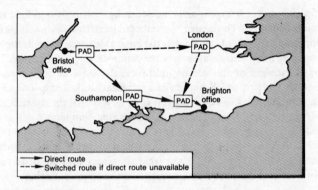

Fig. 8.4 Sending information from Bristol to Brighton using the Public Data Network

8.3.7 Services available

In the UK, the majority of services for the transmission of data are provided by British Telecom, although other companies like Mercury also offer specialist telecommunications facilities. Below is a summary of the main types of service available:

Packet SwitchStream (PSS)   This is the British Telecom packet-switching service that is designed for data communication. Typical uses of this service are for computer-to-computer data access like Telecom Gold and remote order processing.

IPSS (*I*nternational *P*acket *S*witching *S*ervice)   This is the international extension of the PSS that provides direct access to packet-switched networks around the world. Using this service, it is possible to link up to a host computer in North America, Australia, or any one of over thirty countries, for the price of a telephone call to the local PAD.

Cardway   This provides a dedicated link between retailers and credit-card companies for credit authorisation via the PDN.

Leased lines   A leased line is a permanent telecommunications connection between two locations. These lines avoid telephone exchanges, which are the source of most 'line noise' (crackles etc.) that will cause problems with data transmission. Leased lines tend to be most popular when a regular connection is needed or else a lot of data is to be transmitted at high speed. Examples of leased-line services are:

(a) *KiloStream*   This service can provide digital private circuits with full synchronous duplex transmission at speeds up to 64000 bits per second. This service offers high-speed data transmission and is suitable for the transfer of large amounts of data.

(b) *MegaStream* This is a very high-speed digital private circuit that can at present handle transmission speeds of between 2 and 8 megabits per second. By using the MegaStream service in conjunction with multiplexers it is possible to obtain a large number of channels from a single link. The service is able to mix voice and data and it can be used for such applications as videoconferencing (this is explained further in Unit 10), CAD/CAM, and linking together computers located at different sites.

(c) *SatStream* SatStream is a digital communication service that uses satellite and small dish earth aerials to provide fast high-capacity links between the UK, Europe, and North America. It is designed for use by international companies that need to transfer large amounts of data more efficiently than is possible using standard communications links. Typical users of this system would be large international companies which operate worldwide. Data transmission speeds can vary between 56/64 kilobits and 2 megabits per second, according to the type and quantity of data.

Large national and international companies which need to send large amounts of data between their branch offices and main computer are typical users of these services. The cost of these services to the user will depend on the speed of transmission required and the distance over which the link is made.

8.3.8 Data communication using light-waves

One problem with linking together computers by means of the traditional copper cable is that it is subject to electrical interference, leading to corruption of the data being transmitted. As a way of combating this problem, many protocols include an error-checking facility that will cause data to be retransmitted if it is corrupted. A more radical solution is to abandon traditional electrical communications methods and to transmit data as light, either using fibre-optic cable or else with a laser link.

Optical fibres (fine strands of clear glass or plastic surrounded by a protective cladding) are ideal for the transmission of digital data since they do not suffer from electrical interference and can carry far more traffic than conventional copper wire. British Telecom aims to replace much of its main trunk network with fibre-optic cable, and companies like Mercury have established their own networks based on the same technology. In areas subject to frequent electrical storms, computer networks have been set up which operate using fibre-optics to avoid the corruption of data caused by atmospheric interference.

Computers in nearby buildings may also be linked up by using infra-red laser light transmitted from anything up to 1 kilometre away. This data-transmission technique is aimed at large organisations who wish to be able to send information between several offices located in the same area – for example, it is used by a major DIY retail chain to link up buildings in its administrative centre. The rate at which data is transmitted using this technique is high, with speeds of up to 2.5 million bits per second being possible.

8.4 Computer networks

Computer networks are formed by the linking together of computers by means
of communications links, using technology originally developed for use with
large mainframe computer systems. A computer network can vary in size from
a couple of microcomputers in the same room sharing printers and storage, to
the linking of several mainframe computers located on different continents
thousands of miles apart. In the case of large networks that cover one or more
countries, the links between the computers will be established using the
communications techniques discussed in section 8.3. For small-scale local networks involving only short distances, the computers may simply be plugged
together without even the need for modems.

There are two types of computer network: small *local area networks* (LANs)
that link computers in a single building or group of buildings, and large *wide
area networks* (WANs) that link computers nationally or internationally. The
development of an efficient telecommunications network that is able to handle
computer communications has stimulated growth in the number of dial-up
computer services available. These are called *value-added network services*, or
VANS, and provide (usually for a fee) a variety of information, mail, and other
services using the public communications system.

The next three sections will look at each of these in turn.

8.5 Local area networks

A local area network, or LAN, is used to connect a variety of computers over
a limited geographical area, usually a single building or site. Figure 8.5 shows
a typical LAN.

While mainframe- or microcomputer-based LANs have been in existence for
many years, it is only the development of the personal computer that has led
to their widespread use. Indeed, although the majority of LANs in use today
are built around PCs, many will still be linked to the company mini or mainframe computer.

8.5.1 Components of a typical PC-based LAN

Personal computers are generally not designed to be linked up to form a network, so additional hardware and software are required to make this possible.
A PC is likely to require a LAN adaptor card, network software, and the
appropriate LAN cable.

A typical PC-based LAN will also have a powerful dedicated PC, called a
'server', that has a large hard disk and a fast memory. The server will generally
be used to store software or files that need to be available to all users on the
LAN, and it may also handle the flow of output to a shared printer. Servers
are thus sometimes referred to as 'file servers' or 'printer servers'.

There are three main types of cable that are used to connect up the devices
that form a network: coaxial, twisted-pair, and fibre-optic (see fig. 8.6).

With the growth in the number of local area networks, it is becoming

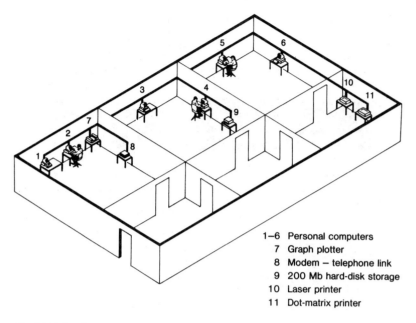

1–6 Personal computers
7 Graph plotter
8 Modem – telephone link
9 200 Mb hard-disk storage
10 Laser printer
11 Dot-matrix printer

Fig. 8.5 A local area network

increasingly common for LANs themselves to be connected together. This is achieved using a 'bridge' (to connect LANs of the same type) or else a 'gateway' (to connect different types of LAN). Using this technology it is now possible for users on widely dispersed LANs to be connected. Practical examples of this are illustrated by the *Guardian* and University of Brighton case-studies in Unit 12.

8.5.2 LAN topologies
There are several methods of connecting computers to form a LAN, each of which is associated with a particular layout or topology. We are now going to look at the three main topologies currently in use: star, bus, and token-ring networks.

(a) Star networks Historically the star network (see fig. 8.7) is associated with mini or mainframe LANs, since it involves a central computer, although PC-based systems are also now available. The central system will generally act as a file/printer server and will handle all links to external systems.

The central computer actively manages all user traffic, inspecting and redirecting messages to the appropriate destination, and for this reason a star LAN is termed an 'active' network. Star networks are widely used and can operate at speeds of up to 10 Mb/s. They may be built around a modern

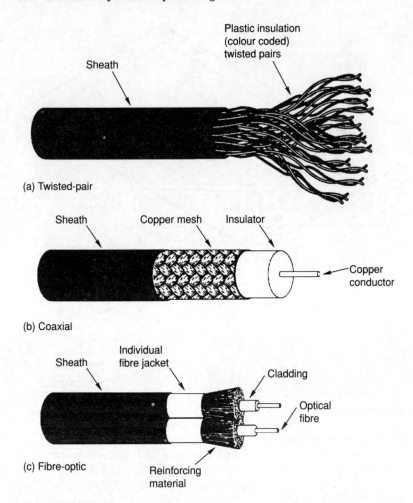

Fig. 8.6 Cable types

high-speed telephone switchboard called a 'private automatic branch exchange' (PABX) – see the University of Brighton case-study in Unit 12.

The two main drawbacks of the star topology are (i) that the speed of the network depends upon the speed at the centre, and (ii) that the LAN is vulnerable to failure of the central system.

(b) Bus networks The bus network (see fig. 8.8) was originally developed by the Xerox Corporation and is sometimes also referred to as 'Ethernet', after the original bus network of that name. Many network products are now based on this system, an example being the Novell Netware network software.

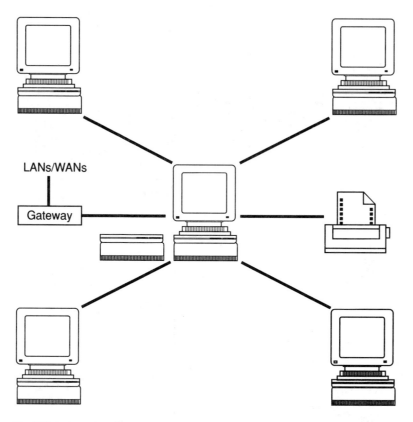

Fig. 8.7 A star network

The bus system is built around a single strand of cable, called the 'bus', to which all devices are connected. The bus simply connects all the devices and does not have any control over the network traffic; instead, devices communicate as required. For this reason, bus LANs are sometimes termed 'passive' networks.

With this system, it is possible for two or more devices to start to transmit over the network at the same time, causing a 'collision' between the two transmissions. To prevent this, network traffic over a bus network is controlled by the use of the CSMA/CD (carrier sense multiple access/collision detection) protocol. To explain how the CSMA/CD protocol operates, we will look at a typical communication sequence.

When a device wishes to communicate over the network, it will first monitor the network to see if there is any other traffic (carrier sense). If the network is free, it will begin to transmit. However, another device may have also started to transmit at the same time (multiple access), so the device will listen to the

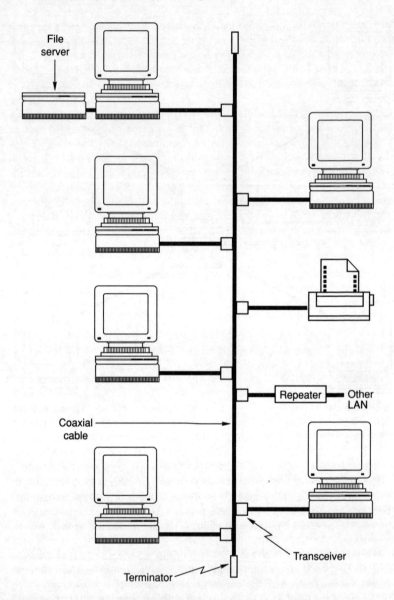

Fig. 8.8 A bus network ('Ethernet') segment

network to check for a collision (collision detect). If a collision has happened then the devices involved stop transmitting and wait for a random period (to avoid repeating the collision) before trying again.

With this system, all communications are broadcast across the network, with devices constantly monitoring traffic and selecting only those messages that are addressed to them.

Data is transmitted over a bus network at speeds of up to 10 Mb/s over coaxial, twisted-pair or fibre-optic cable. The performance of bus networks tends to decline quite rapidly as network traffic rises, due to the increased likelihood of collisions occurring. Bus networks will thus perform best under relatively light traffic loads, and one way of achieving this is to split up a potentially large network into a series of smaller network segments linked by a repeater. Another limitation of the bus topology is that, due to the possibility of collisions occurring, it is not possible to guarantee either access to the LAN at any given time or that a message will be received within a certain period. For this reason, bus networks are not suitable for time-critical applications.

(c) **Token-ring networks**   The token-ring network (see fig. 8.9) organises network communications by means of a special token that is required before a device can transmit. As there is only one token on the network at a time, only one device can transmit at a time and collisions are avoided. All traffic over the network relies upon a token-passing protocol, and to explain how this operates we will now look at the way in which a typical message would be handled.

The token in this type of network is a special communication sequence that circulates continuously. When there is no traffic, the token is said to be 'free' and may be withdrawn by a device wishing to transmit. The device will change the token to a 'busy' state and will transmit its message, the message and token being passed around the network to the destination before returning to the original sending device. Once the sending device receives its own 'busy' token, it will then replace it with a free token so that other devices may use the network.

In common with the bus topology, all communications are broadcast across the network, with devices constantly monitoring traffic and reading only those messages that are addressed to them.

Token-ring networks can handle data at speeds between 4 and 16 Mb/s, usually over twisted-pair cable, although fibre-optic cable systems are available. Since all traffic is regulated with the use of a token, the performance of token-ring networks tends to fall off only gradually, making them suitable for use where network traffic is likely to be high. Another advantage of this type of system is that devices can hold on to the token for only a limited period, thus ensuring that all devices are able to gain access to the LAN on a regular basis.

The major drawback of a ring topology is that the breakdown of one of the devices on the network will cause the whole network to fail. The IBM token-ring network system solves this problem by linking each device to a multi-station access unit (MAU), a number of MAUs then being joined to form a ring

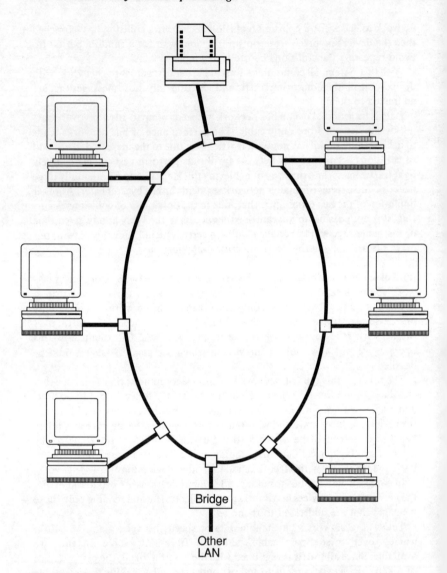

Fig. 8.9 A ring network

as shown in fig. 8.10. As can be seen from the diagram, each MAU will have a number of devices linked to it, and if one of these devices fails then the MAU will automatically disconnect it from the LAN and prevent a total failure of the system.

Just to confuse things, an IBM token-ring LAN may be built around a single MAU in a star layout, giving rise to the 'star-based ring' topology.

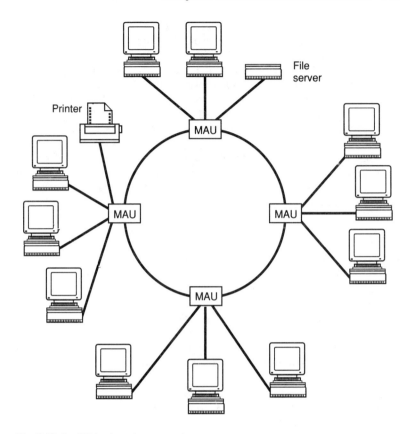

Fig. 8.10 An IBM token-ring network

The FDDI (Fibre Distributed Data Interface) topology is another type of token-passing ring network and is based on two rings of fibre-optic cable. This system makes use of two counter-rotating tokens, one on each of the two rings, and is designed to be fault-tolerant in operation. Operating at data rates of 100 Mb/s and having a maximum size of 100 km, FDDI is suitable for use as a high-speed 'backbone' connecting together other slower networks.

8.5.3 Advantages and disadvantages of LANs
The advantages and disadvantages of LANs may be summarised as follows:

Advantages

(a) Facilitate the sharing of expensive peripherals like laser printers, modems, and file servers.
(b) Enable information held on a central server to be shared by a large number of users.

(c) Applications software may be shared across a network, although some 'network-aware' software will allow only a set number of users at any one time.

(d) In an organisation in which several non-compatible computer systems are used, a LAN may be used to integrate them.

(e) A LAN may be used to offer a wide range of office-automation facilities like electronic mail (see section 10.2.2) to users.

(f) LANs may be used to facilitate 'group working'. An example of this would be allowing a draft document to be accessed over a LAN so that editing suggestions can be attached to it by users other than the author. Once the editing process is complete, only the author is able to amend the document if required. Many users sharing a single database is another example of group working.

Disadvantages

(a) The cost of hardware, software, and cabling.

(b) The complexity of many LANs means that it is often necessary to employ someone to look after the network and solve problems relating to the system.

(c) Security of data (including the threat posed by viruses) may be a problem if adequate procedures are not adopted.

(d) Many LANs can be victims of their own success, in that a large number of users on the system at the same time can cause the response time to become very unsatisfactory.

(e) Once users are accustomed to working over a LAN, they often become dependent upon it to do their jobs. Any failure in the system can often mean that it becomes impossible for users to work.

8.6 Wide area networks

A wide area network, or WAN, will generally use private communications links to connect large numbers of computer terminals over a large geographical area to a mainframe. Large organisations like banks, building societies, and government agencies all use WANs that operate over leased telecommunications lines to link together branches and offices throughout the country. The following are examples of typical WANs.

(a) The automated teller machines (ATMs) provided by banks and building societies to allow access to cash outside banking hours are part of a WAN that is controlled by a computer in another part of the country.

(b) The laser scanners that are used by many supermarkets at the check-outs may also be part of a WAN that collects information on a minicomputer at the supermarket before passing it on to the mainframe located in the company's main computer centre elsewhere in the country. Such a system, illustrated in fig. 8.11, is called a 'hierarchical' network since there are

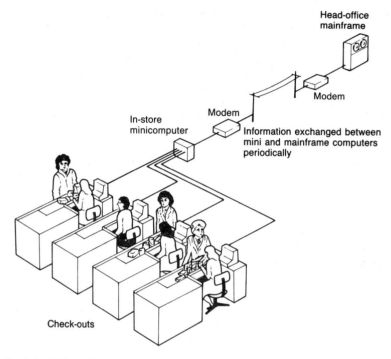

Head-office
mainframe

Modem

In-store
minicomputer

Modem

Information exchanged between
mini and mainframe computers
periodically

Check-outs

Fig. 8.11 A hierarchical wide area network – information from supermarket check-outs assists stock control and provides head office with up-to-date reports on sales.

several layers and only indirect communication between the terminals that collect the data at the bottom of the hierarchy and the main computer at the top. The case-study on Sainsbury's in Unit 12 looks at this system in more detail.

(c) Many banks and retailers are keen to promote electronic funds transfer at point of sale (EFTPOS), a system where money is transferred from your account into the retailer's at the time of purchase – a form of electronic money using a 'debit card'. For this system to be able to work, retailers and banks will need to be linked into a WAN that will carry the information about purchases between the retailers and the banks.

(d) Euronet is an example of a packet-switched data-transmission network (see section 8.3.6) designed for use within the twelve countries of the European Community. Specialist economic, scientific, and technical information on the European Community and other areas is available to users of the system.

8.6.1 JANET (Joint Academic NETwork)

JANET is a network provided to UK universities and research councils by direct funding from the Department of Education. It links over 1000 computer systems in UK academic and research institutions, some academically related institutions like the British Library, and some European Research institutions like CERN (the European Organisation for Nuclear Research). In addition to these institutions, JANET also has gateways to other national and international networks, such as the European Academic Research Network (EARN), the National Science Foundation Network (NSF), and the Space Physics Analysis Network (SPAN).

The JANET network is illustrated in fig. 8.12.

8.6.2 SWIFT (Society for Worldwide Interbank Financial Telecommunications)

SWIFT is a private communications network linking some 1500 member banks and financial institutions around the world. It is used to send electronic messages to correspondent banks overseas confirming that funds to pay for imported goods have been transferred from a customer's account to the exporter's bank account, wherever in the world it may be. No money is actually transferred overseas.

The system is based on two international data centres, in Amsterdam and Virginia, that are linked by fully encrypted international leased lines to processors in each member country. SWIFT has the capacity to handle 1.5 million messages a day and uses a standard format for each message type, including customer transfers, foreign exchange, documentary credits, securities statements, and accounting-entry confirmations.

8.6.3 The Microsoft WAN

Microsoft is one of the world's largest software houses, with operations in America, Europe and the Far East. The worldwide network is currently managed by British Telecom, with the network being centred on London. An idea of the scale of the WAN can be gained from the fact that Microsoft uses 150 Ethernet LANs to link 20 000 PCs, 2000 terminal servers, 700 network servers, 1500 disk/printer servers, nine DEC VAX minicomputers and nine IBM AS/400 minicomputers.

8.7 Value-added network services

While LANs and WANs are ways in which computers are used within a particular company, value-added network services, or VANS, offer information and other services over a communications network like the PDN discussed in section 8.3.6. The term 'value-added network services' comes from the fact that added-value services (that is, services for which people are prepared to pay, over and above the cost of using the network itself) are offered over an existing communications network, like the telephone network.

Some VANS offer a communications gateway to enable users to access

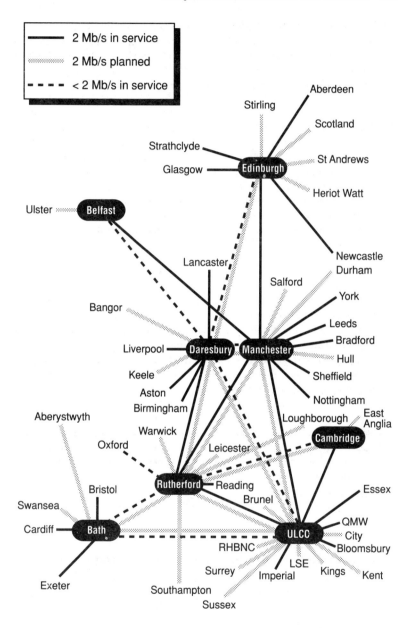

Fig. 8.12 The JANET network

information held in other computer systems. Telecom Gold (see below) for example, has gateways to a number of third-party databases like Datasolve (containing current-affairs information), Petroleum Monitor, and the Official Airline Guide.

VANS will generally fall into one of the four categories below:

8.7.1 Electronic mail (EMail)

This is a service in which each subscriber is allocated an electronic 'mailbox' into which messages can be placed by other users, the contents of each mailbox being readable only by its owner. Messages can be sent to other subscribers, who can read their mail when they next access the system.

The advantages of this service are that it is faster and cheaper than conventional mail and it can be accessed at any time and from any location. Typical users include journalists working from home, travelling salespeople using a portable computer and an acoustic coupler, and large companies exchanging correspondence.

Examples are:

- Telecom Gold – offered by British Telecom using the Dialcom system (a proprietary EMail system).
- Campus 2000 – this is a version of the Telecom Gold service designed for use exclusively within the education system.
- Tradanet – a type of electronic mail service designed to enable companies to exchange orders, invoices, and acknowledgements electronically, and thus speed up transaction processing. Each user of the service is allocated a private postbox, in which outgoing trading information to other companies can be 'posted', and a private mailbox in which incoming information can be collected. Tradanet acts as a clearing house by sorting all the mail left in postboxes and sending it to the correct mailboxes. The service is faster and cheaper than the conventional postal system, and can increase the efficiency with which orders are processed.

EMail is discussed at greater length in Unit 10.

8.7.2 On-line databases

These services offer up-to-date information in a number of general-interest and specialist areas. Subscribers are able to access the system and search the database for particular items of information.

On-line databases can be divided into three types:

(a) *full-text databases*, which allow entire articles to be retrieved and viewed;
(b) *bibliographic databases*, which contain pointers as to where the full information can be found;
(c) *interactive information services*, which offer information relating to specific topics.

Examples are:

- Jordans – holds financial information on over 1.6 million UK-registered companies, as well as their precise name, registered office, and date of last filed accounts.
- Lexis – contains the full text of US and UK case law and other legal documents, and also a section on European case law.
- World Reporter – contains the full text of information published by news services (such as the Associated Press Newswire) and major world news-papers such as the *Financial Times*, *Tass*, the *Washington Post*, and the *Guardian*.
- Datastream – contains business and financial information consisting of six databases relating to equities, securities, company accounts, interest rates, exchange rates, and historical economic information.
- Crude – contains information on spot crude oil prices, in time-series format, for two major crude oils.
- Jokes – a full text database containing jokes, anecdotes, and humorous say-ings by well-known figures in all public fields.

Details of other UK databases are given in Brit-Line's *Directory of British Databases* and American databases are listed in the *Directory of On-line Databases*.

8.7.3 Electronic payment systems
These allow the transfer of funds between banks, companies, and individuals – both nationally and internationally. Examples are:

- *BACS* (Bankers' Automated Clearing Services) – set up to reduce or eliminate the high costs of handling cash transfers between accounts in the UK banking system, by moving all funds electronically. BACS has over 50 000 users and each month handles around 150 million entries valued at about £60 billion. Over 80% of all life-insurance premiums are collected using BACS, as are all direct debits and standing orders, and 90% of all salaries paid in the UK.
- CHAPS (Clearing House Automated Payment System) – set up to enable financial institutions to transfer large sums of money from one account to another on the same day, thus avoiding the three days usually required to clear a cheque. CHAPS is based on Tandem front-end processors running software provided by Logica and uses the British Telecom PSS for all com-munications. Security is very important in all financial systems, and the messages passing around the CHAPS network are protected in a number of ways. All transmissions on the system are encrypted, and all payments messages are authenticated before transmission and reauthenticated when they reach their destination, to ensure that sensitive fields within the pay-ment cannot be altered between source and destination.
- SWITCH – an EFTPOS system launched by NatWest, Midland Bank and the Royal Bank of Scotland in 1988. The aim of the system is to give

cardholders the option of paying for goods and services using EFTPOS, by generating a debit entry to their current account that is cleared in around the same time as a cheque but electronically.

8.7.4 Other services

These are services that are aimed at specific sectors, and include such things as:

- Travicom (Travel Automation Services) – links together airline reservation systems, provides up-to-date information on the availability of holidays and flights, and is widely used by travel agents.
- Bulletin boards – these are the equivalent of electronic notice-boards that may be dialled up and examined, usually at no cost other than that of the telephone call. There are a large number of such boards run by enthusiasts and organisations, and such services as EMail, free software, and computing advice may be offered.

8.8 Conclusion

The ability to link computers together into networks relies upon the availability of efficient communications facilities. The growth that has taken place in the numbers of networks and network services has been made possible only by the existence of a fully developed and efficient telecommunications network.

The move towards a cashless society with the advent of EFTPOS (electronic funds transfer at point of sale) will be possible only with the use of a high-speed communications network.

Once standard communications protocols have become adopted, it will become possible for computers of all makes to exchange information and become part of a vast network.

The fall in the cost of microcomputer hardware and software is likely to cause an increase in the demand for dial-up VANS that will offer information, EMail, or other services. It is in this area of VANS that there is likely to be the greatest growth, since access to the ever-increasing amounts of information available on-line will become vital for organisations and useful for individuals.

8.9 Glossary of terms

Baud　A rate of data transmission of one bit per second.

Modem　A device to convert digital computer signals into analogue signals to enable transmission by the telephone system, or to convert the transmitted analogue signal back into digital form.

Acoustic coupler　An alternative to the modem that makes use of a telephone handset as a connection to the telephone system for data-transmission purposes.

Synchronous　Describes a data-transmission system in which the sending and receiving computers transmit bits according to a given time sequence.

Asynchronous Describes a data-transmission technique in which additional bits are sent to signify the start and end of each byte transmitted.

Multiplexer A device that allows the sharing of a single communications link between a number of users.

Protocol A set of conventions governing the format of data transmissions between two communicating computers.

OSI Open Systems Interconnection – a set of standards that define communications protocols.

LAN Local area network – describes the linking together of computers within a single building or group of buildings to enable the sharing of information and other resources.

WAN Wide area network – describes the linking together of computers so that information and other resources can be shared nationally or internationally.

VANS Value-added network services – describes the information, EMail, and other services offered to computer users and available over the telecommunications system.

Bridge A device that connects two separate LANs.

Bus LAN A LAN in which PCs, printers, etc. branch off a single strand of cable.

CSMA/CD Carrier sense multiple access/collision detection – a widely used protocol for bus LANs.

Ethernet A type of bus LAN developed by the Xerox Corporation.

FDDI Fibre Distributed Data Interface – a high-speed token-ring LAN topology based on a double fibre-optic ring with counter-rotating tokens.

File server A high-volume disk storage unit that is used as a shared resource over a LAN.

JANET Joint Academic NETwork – a WAN linking academic and research institutions in the UK and elsewhere.

MAU Multi-station access unit – a device used to connect a number of PCs, printers, etc. to a token-ring LAN.

Printer server A disk storage unit that may be a subsystem of a file server, available over a LAN and used for spooling print jobs.

Repeater A device used to extend the size of a LAN by joining two lengths of cable and repeating the signal.

Ring LAN A LAN in which PCs, printers, etc. are each connected to a common loop around which signals circulate.

Star LAN   A LAN in which PCs, printers, etc. radiate from a central hub or network controller.

SWIFT   Society for Worldwide Interbank Financial Telecommunications – a private communications network linking some 1500 member banks and financial institutions worldwide.

Token-ring LAN   A ring LAN that makes use of a circulating token to control data traffic.

8.10 Exercises

1 What is the difference between a LAN, a WAN, and VANS?

2 Explain the main features and benefits of a LAN. What are the main types of LAN available?

3 What is a WAN? Explain the ways in which organisations may make use of a WAN.

4 What are the main types of value-added network service available? How might a business make use of each of these types of service?

5 Describe the function and potential use of each of the following

(a) a multiplexer,
(b) a local area network, and
(c) a modem.   (AAT, Elements of information systems (pilot paper))

6 Give a brief explanation, which would be suitable for a manager, of the following telecommunications terms:

(a) Private Automatic Branch Exchange
(b) Protocol
(c) PSS
(d) Baud rate
(e) Asynchronous   (AAT, Elements of information systems)

7 Define the term 'local area network' and outline the range of structures and technologies used in different types of local area network.
   (ACCA, Systems analysis and design)

8 Sketch the main elements of a long-distance communications network and describe functions.   (IDPM, Data processing I)

9 Explain the following terms used in connection with data-transmission networks:

(a) Duplex and half-duplex methods of data transmission
(b) Protocol
(c) Packet switching
(d) Multiplexer
(e) Hard-copy terminal   (IDPM, Data processing II)

10 A company is considering installing an interactive data transmission system to link the existing mainframe computer to the regional sales offices and warehouses. Describe the additional hardware and software required and how the remote sites will be linked. (IDPM, Data processing II)

Project

Many large public reference libraries subscribe to a number of VANS like World Reporter, Lexis, and Prestel. Pay a visit to your local reference library and find out what on-line information services it subscribes to. Ask if it is possible to arrange a demonstration of some of these services, and find out how much they cost to use.

Case-study

BES Electronics produces a range of peripherals designed for use with all sizes of computer. BES does not sell directly to the public but to suppliers of computer systems who rebadge the peripherals and sell them as part of a complete system. At present, the sales force communicates with head office over the telephone, with salespeople phoning in for guidance over pricing, technical matters, and possible new sales contacts. Due to the nature of the work, salespeople are likely to call in at any time during office hours, and situations often occur when information is sought from someone who is not available at the time of the call. Although messages are left, they tend to go astray and it is almost impossible to contact the salespeople with the replies since they are constantly on the move. This is obviously very unsatisfactory, and the sales manageress is looking for a way to remedy the situation.

Most of the business done by BES is with a few large companies who purchase a large number of different items of hardware. The orders for these purchases are all processed manually, both by BES and by their large customers, the whole process being very labour-intensive and time-consuming. The rate of growth of sales is such that the order-processing department will either have to move into new offices or else find another way of handling these large orders.

1 (a) What value-added network service would you suggest could solve:

    (i) the communication problem with the sales staff?
    (ii) the problem with the growth in the number of sales orders to be processed?

  (b) Make a list of the hardware and software necessary to implement your answer to (a)(i) above.

  (c) Using computer trade magazines, British Telecom, and local computer dealers, find out the total cost of the hardware and software to be purchased in (b) above.

2 BES plans to purchase a large number of desk-top microcomputers at its head office, and the DP manager is anxious not to duplicate the printers, plotters, and hard-disk storage necessary.

    (a) What would you suggest as a way to avoid the unnecessary duplication of peripherals?

    (b) Using the resources mentioned in 1(c) above, find out the likely cost to BES of linking up fifteen microcomputers.

    (c) What other benefits is your solution likely to offer to BES?

3 BES is considering setting up an office in Coventry to cover the north and would like this office to have on-line access to the information held on its main computer in Slough, 80 miles away. The Coventry office will probably have five terminals linked directly into the Slough system.

    (a) What hardware will be necessary for such a link to be effective?

    (b) What services are offered by British Telecom that might speed up the rate at which information can be sent between Slough and Coventry?

Methods of information processing

9.1 Introduction

Information may be stored in computer systems in the form of 'files'. The files containing the main records on, say, personnel, stock, or any other system are called *master files*, and these are updated from time to time with new information that may be held on *transaction files*. The way in which this updating takes place is called *information processing* (IP), *data processing* (DP), or sometimes *transaction processing* (TP), and may be organised in a number of ways.

Once it was possible to process information only at set times, but today it may be processed as soon as it is received. The method by which information is processed by your own organisation, or by another company on your behalf, is partly determined by the nature of the application the information is being used for. The more up-to-date the information needs to be, the faster it needs to be processed – that is, the faster the master file needs to be updated.

Before information can be processed, however, it is vital that checks are made to ensure that it is correct. The first section in this unit describes some of the ways in which it is possible to check that information being entered is correct.

9.2 Control over the input of data

Information processing has three distinct and related stages:

input → process → output

There is an old saying in computing: 'garbage in – garbage out' (GIGO for short). This means 'If the information that you enter is incorrect, then the results you will get out after it is processed will also be incorrect'. This saying is a reminder that it is vital to build checks on accuracy into the first stage of information processing.

There are two types of input check that may be made upon information that is to be processed: validation checks and verification checks. We will now look at each one of these in turn.

9.2.1 Validation checks

Validation checks are designed to test input data to see if it meets certain criteria. This type of test does not ensure that the data is correct, but rather that it is reasonable, and for this reason it is sometimes called a 'reasonableness check'.

The ways in which it is possible to 'validate' input include the following:

Range check   Does the data fall within the acceptable range? For example, on a date field, does the month number fall between 1 and 12? For a telephone number, is the input numeric?

Limit check   Does the data fall within the predetermined limit? For example, on a payroll, are hours worked less than or equal to 60, the maximum possible? On a customer reference, is the value less than or equal to 10000, the highest number?

Cross-field check   Do the related data fields produce compatible results? For example, on an invoice, do the individual charges produce the same amount as the invoice total? On a personnel record, if 'Sex = Male', is the title 'Mr' or 'Doctor'?

Validation of input data will usually be programmed into the system so that the data is checked as it is entered. The purpose of this kind of check is to highlight obvious errors automatically, faster and more efficiently than can be done by a human operator.

9.2.2 Verification checks

Verification checks are designed to check the correctness of the input data. If data passes a verification test it can be assumed to be correct. Some of the ways in which input data can be verified are shown below.

Visual check   This is one of the main ways of verification. It is often necessary to visually check and correct errors in data that have been located by some of the methods below.

Rekeying   This is where data is entered twice by different people, one after the other, with a character-by-character comparison being made automatically by the computer. If there is any difference, the system will ask the operator to visually verify and correct the data before proceeding. Rekeying is commonly used with the batch-processing method described in section 9.3.

Check digit For certain types of numbers, such as VAT numbers or payroll references, check digits may be calculated by applying a particular formula to the number. By adding a check digit to the number, verification is achieved by recalculating the check digit, since an incorrect value will generate a different check digit. This type of verification technique will cause an operator to visually check and correct the data. The ISBN (international standard book number) of this book has a unique ten-digit number that contains the country of origin, publisher code, and title code, with a single check digit at the end.

Control total A value obtained by adding up the contents of same field (for example the 'Amount Payable' field on a batch of invoices) of each document in a batch.

For example, in a batch of invoices, a control total may be the overall total of all the invoices, and this will be calculated manually before the data is entered. On entry, the computer will automatically generate its own control total, which can then be compared with the manual calculation. This acts as a cross-reference and can highlight errors in data entry, although it will not tell you which value has been entered incorrectly, only the batch in which the error occurred.

Hash total A value made up by adding up the same value (for example the invoice number) on each document in a batch. The main difference between this and a control total is that a hash total will not be of any use other than as a verification check that all documents in a batch have been processed.

For example, in a batch of invoices, a hash total may be calculated by adding the invoice numbers together manually before entry. On entry, the computer will automatically generate its own hash total, which can then be compared with the manual calculation. Like the control total, this also acts as a cross-reference, highlighting errors in data entry, but will only tell you the batch in which the error occurred.

Each one of these verification techniques is designed only to indicate that something is wrong. They will not say exactly what is incorrect – that must be found by a visual check by the human operator.

9.3 Batch processing

Batch processing involves the collection of all transactions up to a specified time into a batch, which is then used to update the master file. A purchases-ledger system might be updated once a day at 4.30p.m. with a batch composed of all purchases invoices received between 9a.m. and 4p.m., when the batch is made up. Invoices received after this time must wait until the next day before they are processed. This form of processing is particularly suitable for the processing of large numbers of similar transactions which require careful checking.

The main feature of batch processing is this delay in the updating of the information held on the master file with the most recent transactions. Since the updating of the master file is delayed in this way, the information held on it will always reflect an out-of-date position, rather than the current situation. In the above example, the purchases-ledger file could only show the state of the purchases ledger at 4p.m. the previous day and so could only provide out-of-date information. This would be a problem for a travel agent selling holidays, since there would be a risk of selling the same holiday twice, but for some applications that do not always need to be so up-to-the-minute this is not so important.

The kinds of application for which batch processing is likely to be suitable include payroll, which need be updated only once a week (or even once a month), and personnel files which will only need to be updated as the information they contain changes, rather than every day. Small-scale businesses may also run their entire system on a batch-type method, since the size of their operation may not need all information to be totally up-to-date all of the time.

Batch processing was the main method of processing information in the early days of business computing and is typified today by applications with high volumes of input and output requiring large-scale processing. This makes it ideal for mainframe computer systems which are equipped to read data in, and print data out, at much higher speeds than is possible with smaller local computers. Typical applications include payroll, large-scale invoice production, and the cheque-clearing system.

9.3.1 Small-scale batch processing

In small-scale applications where the sole trader does the books using a personal computer, batch processing may be the most efficient way of operating. There are two reasons why this form of processing may fit in with the way in which a small business may be run. Firstly, there is no need for information held in the computer to be up-to-the-minute, because the business is small enough for the owner to be in touch with what is going on. Secondly, batch processing fits in with the way of working, with the business being carried on during the day, leaving the accounts to be updated at the end of the day or week.

Before the transactions (purchases invoices and sales receipts) are entered into the system they will be sorted into date order, validated, and then verified to ensure that they are correct. These are exactly the same types of check as would be made on data being used to update files held on large mini and mainframe computers.

9.3.2 Large-scale batch processing

Modern large-scale computer systems will use batch processing for only some applications, on-line processing (see section 9.4) being preferred for those areas which demand up-to-date information. While it is important to have up-to-date information on stock levels, for example, applications like payroll and purchases may only need to be updated periodically. It is for applications like these that batch processing is still used.

A typical batch-processing sequence for a purchases-ledger system that is updated twice a day might have the following stages:

1 The purchases invoices received up to 12.30p.m. are made up into batches of 50 invoices.
2 A control total (the total value of all the invoices) is calculated manually for each batch.
3 The information contained on each batch of purchases invoices is keyed-in by data-preparation personnel, the data being automatically validated on entry and stored on disk.
4 At the end of each batch the control totals produced manually and by the computer are compared to check for errors.
5 The purchases-invoice information is then typed in again, with each new keystroke being compared with the existing data as an additional check for errors. This, in addition to cross-checking with the manually calculated control total, effectively verifies that the data is correct.
6 The purchases-invoice information on disk is now sorted by the main computer into master-file order, since it is faster to use sorted data when updating.
7 The information is now used to update the purchases-ledger master file, creating a new master file.
8 Transaction summaries and management reports are produced and printed out.

This is illustrated in fig. 9.1.

9.3.3 Security of batch-processing systems

A batch-processing system updates the master file using new information held on a transaction file. A standard security method in use with batch systems is to keep several sets of master and transaction files and to reuse them on a rolling basis. This is called the *ancestral-files* (or Grandfather–Father–Son) system and it involves keeping three or more 'generations' of files. The system is illustrated in fig. 9.2.

If we assume that we are starting a new system in which the master file (MF) is updated from the transaction file (TF) in a batch process at the end of each working day, the system would work as follows:

Day 1 MF1 is updated with the day's transactions held on TF1 to produce the next day's MF called MF2. MF1 and TF1 are both stored in a safe place.

Day 2 MF2 is itself updated with the day's transactions held on TF2 to produce MF3. MF2 and TF2 are both stored in a safe place.

At this stage we have three versions of the master file: MF1, MF2, and MF3. MF1 is called the Grandfather file, MF2 the Father, and MF3 the Son.

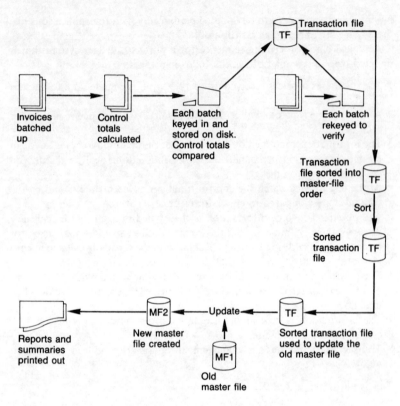

Fig. 9.1 A typical batch-processing system

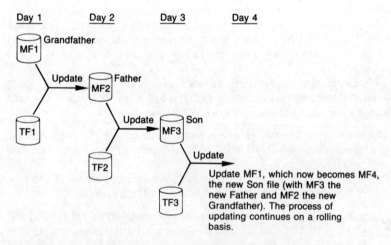

Fig. 9.2 The ancestral-files system of taking back-up copies of data

Day 3 MF3 is in turn updated with the day's transactions stored on TF3, the results being placed into the old MF1 disk which now becomes MF4, the new Son file. MF3 is now the Father file. MF2 (the new Grandfather file) and TF2 are both stored in a safe place, possibly in another location.

Day 4 MF4 is updated with the day's transactions stored on TF4, the results being placed into the old MF2 disk which now becomes MF5, the new Son file. MF4 is now the Father file, and MF3 (the new Grandfather file) and TF3 are both stored in a safe place, possibly in another location.

This process is repeated on a rolling basis, with each master disk taking it in turn to become the Grandfather, Father, or Son File. The justification of this method is that if one or two of the master files are lost for any reason, it is still possible to recreate them by using a previous set of master and transaction files.

In everyday use, the updating period might be more frequent than once a day, depending on the application, but the principle will remain the same.

9.3.4 Features of batch processing

(a) Information held in batch-processing files is always out of date, since it is only as recent as the last time a batch of transactions was submitted for processing. This may not be important for some applications.

(b) Batch processing lends itself to the processing of large numbers of similar transactions which require careful checking.

(c) Transactions are passed to the computer centre for processing by specialist computer staff, with output being returned to the user to be stored or used at will.

(d) It is easy to schedule processing at set times and therefore easier to organise work on a large computer with many competing users.

(e) It is easier to control the input and processing of data with batch processing than with the on-line or distributed methods described below.

(f) Batch processing has been declining in use as on-line and distributed processing have been installed for applications requiring up-to-date information or decentralised computing facilities.

9.4 On-line processing

'On-line processing' describes the situation where the user is able to enter information directly into a computer for immediate processing. If the computer is located some distance away it will be necessary for some form of communication link to be used, as described in Unit 8. These same links can also be used to retrieve information from the files held at the central computer as part of an on-line enquiry system.

On-line processing may be associated with fairly low volumes of input from a number of separate locations that are linked to a central computer. An example of this would be the on-line access to investors' records from the geographically dispersed branch offices of a large building society. On-line processing by definition operates in real time – that is, the transactions are used to update the master file as they are entered. For this reason, on-line processing may also sometimes be referred to as *real-time processing*.

Some applications must use on-line processing, since it is important that the information held by the master file always reflects the current situation. An example of this is the way in which many holidays are booked by travel agents for their customers by using a computer terminal linked into the holiday-company computer. Once the holiday has been booked by the travel agent it must not be sold to anyone else, and for this reason on-line processing of bookings is essential to avoid selling the same holiday more than once. Another application which requires on-line processing of information is the SEAQ (Stock Exchange Automated Quotation) system which provides dealers with information on the changes in prices of stocks and shares traded on the London Stock Exchange.

There has been a movement towards on-line and away from batch processing as the hardware and software have been developed to be able to cope with the heavy demands this type of processing makes upon a computer system. In a typical on-line processing system, data may be input randomly from a large number of dispersed terminals, validated and accepted or rejected on input, and then processed. Such a system needs a powerful multi-user multi-tasking computer that has large amounts of direct-access storage and a fast response time. In addition to this, since the organisation is dependent on the operation of its computer, the system must be very reliable and the possibility of total system failure must be planned for.

The big advantage of on-line processing is that it enables the user to control when and how processing will take place. Thus the computer system fits in with the way the business operates, rather than the business fitting in with the computer.

9.4.1 An on-line order-processing system
The advantage of an on-line processing system is that the master files within the system will always contain the most up-to-date transactions, so that management always has access to the most recent information. An on-line order-processing system which deals with all sales orders will update both the customer and stock master files. A simplified on-line order-processing system for a company that makes a large number of sales over the telephone would operate as follows:

1 The sales data is input at each of the data-entry terminals as it comes in.
2 As the order is placed, the system automatically checks the stock file to see if there is enough stock to fill the order. If there is sufficient stock, the order may be taken; if not, the operator is told to offer the customer a longer delivery date.

3 If there is sufficient stock, the system checks the customer file to make sure that the order will not take the customer over the agreed credit limit. If this is satisfactory, the order may be accepted.

4 Operators are required to sight-verify each order before it is accepted by the system.

5 Accepted transactions are used to update the customer file with the value and date of the sale, and the stock level in the stock file is reduced for the item purchased.

6 The accepted-orders file is also updated, this file being later used as a basis for printing invoices, picking lists (lists of goods to be drawn from the store) for the warehouse staff, and delivery notes for the van drivers.

This is illustrated in fig. 9.3.

9.4.2 Security of on-line processing systems

If an extensive on-line system fails, it is likely to paralyse the operations of the organisation to which it belongs. For this reason, when a large-scale on-line processing system is adopted, elaborate precautions are usually taken to guard against total system failure. Measures taken can include the following:

(a) Regular back-up copies of all master files and transaction summaries should be taken to ensure that if the current working copy is lost it can be recreated and operations can proceed.

(b) For applications like manufacturing, EFTPOS, and air-traffic control which cannot afford to have a computer failure, it may be necessary to have a duplicate computer on stand-by. In the event of the primary computer failing, or 'going down', the duplicate is able to take over processing operations.

(c) For applications like stock control and order processing, in which a pause in processing may not be disastrous, it may be possible to transfer processing to another computer. In this system the second computer is engaged in batch processing which can be interrupted to allow the on-line system to take over use of the computer until the problem is solved.

9.4.3 Features of on-line processing

(a) No delay in the processing of information, so that output can be received back as soon as processing is complete.

(b) Associated with fairly low volumes of input and output from many separate locations combining to produce a high level of processing at the central computer.

(c) Master files will always be up-to-date and reflect the current state of the business.

(d) The system will usually enable on-line enquiries to be made to the master file, requesting information on customer account balances etc.

(e) It is harder to control the quality of data input, since non-specialist users may be entering the data.

Order received

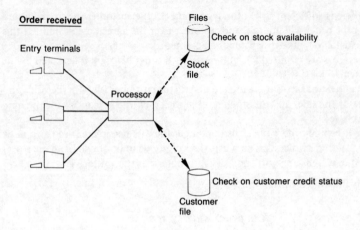

Order accepted

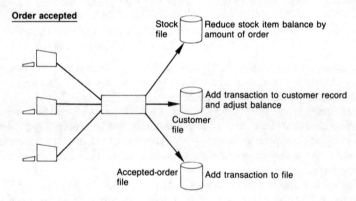

End of day

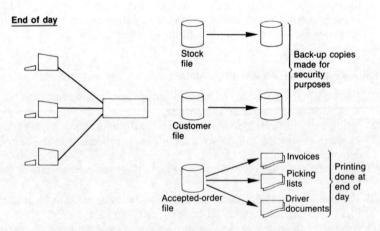

Fig. 9.3 A typical on-line order-processing system

(f) Increasingly used.

9.5 Distributed processing

Distributed processing is where information is processed at a number of separate locations which may then share their results and work in a co-operative manner. This differs from centralised processing, where a number of terminals are connected to a single computer, and it uses local or wide area networks (LANs or WANs) to link up computers and enable information to be exchanged.

Distributed processing represents a movement away from the concept of computing at a centralised single location, enabling users to take far more control over their own information processing. When companies originally introduced computers for business data processing, the applications computerised were those requiring large-scale processing like accounts and payroll. The cost of the computer system and the scale of the operations meant that processing tended to become centralised, and control over processing was taken away from the users and given to the computer department. This centralisation led to problems concerning the time taken to develop new programs and the responsiveness to the demands made by users. The development of mini and later microcomputers enabled users to take more control of their processing and fuelled the development of distributed processing systems.

It is not usually efficient to decentralise all processing, since some applications by their very nature need to be controlled centrally. Information on sales, purchases, and stock levels may be best kept centrally, but departmental planning and budgets and specialist applications may be best suited to a distributed approach. Distributed processing may be applied efficiently to a number of application areas, some of which are discussed below.

9.5.1 Applications of distributed processing

Office automation Staff are provided with their own powerful microcomputers which are used for such applications as spreadsheets and word-processing (see Unit 6). Communication facilities between the microcomputers are required for electronic mail, document distribution, data storage, and access to on-line databases (see Unit 10).

Data collection Point-of-sale (POS) terminals using laser readers to read bar codes on grocery products in supermarkets are an example of the use of distributed processing for data collection. In this case, the POS terminals collect the coded information for the supermarket minicomputer which stores it to be sent on (via a WAN) to the central computer at regular intervals. (See section 8.6 and the case-study on Sainsbury's in Unit 12.)

CAD   Computer-aided design requires so much processing power that a dedicated processor is often the best way of providing the fast response time needed by each workstation. In a CAD/CAM system these workstations may pass the detailed design drawings over communications links to other dedicated computers which control the CAM (computer-aided manufacturing) process and stock levels, as described below.

Factory automation   In modern factories, robots and specialised materials-handling machinery are controlled by their own dedicated computers. These dedicated computers are in turn co-ordinated by a central factory computer which controls the work flow and which may itself be linked to another computer which monitors the stocks of raw materials and finished goods.

Applications requiring a high level of reliability   Some applications demand a high level of reliability and a minimum of disruption in the event of computer failure. The signalling for trains on the London underground is carried out by a network of minicomputers – if a single computer fails, the other computers can take over. Newspaper production, which cannot afford to be delayed, is also often controlled by a network of minicomputers so as to minimise the risk of total system failure and the missing of a publication deadline – see the *Guardian* case-study in Unit 12.

Geographically dispersed processing   Some large organisations use separate computer systems for a variety of information-processing applications in different parts of the country. For example, the branch offices of an investment company may each have a small minicomputer for entering client details, assessing investments, and wordprocessing. These minicomputers are all linked to a central computer which collects all client data for centralised investment analysis.

A possible distributed-processing system for a design, manufacturing, and warehousing application is illustrated in fig. 9.4. (The Benetton case-study in Unit 12 describes a system similar to this.)

9.5.2 Security and distributed systems
The nature of a distributed system is such that processing may take a number of forms and be spread over a large geographical area. For this reason, security may take a number of forms, including the following:

(a) Regular back-up copies of all data should be taken at all processing sites.
(b) On vital applications it may be necessary to have a duplicate computer ready to take over processing in the event of the failure of the primary computer.
(c) It may be possible for other computers in the network to take over the processing tasks of a computer that has failed. In this way, processing can continue with other parts of the network sharing the additional load.

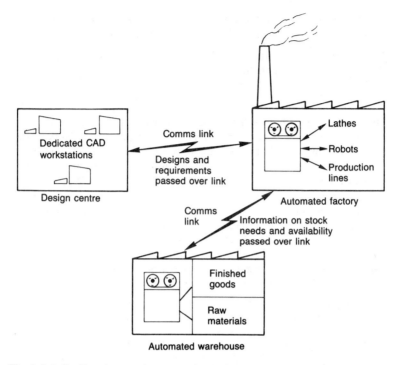

Fig. 9.4 A distributed-processing system for design, manufacturing, and warehousing

9.5.3 Features of distributed processing

(a) Information may be processed at more than one location, with sharing of information and other resources.

(b) Distributed processing may not be suitable for applications, like accounts, that require a high degree of central control.

(c) Faster response time, since users do not have to share time on a central computer.

(d) Users may be more involved in the development of their own computer systems, since they tend to have more control over their own information processing.

(e) Possible loss of central control of processing and also duplication of effort, with individual departments pursuing their own policies.

(f) It may not be possible to offer the same sophistication of software on smaller computers as is available on the larger central computer.

(g) Security may be harder to achieve, due to the geographical spread of a distributed system.

9.6 Using a computer bureau to process information

A computer bureau is a company which specialises in the provision of computer-related services to other organisations. The services offered will vary, but it will usually be possible for a bureau to take over all or some of an organisation's processing for a fee.

9.6.1 Processing information using a bureau

It is usually possible to arrange for any type of processing to be done by a bureau. The major functions of accounts, stock, and payroll may all be processed using either a computer bureau or another company offering a bureau service due to spare capacity on its computer system. The information to be processed, and the results of the processing, may either be transferred between the bureau and its client by courier or else be transferred directly using one or more terminals connected via communications links with the bureau computer. The latter method is preferable, since it reduces the data-transfer time.

There are a number of reasons why an organisation might decide to use a computer bureau to process information:

(a) For some complex or sensitive applications like payroll, it may be cheaper, easier, and more secure to pay a bureau to do them, rather than employ specialist staff.

(b) For applications like sales and purchases ledgers it may be safer to set up and test a new system using a bureau, before transferring to running it in-house.

(c) Small companies may find it more efficient to pay a bureau to do their book-keeping and so free more time to be spent on the development of their business.

(d) One-off applications, like circulars and compilation of mailing lists, may be more efficiently done by a bureau.

(e) Seasonal fluctuations in work may make it necessary to use a bureau to deal with some of the processing load.

Drawbacks of using a bureau for the processing of information may be a loss of control over processing, and the cost of the service.

9.6.2 Features of bureau processing

(a) Data may be processed efficiently without the high capital outlay involved in purchasing a computer.

(b) May be used to help deal with seasonal variations in the amount of work to be processed.

(c) Involves a degree of loss of control, since the processing of data is done outside the organisation.

(d) Use of a bureau to process data may work out to be very expensive in the long term.

(e) The use of a bureau may give the owners of a small business more time to concentrate on developing their trade.

9.6.3 Other bureau services

Most bureaux will offer many more services than just the processing of clients' data, which may only be a small proportion of their work. The types of service that may be offered in addition to the processing of clients' data include the following:

(a) *Consultancy services*   These will include specialist information and advice on a wide range of areas relating to computer systems, including data communications, networks, programming, and system analysis.
(b) *Systems development*   This may involve the development of a new computer system from its initial specification, writing of the programs, installation, and operation (see Unit 13).
(c) *Data entry*   It may be possible for bureaux to offer specialist data-entry personnel to key-in client data on payroll, sales, and purchases ledgers, or as preparation for changing to a new system. The use of bureau data-entry services dispenses with the need for a company to have its own data-entry staff.
(d) *Computer time*   Bureaux, or other organisations with spare processing capacity, may rent out computer time to those companies who wish to develop their own programs.
(e) *Stand-by facilities*   Bureaux may be willing to provide stand-by processing facilities to act as a back-up in the event of the client's computer being out of action for a long time.
(f) *Printing*   With the use of high-speed line and laser printers, bureaux can offer a mass printing service for the production of circulars and mail shots.

9.7 Glossary of terms

Master file   The file containing the main source of information on an application that is updated periodically.

Transaction file   A file containing information on transactions that is used to update the master file.

Updating   The process by which the master file is brought up to date with the information contained in the transaction file.

Ancestral files   Files generated from each other to ensure that the information held on master files is not lost.

Back-up   A copy taken of a file of information for security reasons.

Validation check   A check on data to be input to ensure that it meets pre-set criteria. Also called a 'reasonableness check'.

Verification check A check on input data to ensure that it is correct.

Batch processing A method of periodically updating a master file which involves a delay during which transactions are collected.

On-line processing A method of processing in which the master file is updated as soon as the transaction data is entered.

On-line enquiry The use of on-line facilities to extract information from a master file.

Distributed processing A method of processing in which a number of geographically dispersed computers co-operate in the processing of information.

Real-time Now.

Computer bureau A company that specialises in the provision of processing and other services to other organisations.

9.8 Exercises

1 What is the difference between verification and validation? Give three examples of each technique.

2 (a) Define the term 'validation' when used in connection with computer application systems.
  (b) Identify *three* stages in an application system where the use of validation is pertinent.
  (c) Describe *four* validation checks which may be used in application systems, and the types of error which each may detect.

(IDPM, Data processing II)

3 Using a VDU and keyboard, with direct access to a master file on disk, what *validation* routines would be used for entry of a transaction such as:

Transaction type   Account-Code   Date
Customer-name   Product-Code   Description
Quantity   Price each   Total value

(IDPM, Data processing I)

4 Business transactions can be processed either in batches or on-line. Compare the respective features of each of these two approaches.

(AAT, Analysis and design of information systems)

5 (a) A magnetic-tape-based system uses the 'Son–Father–Grandfather' technique for security. Explain with the use of a diagram how this is done and how the files are recovered after a breakdown.
  (b) What technique is used for files in an on-line transaction-based system?

(IDPM, Data processing II)

6 Examine the reasons behind the trend in many organisations to move away from centralised mainframe computing towards distributed data processing. (ACCA, Systems analysis and design)

7 What is a 'computer bureau', and in what circumstances would one be used?

8 What types of services may be available from a computer bureau?

9 The organisation for which you work uses a mainframe computer for many of its accounting systems. At present it operates mainly on a batch-processing basis, but senior management is keen to take advantage of the developments in information technology which have taken place in the last few years.
You are required to:
Describe these developments and their possible implications for the organisation. (ACCA, Systems analysis and design)

10 You have been called upon to act as a consultant on the application of computing to the business of a client company.
Required:
Explain what is meant by *three* of the following terms, giving an example which may be applied to a business situation: Real-time processing, Time sharing, On-line processing, Distributed processing.
(ACCA, Numerical analysis and data processing (part))

11 What is distributed processing and why is it implemented by many large companies? (IDPM, Data processing II)

12 (a) What is Distributed Data Processing? Illustrate your answer with a diagram.
(b) Describe how mini and microcomputers are used in such a system and the additional equipment required. (IDPM, Data processing II)

13 (a) Describe briefly the term 'real-time updating'.
(b) You are designing a large master file of data to be accessed in real-time. Discuss the following important aspects of your design:
(i) the form of file organisation you would recommend,
(ii) the file media you would choose,
(iii) the procedures you would recommend to ensure confidentiality of the data,
(iv) the precautions you would expect to protect the data from loss, damage or corruption. (CBSI, Management services)

14 One of your smaller clients is planning to expand in the near future by making use of the latest features of information technology.
Required:
(i) List and explain to your client some of the facilities that can be offered by using a wordprocessor.

(ii) Outline some of the advantages that your client as a small concern could gain by using the services of a computer bureau.

(iii) Your client has decided to purchase a microcomputer system which uses floppy disks (diskettes) on which to store files. Outline some of the security measures which the client should institute to protect those files.   (ACCA, Numerical analysis and data processing)

Case-study

You are an assistant systems consultant employed by a firm of computer consultants. Knowing that you are an expert on the methods of information processing, your manager has asked you to handle a contract from Exploit Travel Ltd to analyse its processing requirements and recommend the way in which it should operate its system.

Exploit Travel is a growing firm of travel agents specialising in adventure holidays. Its growth has meant that, in order for it to be able to co-ordinate the activities of its seven offices, it will need to install a computer. No decision has yet been made on the type of computer to be installed, but it has a list of the type of activities it would wish the computer to be able to handle, as follows: payroll; the booking of holidays from large holiday companies; keeping track of all bookings made; periodically sending out catalogues to selected customers; the printing of bills to send to customers; producing reports of the amounts due to holiday companies; keeping personnel records; keeping a database of customer feedback on holidays; keeping track of all income and expenditure; sending messages between branch offices.

Your job is to produce a report which does the following:

(a) Analyses the applications listed above and states whether each will be most efficiently handled by batch, on-line, or distributed processing.

(b) For each type of processing, recommends the security methods which should be adopted when the system is running.

(c) Discusses which applications could usefully be handled by a computer bureau, and explains the advantages and disadvantages of this approach.

Office automation

10.1 Introduction

'Office automation' (OA) is a term used to refer to the use of technology to support office communications and information-related activities. Sometimes also called 'the electronic office' or 'the paperless office', it involves a movement away from paper as the main way in which information is communicated and stored, towards the use of electronic methods of communication and storage. This movement inevitably has an impact upon the way in which information is handled and used.

Information is the life-blood of any organisation, and good communication links will ensure that the flow of information is not interrupted. The information that comes in to a trading company may include orders from customers, quotes for materials to be supplied, enquiries about prices, demands for payment, and so on. Different types of information will be received by each of the departments in the organisation – orders go to the Sales department, invoices go to the Finance (or Accounts) department, and so on. In order for any organisation to operate, information will have to be exchanged between departments as well. As we saw in Unit 1, information must flow between Sales and Finance, Finance and Purchases, Purchases and Sales if the business is to be efficient.

There is thus a need for good *external* communications (between the organisation and the outside world) as well as good *internal* communications (between various departments and individuals within the organisation). This information may be used as a basis for making operational decisions (and will then give rise to further information flows) or it may be stored for later use.

This unit will look at the facilities of the electronic office, how they may be used, and their impact upon office work.

10.2 OA and external communications

This section will examine how the facilities of the electronic office can increase the efficiency of external communications.

Efficient external communications has always been one of the key factors in the success of any organisation. The standard methods of communication – the postal service and the telephone – both have certain disadvantages. The postal service can be slow and erratic. It may not always be possible to reach the person you want using the telephone. There is a need for external communications services that do not suffer from these disadvantages, and a number of fast and accurate services have been developed.

Electronic mail, in a general sense, is the sending of messages electronically over a communications network, but the term is generally taken to refer to EMail.

10.2.1 Telex

Telex was designed to provide a fast and efficient means of exchanging written messages between organisations using the telephone network. Since it was started in 1932, the telex service has been constantly updated and now offers many of the features associated with modern telephone communications, such as an on-line directory, automatic dialling, and last-number redialling.

The telex service is a system in which each user has a unique code number. A telex message would be sent as follows:

1 The user types or dials the number of the terminal for which the message is intended.
2 Once connected, the message is then typed – a copy of the message being produced by both the sending and receiving terminals.
3 Proof that the call was made to the correct telex terminal is given by the exchange of an 'answerback' code.

The main advantage of the telex system is its wide acceptance within the business community, with a large number of users in the UK and worldwide. The limitations of telex are that it is based on a five-bit code that allows only a restricted character set, and all messages appear in upper case (capital letters) only. These limitations are, however, outweighed by its large number of users and the ease with which telex enables organisations to communicate. Telexes might be sent from a prospective customer to a supplier to confirm an order, from the head office of a company to a regional office to advise on company policy, or from a supplier to an overseas customer informing it of the despatch of an urgent spare part, for example. Although telex has been replaced by fax for many inter-company communications in the UK, it is still widely used for international communications.

10.2.2 External EMail

External EMail – short for 'electronic mail' – is a telephone-network-based communications service in which each user is allocated a 'mailbox' in the central computer of the service provider. The mailbox is the receiving point for messages sent by other users, the contents of each mailbox being private and accessible only by the use of a password. To find out if any mail has been received, the user must 'sign on' to the system and look in the mailbox. An EMail system is illustrated in fig. 10.1.

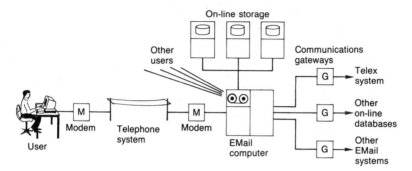

Fig. 10.1 An EMail system

The sending of a message using EMail involves several stages:

1 The message may be prepared on a wordprocessor and stored on disk.
2 The user dials up the EMail service and signs on to the system, using a password.
3 The user can read any waiting mail, perhaps saving some on to disk for later use, before sending the prepared message.

The message will be placed into the receiving mailbox immediately.

One feature of EMail is that it is possible to arrange for a single message to be sent to a large number of other users simultaneously.

In the UK, EMail was first offered by British Telecom in 1981 with Telecom Gold. The total number of EMail users in the UK is approaching that of telex users, but EMail is only beginning to offer the same degree of widespread connectability. To take advantage of the widespread use of telex, it has been made possible to send and receive telexes via an EMail mailbox. The problem of knowing when a telex has been received is solved by linking the mailbox to a radiopager which beeps whenever an incoming telex message arrives.

In addition to electronic messaging, EMail can provide the user with access to a number of on-line databases like the World Reporter news service, Jordans, and the Official Airlines Guide, among others.

Examples of the way in which EMail can be used include communications between offices in different time zones; between people who do not work from an office, like sales representatives and journalists; between people who 'tele-commute' or work from home; and between large companies exchanging correspondence.

10.2.3 Facsimile transmission

Facsimile transmission, or 'fax', is essentially long-distance photocopying. Like telex terminals, fax machines communicate directly with each other – the sending fax machine converts any image into a stream of electrical impulses that are transmitted over the telephone system, to be reassembled by the receiving fax machine. Fax machines are able to transmit graphics as well as text, something that no other electronic mail service can do.

A document can be 'faxed' to another part of the country, or another part of the world, with each transmission being identified with the time, the date, and the sender's or receiver's identifier. A receiving fax machine can collect documents from other units by calling them up, identifying itself, and asking them to transmit.

With the introduction of internationally recognised transmission standards (Groups 1, 2, 3, and 4), fax is widely used and accepted as a means of business communication. Fax communication is illustrated in fig. 10.2.

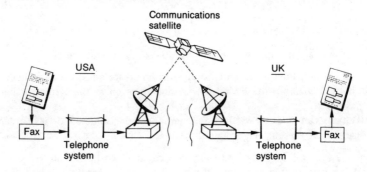

Fig. 10.2 Fax transmission

Examples of use include designs being faxed from a designer to a production centre, contracts being faxed from a company to one of its subcontractors, and photographs of a suspected criminal being faxed from Interpol in Paris to Scotland Yard in London.

It is interesting to note that fax is widely used in the Far East for business communications, because a written language which uses a large number of separate pictorial characters precludes the use of equipment of the word-processor type.

10.2.4 Electronic data interchange

Electronic data interchange (EDI) is the passing of orders, invoices, and other trade transactions directly between company computers. EDI avoids the need to print out documents at one end, post them, and then key the information in at the receiving company, and can thus be a faster and cheaper method of exchanging information.

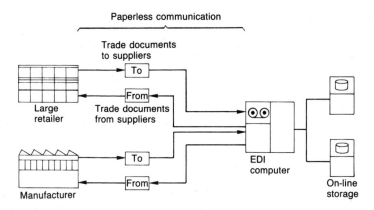

Fig. 10.3 Large-scale electronic data interchange between companies

Although EDI has taken place for some time – BACS (the Bankers' Automated Clearing Service) being an example – it is only recently that large-scale paperless business communication between companies has become possible. The use of EDI is illustrated in fig. 10.3.

Tradanet, offered by International Network Services Ltd, is an example of an EDI service that operates on similar lines to EMail. Each user of the service is allocated a private postbox and mailbox and can post outgoing trading information to other companies in its postbox, and collect incoming information from its mailbox. The Tradanet computer then acts as a clearing house by sorting all the mail collected in postboxes and sending it to the correct mailbox. The trading data then received by companies is fed directly into their computer systems, thus avoiding the need to rekey it.

Users of EDI include companies in the financial, health, travel, and leisure sectors, and also the government. The UK government has set up its own data network – the Government Data Network (GDN) – designed to link together the computing facilities operated by various departments. This will enable paperless communication between government agencies, and is intended to increase the efficiency of their operations. Other areas that have set up their own EDI networks are the Lloyd's insurance market in London (LIMNET), the British shipping industry (to handle import/export documentation), and the Electronic Record Ordering Service (EROS), set up to enable record shops to respond quickly to changes in demand.

The benefits claimed for EDI may be broken down as follows:

(a) *Operational benefits*:

● reduction in paperwork,
● improved accuracy,
● handling of paper invoices and statements eliminated,
● greater security.

(b) *Cost savings*:

● reduction of data-entry overheads,
● reduction in amount of stationery used,
● elimination of duplicated processes like the rekeying of data.

(c) *Logistical benefits*:

● reduction of order/despatch time-lag,
● improved delivery time,
● reduction in inventory levels,
● improved planning and forecasting.

It should be noted that, due to economies of scale, only big companies with a large number of trading partners are able to maximise the operational and cost benefits. However, both large and small firms are able to benefit by the fact that EDI will tend to bring companies closer together in terms of trust and understanding.

10.2.5 Viewdata

The term 'videotex' is used to refer to both teletext (a broadcast television-based service) and viewdata (a telephone-based service). Both these services offer access to information held on a central database, but only viewdata is designed to be used by business organisations.

Viewdata is a text-based service that is designed to display a single 'frame', or screenful, of information at a time. All information is held by a central computer system, and the user must use the telephone system in order to sign on to the system and access information. Viewdata will usually operate at 1200/75 baud – that is, it transmits to the user at 1200 baud and receives data at 75 baud. This speed difference means that, although it is an interactive service, it is designed to send more information (in the form of screens of text) to the user than it receives (the numbers of the pages selected).

Prestel, a viewdata system operated by British Telecom, was started in 1981 and contains information provided by over 1000 independent sources called information providers. The information available from these providers includes the latest share prices from the London Stock Exchange, train and airline timetables, consumer advice, and weather reports. Depending on the type of information viewed (financial information can be expensive), the user's Prestel account may be charged for accessing the information. It is also possible to book holidays and order goods from high-street shops by using special 'response screens' that feed directly into the company computer by means of Prestel Gateway. Prestel Gateway is designed to enable users to access directly into a company computer, providing direct access to the information that may be held there and allowing goods or services to be ordered.

Prestel also offers the ability to send and receive telexes as well as to send messages to other Prestel subscribers by using the mailbox service. The Prestel service is illustrated in fig. 10.4.

Viewdata is extensively used in the travel industry, with many of the large

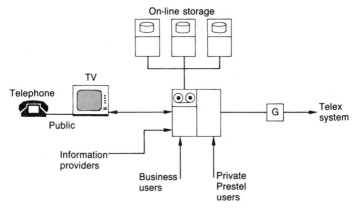

Fig. 10.4 A Prestel system

Fig. 10.5 A Sony KTX 1000 viewdata terminal

tour operators making it possible for travel agents to access their central computers to check on holiday availability and make bookings. Other users of viewdata as a way of obtaining information include doctors, farmers, and motor traders. Austin Rover, for example, operates a viewdata system (called Dealer File) for its dealer network that provides finance, sales, order, and service information that aims to eliminate much of the paperwork generated in day-to-day business. See fig. 10.5.

10.3 Internal communications in the electronic office

A high proportion of all communications take place *within* organisations, in the form of messages between individual departments and staff. The use of paper or the telephone as a means of communicating can be slow and subject to error, and this has led to many organisations moving towards electronic systems as a means of streamlining internal communications.

Internal written communications can be easily handled by some form of electronic mail system that stores all mail in a mailbox until it is collected. Internal spoken communications can be handled by voice mail (VMail), the speech equivalent of electronic mail, in which spoken information is digitised and stored for later retrieval. Internal EMail and VMail systems may be operated from a local area network, or else from a central computer system. Such systems increase the speed and accuracy with which communications take place within an organisation, and should enable information to be dealt with more efficiently. Figure 10.6 shows the screen for an internal EMail system called Microsoft Mail that is designed to operate over a LAN.

Internal communication systems may be just a small part of a larger office-automation (OA) system that offers a large number of facilities. In addition to an electronic or voice mail system to communicate with other users, such systems may offer such facilities as an on-screen calculator, a diary and networking calendar system for arranging meetings at different sites, word-processing, a database and spreadsheet, and access to information held on the main company files. Such systems will usually run from a mini or mainframe computer and are an attempt to offer electronic, or 'automated', office facilities for an entire business.

Digital Equipment Co. (DEC) offers such an automated office system in its 'ALL-in-1' package which runs on its VAX minicomputer range. IBM offers DISOSS (*DI*Stributed *O*ffice *S*upport *S*ystem) and PROFS (*PR*ofessional *OF*fice *S*ystem), both of which run with IBM computers and provide a range of office-automation services.

An example of how a sophisticated internal office-automation system might be used to resolve a problem might be as follows. It is coming to the end of the financial year and Dave from Personnel wants to know how much is left in his training budget. From his workstation, which is linked in to the company office-automation system, he sends a message to Janice in Finance, who handles departmental budgeting, asking what remains of his training budget.

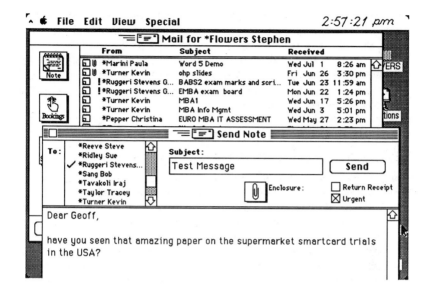

Fig. 10.6 A Microsoft Mail screen display

Janice receives the message, accesses the financial records system, and downloads the relevant information into her on-line spreadsheet facility. She prepares a memo to Dave telling him the latest date by which his budget must be spent, and sends the memo and the spreadsheet file to Dave.

Having read the memo from Janice, Dave switches to his spreadsheet facility and examines the figures on the spreadsheet. Dave knows that a number of other departments in the company have staff that need training in advance office systems, and that there is enough money left in his budget to send five people on such a course. Dave uses his wordprocessing system to write a memo to all department heads, explaining the situation and asking for nominations. In order to help the busy department heads, Dave accesses the company personnel database to search for suitable staff. The memo is sent to each department head with a list of suitable staff in each department, using the EMail system, with a priority tag that demands that an answer be sent urgently.

Dave is anxious to reserve the five places on the advanced office systems course and uses a communications gateway on the company EMail system to send a telex to the training company, reserving the places.

In order to plan ahead for the next financial year, Dave decides to set up a meeting between himself and the department heads to discuss future training needs. To do this he goes into the on-line diary system, which holds the commitments of all senior staff for the next year, and asks it to find the earliest possible date when all the department heads and himself are free for a one-hour meeting. The system searches the diaries until a mutually convenient time and date are found. Dave then books this time and date, and sends another memo on the EMail system to all department heads, informing them of the time, place and subject of the meeting.

Dave then sits back and starts to play one of the many executive games available on the system, to help him relax after so much work.

10.3.1 Private viewdata

Private Prestel is designed to enable businesses to maintain links between dispersed branches. Private Prestel operates within the Prestel network and can be accessed only by specified company personnel. Information on stock availability, prices, and other company business can be exchanged between staff and head office using the mailbox facility.

Organisations can use Private Prestel for a wide variety of purposes, including entering sales orders and issuing timetables and price lists, job schedules, and company news.

10.3.2 Videoconferencing

Videoconferencing is a system in which groups of people unable to meet at the same location can be linked in both sound and vision for face-to-face meetings. A typical videoconferencing system is able to handle meetings of six people in each of two locations that may be hundreds or thousands of miles apart.

The benefits of videoconferencing are that it avoids tying up key personnel in travelling to a central meeting place, and it speeds up the decision-making process. It is good for discussions and provides the means to solve problems quickly, but it is not thought to be so useful in situations in which persuasion or selling needs to be done. In addition to this, unless an organisation has its own facilities, there is the issue of the confidentiality of the discussions, since telephone-company employees will monitor the meeting. A typical videoconferencing system is illustrated in fig. 10.7.

British Telecom offers two videoconferencing services: Confravision, in which company personnel must travel to one of ten Confravision studios, and Videostream, in which companies are able to set up their own videoconferencing studios.

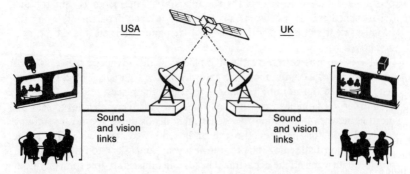

Fig. 10.7 A typical videoconferencing link-up

Typical users of videoconferencing are likely to be large national and multi-national organisations whose staff are too widely dispersed to be able to travel to one location for a meeting.

10.4 Flexible communications networks

Two major drawbacks of the use of electronic office facilities for external communications were their inability to be moved out of the office and the inability to communicate with many other users because of incompatible equipment. These drawbacks have been largely overcome with the introduction of the cellular-radio mobile-telephone system and intelligent communications links. The introduction of these two systems has enabled communications to be opened up to all users of electronic messaging systems using many types of equipment, wherever they might be. These two systems are considered below.

10.4.1 Mobile telephones

The mobile telephone system is a computer-controlled cellular radio communication network that uses radio to transmit telephone messages. The 'cellular' part of cellular radio refers to the way in which the country is divided up into a number of 'cells', each of which is covered by a low-powered radio transmitter. Each transmitter operates on a set of frequencies that is different from those of other transmitters around it, so that they do not interfere with each other's transmissions but the same frequencies can be reused across the country.

The computer control is needed to reroute calls automatically from one transmitter to another as users move between cells. This means that calls can be made while on the move without any loss of contact. The coverage of one system is illustrated in fig. 10.8.

In addition to transmitting voice messages, cellular radio can also be used for computer communications with the use of a modem. This opens the way for the use of portable computers to access a company's central computer without the need for standard telephone lines. The electronic office can now move with the person, rather than being located in an office block.

Typical users are people who need to be in constant touch with their office and who tend to lead a highly mobile working life. Sales representatives, architects and builders on site work, and executives who spend a lot of time travelling are all likely users.

10.4.2 Integrated Services Digital Network (ISDN)

The telephone system is the means by which most of the devices discussed above are linked together. At present, the UK telephone system is moving from one that was designed solely for speech to a digital network called 'System X' that is capable of handling a wide range of other types of communication. In the new type of network, communications will travel in digital form and the whole system will be under the control of computerised digital exchanges. This combination of computers and communications makes it possible to build

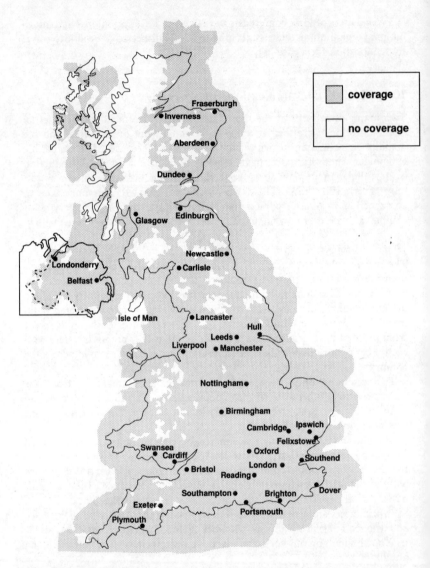

Fig. 10.8 The Vodaphone cellular radio network. The cells in fact vary in size according to location, with cells being smaller in areas of high usage (such as London) and larger in rural and coastal locations.

intelligence (the ability to cope automatically with a wide variety of devices and situations) into the system, and will enable a far wider range of services to be offered than is possible at present. The term given to this new network is ISDN (Integrated Services Digital Network), referring to the fact that all services will be available down a single communications link.

The new system will be used as a means of sending voice, computer data, and audio and video signals. It is envisaged that such services as data encryption (the automatic coding of data for secure transmissions), electronic mail, and automatic format conversion to enable different types of computer to communicate with each other will be automatically provided. It may also be possible to provide on-line database users with automatic cross-referencing to other databases. These services will be of great use to business users, but the system will also enable a range of new services to be offered to the domestic consumer as well. This is illustrated in fig. 10.9.

As a step towards this intelligent network, British Telecom offers a facility called Gold 400 to users of the Telecom Gold EMail service. Gold 400 is designed to connect public and private EMail systems and enable messages to be sent between them and the telex and fax systems. This service is based on a special protocol (ISO X400) that allows all types of electronic messaging systems to communicate with each other. This means that the compatibility of the sender's and receiver's equipment is no longer a problem, and communication with other organisations using different equipment becomes possible. Using this system, a subscriber to the public Telecom Gold EMail system should be able to send messages to a user of a private DEC ALL-in-1 EMail system, for example. It should also be possible for the same Telecom Gold user to send messages to a telex or fax machine in some other organisation. These types of facility will make the task of communicating with other organisations much easier.

10.5 The impact of OA on information handling

Once information comes into an organisation, it must be dealt with in some way. The action that is taken will depend on the type of information – orders for goods or services demand further communication to the Finance and Despatch departments, whereas a general enquiry may only require a company brochure to be sent out and the request to be put on file. The communication of information is, however, only one aspect of the impact of OA upon organisations. Work in an office can be divided into two broad types: clerical work (which involves the handling of information/data – document preparation, filing, etc.) and management work (which involves co-ordination of staff activities, and using information as a basis for planning and decision-making). The next two sections look at the way in which the facilities of the electronic office can be used in both clerical and management activities.

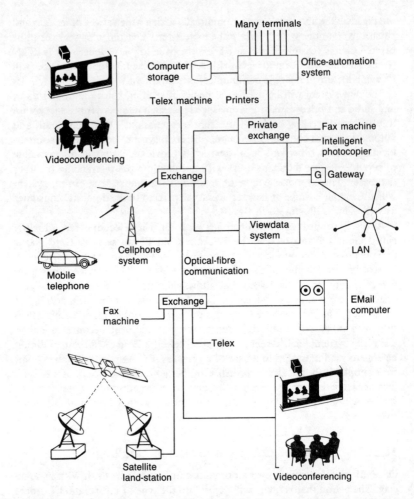

Fig. 10.9 Facilities that may be available through the Integrated Services Digital Network

10.5.1 Clerical work

The effect of information technology in the office has been to automate the routine clerical work of information-handling. Text-preparation has been revolutionised by the introduction of wordprocessors into the office. The word-processor enables text to be created, stored on disk, and reused at a later date, as discussed in section 6.3.2. The need for people to be employed to copy text (copy-typists) or retype letters has largely disappeared. The nature of the job of text-preparation has changed from being mostly concerned with the sub-sidiary activities of retyping, correcting errors, and handling paper, to concen-trating on editing old text and the creation of new text.

The updating of records has also largely become automated with the wide-spread adoption of computerised accounting and information-handling systems. Entering information is still likely to involve using a keyboard (although bar-code and optical-character readers may be used), but the extraction of end-of-month summaries and reports is likely to have been built into the system and be fully automated.

The use of integrated computer systems, as discussed in Unit 1, has replaced much of the paper communication between departments, with the computerised system providing a faster and more efficient means of communication.

10.5.2 Management work

Management work is as varied as the organisations for whom the work is done, and it is difficult to generalise about the impact that office automation will have upon it. In general terms, higher levels of management are concerned with the long-term development of an organisation and are not involved with decisions involving its day-to-day running. High-level management may not be as affected by OA as those lower-level managers and supervisors who are concerned with running the organisation on a daily or weekly basis. Such managers and supervisors need to base their decisions on the most up-to-date information available, and it is in providing this information that OA facilities are of use.

The use of computers in the office can bring positive benefits to the way in which managers work. The communications facilities discussed in section 10.2 enable up-to-date information to be obtained from other organisations as well as from the company computer system. This use of the latest information can take some of the guesswork out of decision-making by providing a more complete picture of what is happening.

In a similar way to the wordprocessor's effect on text-processing, the spreadsheet has revolutionised the way in which numerical information is processed. Using such software (see section 6.3.4) it is possible for managers to see the effects of changes in price, quantity, etc. upon their business. Spreadsheets have become an essential aid to the manager's decision-making process, with the effect of each change being checked upon the spreadsheet before a decision is taken. The use of graphics to present numerical information, either as a part of a spreadsheet package or else as a separate package, can aid decision-making by presenting the information in a more easily understood form.

Sophisticated programs called 'expert systems' (see Unit 15) can be used as a way of assisting the manager to make decisions about complex issues. Expert systems are special programs that are designed to imitate the way in which human experts make decisions on specific areas of knowledge. A stock-control expert system would be able to take in information about the ordering of certain stock items, for example, and make recommendations on what should be ordered, and also explain why it came to those conclusions. This would be of great use to a manager running a large supermarket with 15 000 different stock items who needs to maintain minimum levels of stock and avoid wastage. These programs are being increasingly used to support the decision-making process in such areas as financial management, general administration, and design.

'You'll have to start at the bottom on a remote VDU, my boy, and work up to a management workstation'

Such programs also enable access to the expertise contained in the program to be spread between the staff, who are able to use it to support their own decision-making.

10.6 Storage and retrieval of information in the electronic office

Office automation cannot dispense entirely with paper as a means of holding information – nor is it ever likely to – but information is stored in a number of different forms. One aspect of the automation of many of the manual office systems like text-preparation and record-keeping has been the use of non-paper methods of storing information. Much of the information needed to run the electronic office will be stored upon magnetic or optical disks that are held on-line to enable rapid access to the information held there (see Unit 5). These disks will in turn have been copied and the copies stored elsewhere for security reasons (see Unit 9). Other systems like microfilm/microfiche (see section 4.3.4), in which the documents are stored in a much reduced form, are also used – particularly for the keeping of archival copies of documents and records of transactions or balances.

The way in which information is stored will depend upon the size and type of the organisation. Information may be held on a large-scale database that is able to provide access to all information held by the company. Such a system provides an integration of information from differing areas that is not possible with other systems and can provide management with a much wider view of company operations. Microfilm may also be stored in a computerised document-retrieval system that acts like an intelligent filing cabinet, but with many more times the capacity.

10.6.1 Document image processing (DIP)

Document image processing (DIP) is a system that aims to avoid the costs and problems associated with handling and storing paper documents by using magnetic or optical disks to record document images in digital form which can be accessed and displayed on VDUs.

A DIP system can capture document images by use of an image-scanner or else as inputs from another computer system or a fax machine. Once captured, an image will be indexed to enable it to be easily retrieved, with images being stored either on a magnetic disk or, more usually, on an optical (WORM) disk. To enable fast retrieval of information, the optical disks are often stored in a 'jukebox' which is able to auto-select the required platter when a document is requested. The structure of a typical DIP system is illustrated in fig. 10.10.

A DIP system can offer the following facilities:

(a) *Work allocation and work-flow control* This enables work to be automatically routed according to a set of predefined criteria. For example, work can be prioritised according to the date received, so that the most urgent work is completed first.

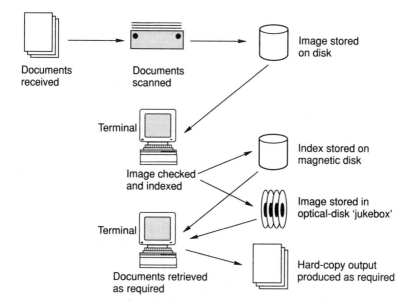

Fig. 10.10 Document image processing

(b) *Image annotation* Documents may be electronically annotated in a way that does not alter the original image and then be transferred, together with the annotation, to someone else on the system – a manager, for example.

(c) *Integration with existing computer systems* If integration with existing computer systems exists, data can be transferred between a DIP system and other applications software.

(d) *Management information* Information can be made available on the performance of whole departments or else on individual members of staff.

The main benefits claimed for DIP systems include:

● space savings,
● savings in photocopying costs,
● savings in microfiche costs,
● productivity gains,
● faster access to documents,
● reduction in lost or misfiled documents,
● improved customer service,
● time savings.

Some problems associated with DIP include:

● high cost,
● complexity,
● need to explicitly identify, or index, each document when it is received – retrieval difficulties may arise if a document is wrongly indexed,
● lack of paper copies, and the need to print one if a hard copy is required.

Examples of organisations using DIP include the Britannia Building Society, the Norwich Union insurance company, and the Co-operative Bank.

Case-study – the Britannia Building Society The Britannia Building Society has around 250 000 mortgages and has moved from holding documents in original form or microfiche to the use of DIP as a way of eliminating the huge amount of paper it has to store. The volumes involved are very large, with around 10 000 or so documents per day being committed to optical disk on to the FileNet system.

Once received, documents move through a series of stages before they are finally stored on optical disk. Firstly letters are opened and sorted, staples are removed, and then the letters are placed into batches of work. Each document is then put through an optical scanner, and the scanned image is checked to ensure that it is legible. The document images are then indexed and committed to disk, with the paper originals being shredded and finally recycled.

The documents are held on 12 inch WORM disks that are held in one of two OSARs (optical storage and retrieval systems) in the computer room, resulting in a vast amount of storage space being saved in comparison with paper files. Using this system, documents can always be retrieved, and it is also possible for documents to be viewed by more than one person at the same time.

Specialised Workflo software enables documents to be routed through the system to the people who need to see them, with other relevant information held on the mainframe files being displayed in a separate window on the screen. This means that, for example, when the Insurance department needs to finalise insurance arrangements on the closure of a mortgage account, all the relevant documents will be automatically extracted and displayed.

It is anticipated that, as a result of the FileNet Workflo Project, the productivity of the clerks who work within the Britannia Building Society could be increased by between 15 and 20%.

10.7 An automated office

The automated office described below might be part of a large multinational company. We will look at one office of that company and examine the links it might have with the rest of the company and with other organisations.

Within the company the vast majority of internal mail is handled by the EMail part of the company office-automation system. In addition to EMail, this system provides voice mail, wordprocessing, a spreadsheet, a personal database, an on-line diary and meetings scheduler, access to company financial information for senior staff, and a communications gateway to outside services.

Most staff will be provided with a workstation linked into this system, and all users will be able to use the keyboard to send their own memos and messages. There will still be a need for some wordprocessing staff to prepare documents, but the role of the secretary will have changed to resemble far more that of a personal assistant. Managers, in their turn, depend upon the system to provide them with the up-to-date information they need to make decisions, and to keep them in touch with their customers and each other. The more mobile of the managers will be provided with a mobile telephone and a portable computer to enable them to make use of the range of electronic office facilities while they are out of the office. The office itself will have a fax and a telex machine, and videoconferencing facilities linked to head office in London, as well as a range of shared printers and storage devices.

The company will have encouraged most of its suppliers and customers to move on to EDI (electronic data interchange) as a way of exchanging invoices and other trading documents.

The dependence of the organisation will be such that its computing facilities will be split over two sites, each with a back-up generator to avoid the disastrous effects of a power cut (see the Sainsbury's and NatWest case-studies in Unit 12).

Office automation is illustrated in fig. 10.11.

The effects of office automation on such a scale will be increases in individual productivity (as was achieved with wordprocessing) as well as in the performance of the business as a whole. This will be due to the improvements in the management information systems and in managerial effectiveness. At its best, OA provides management with a greater number of options and the ability to

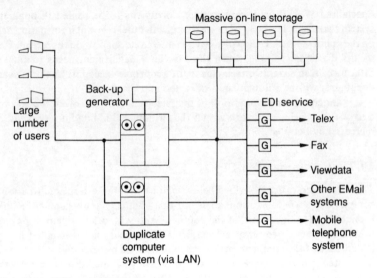

Fig. 10.11 Office automation

respond faster and to make more informed decisions. At its worst, an inadequate or inefficient system will cause a business to collapse through lack of information.

10.8 Glossary of terms

Electronic mail   A global term covering all forms of electronic messaging, although sometimes used to refer solely to EMail.

Telex   An international messaging service that operates over the existing telephone network to produce a printed message.

DIP   Document image processing – a method of document storage that involves images of the originals being captured using an optical scanner, indexed to facilitate future retrieval, and stored on a WORM (write-once read-many) optical disk.

EMail   A messaging service that allocates each user a 'mailbox' into which 'mail' in the form of electronic signals can be placed by other subscribers, for subsequent display or printing out.

Fax   The transmission of images by using a fax (facsimile) machine to convert them into digital form for transmission to be reassembled by another distant fax machine. May be thought of as long-distance photocopying.

Videotex   A menu-driven service which provides access to a large central database of information that is divided into pages. The term 'videotex' is used to describe both teletext and viewdata.

Teletext   A broadcast television-based videotex service, such as Ceefax and Oracle.

Viewdata   A telephone-based videotex service, such as Prestel.

EDI   Electronic data interchange – the electronic transmission of business information, invoices, orders, etc. between trading partners – by Tradanet, for example.

Videoconferencing   The use of sound and vision links to connect up two distant locations.

Cellular radio   A radio-based mobile-telephone network.

ISDN   Integrated Services Digital Network – the term given to a future network which will be able to provide a number of services (including fax, EMail, and video) down a single communications link.

Expert systems   Special types of program that attempt to embody human expertise in decision-making in a specific area of knowledge.

10.9 Exercises

1 In addition to internally generated information, businesses need access to external information sources.

   (a) Compare and contrast the services offered by Teletext and Viewdata giving an example of each.
   (b) Explain how private Viewdata can be used as an alternative to conventional computers as an information collection and distribution vehicle.

                           (AAT, .Elements of information systems)

2 (a) Briefly explain the nature and importance of office automation.
   (b) Describe the typical facilities which would be available in an organisation which makes extensive use of office automation aids.

                    (AAT, Analysis and design of information systems)

3 The local area network has been described as 'the glue which will hold together the electronic office'.

   (a) Explain what you feel is meant by this statement.
   (b) Briefly describe the technical features of a local area network.

                    (AAT, Analysis and design of information systems)

4 Explain the difference between the following systems:

   (a) viewdata and teletext,
   (b) EMail and VMail,
   (c) fax and EDI.

5 What advantage does fax have over EMail?

6 A very large mail-order company may house a mainframe computer yet also have a wide variety of other computer hardware in various departments. Name and describe five items of office equipment which you could expect to find in a specialist electronic office.   (LCCI, Information processing)

7 What is EDI, and what are the advantages to the business community of its large-scale adoption?

8 Which office automation system would be of most use to each of the following?

 (a) A travelling sales representative who wants to call in to the office from time to time
 (b) Divisions within a multinational company in different time zones who wish to be able to exchange information
 (c) A designer in the UK who wishes to send a technical drawing to a company in Germany
 (d) A UK company that wishes to send an urgent message confirming the placing of an order to a supplier in Taiwan
 (e) A large company that wishes to streamline the way in which it sends and receives invoices and other trading information to and from other companies
 (f) An old person who wishes to be able to book holidays and order goods without leaving home
 (g) A large company that wishes to hold meetings between key personnel located in different parts of the world, without the need to make them all travel to the same location

9 You want to set up a fully 'electronic' business that uses all the facilities of office automation. You already have a modem, a microcomputer, and an outside telephone line.

Find out how much it would cost to have each of the following: a facsimile machine, an EMail (Telecom Gold) mailbox, a telex machine, an EDI (Tradanet) subscription, and videoconferencing facilities (from British Telecom). To get this information, contact British Telecom or International Network Services.

Case-study
You are employed by a firm of computer consultants as an assistant systems consultant, specialising in microcomputer applications. Your manager, Ms Sykes, has given you full responsibility for the new International Services contract. The contract is to produce a report discussing how the International Services Group could make use of 'electronic office' facilities to improve its operations.

Background   International Services Group Plc is a holding company that grew out of the rapid growth of Burnton Office Suppliers over the last ten years. This growth has largely been fuelled by mergers and the acquisition of other companies in related areas. The result is that ISG Plc now controls some fourteen businesses that all trade in the service sector of the European market. In order to improve the group's effectiveness, it has been decided to investigate the use of so-called 'electronic office' technologies.

Task Produce a report that investigates each of the following electronic office facilities: viewdata, electronic mail, Prestel, facsimile transmission, telex, and integrated office-automation systems.

For each of these electronic office services you should find out:

(a) what facilities the service would offer to ISG;
(b) how the service could be used to co-ordinate the work of the group as a whole;
(c) the advantages/disadvantages to ISG of using the service;
(d) examples of the service offered;
(e) costs of the service.

Note Using the *British Humanities Index*, make a list of the articles that have been published in papers and magazines on this area. Look under the category of 'Computers' (as well as the items mentioned above) and see if you can locate and read some of these articles.

Computer personnel and their work

11.1 Introduction

The most important of all computer personnel are the *users*. The users – sometimes also called 'end-users' – may be reliant upon a computer system to process information, and will need the assistance of specialist computer personnel to do this. These specialist computer personnel are employed simply to ensure that the users are able to use the computer system to help get the job done.

Computer personnel can be divided into the three categories of development, operations, and support.

The development staff create and maintain the computer programs needed by users.

The operational staff are needed to run these programs for the users on larger mini and mainframe computer systems.

The support staff help the users choose new systems and operate existing ones efficiently.

The users can be thought of as being at the top of an inverted pyramid of highly trained and highly paid staff whose sole purpose is to make sure that the computer system does what the users want it to do. This is illustrated in fig. 11.1.

This unit will look at the work and responsibilities of each category of specialist computer personnel before looking at the ways in which these staff may be structured into specialist departments.

11.2 Development personnel

Development personnel are involved in the creation of new computer programs. A collection of individual programs linked together to perform a complex job (like order processing, payroll, or stock control) is usually called a *system*. Part of the work of development personnel is producing new systems in, say, Finance or Personnel. Another aspect of their work is in the 'main-

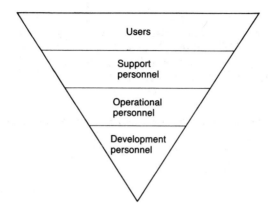

Fig. 11.1 Large numbers of users are supported by smaller numbers of specialist computer personnel.

tenance' of existing systems – that is, modifying and updating systems that are currently in use.

Development personnel are usually associated more with mini and mainframe computer users rather than with microcomputer users, who tend to use packaged software. This is because many larger businesses may have their own unique needs and ways of doing things and want a computer system that will mirror these existing methods. For this reason, development staff will be needed to create and maintain this 'custom' software. Organisations that use software that is not subject to continual development will not employ development personnel on a permanent basis but will hire them on temporary contracts to do specific tasks. It is quite common, even for organisations that do possess an in-house development facility, for new projects to be undertaken by outside contact staff.

There are two types of development personnel: systems analysts and programmers.

11.2.1 Systems analysts

Systems analysts are responsible for the design, testing, and implementation of new systems. At all stages in the development of a new system, the systems analyst should work closely with the staff who will use the system – the end-users.

Systems analysts need to understand both the ways in which organisations handle their information (their internal information systems) and the capabilities of the hardware and programming languages available. The primary task of a systems analyst is to translate the wishes of the users into a viable system design that will do what the users want.

The main tasks of a systems analyst involved in the creation of a new system will be as follows:

Analysis and design   In order to design the new system, the analyst must discuss with the users what they require it to do. A great deal of investigation into the existing system (if there is one) and the operation must be done before a design can be finalised. Throughout the entire design process the analyst will work very closely with the eventual users of the system, to ensure that the design is based on what they want, rather than what the analyst thinks they want.

Testing   Once the various programs that make up the new system (sometimes called a 'suite' of programs) have been written by the programmers, the analyst and the users must test the system. This is to ensure that the system operates as expected, in line with the original design.

Implementation   Once the testing is finished, and any errors have been corrected, the system will need to be installed before being used. This will include moving from the old system to the new one, training staff, and writing operational manuals.

Unit 13 contains a more detailed explanation of the work of the systems analyst.

11.2.2 Programmers
Computer programmers write the programs that instruct a computer what to do according to specifications that have been laid down by the systems analyst. The analyst and the programmer have the same kind of relationship as exists between an architect and a builder, with the original design created by the architect or analyst being implemented by the builder or programmer. Just as there are the two types of software – systems and applications software – so there are two types of programmer – systems programmers and applications programmers.

Systems programmers   Systems programmers specialise in writing the software that deals with the running of the computer system itself – its operating system and utilities (see section 6.2). They are generally involved in correcting problems, setting-up new software from manufacturers, and fine-tuning of the systems software in order to increase operational efficiency.

Applications programmers   Applications programs, like accounts and databases, are written by applications programmers. Most programmers are concerned with either maintaining or developing a range of applications software that is as varied as the uses to which computers are put.

11.3 Operational personnel
In larger organisations that use mini and mainframe computers that may serve the needs of many users, specialist staff are needed to operate the computer

systems. The operational staff will tend to specialise in one particular aspect of the running of the computer system. This section will look at the work of three types of specialist operational staff: computer operators, data-preparation clerks, and data-control clerks.

11.3.1 Computer operators

The computer operators are concerned with looking after the operation of the computer hardware. The kind of tasks done by operators include loading and unloading disks and tapes from drives in response to instructions from the systems software, loading paper into printers and removing the output, and making back-up copies of disks and tapes for security purposes. They will also monitor the overall performance of the computer system, and order maintenance and take corrective action when necessary.

Many large computer systems are operated for 24 hours a day, with operators working on two shifts and leaving the computer to run unattended overnight.

11.3.2 Data-preparation clerks

Data preparation is the conversion of data into computer-readable form. Data-preparation clerks are responsible for typing, or 'keying-in', the data (held on documents) that will be used to update the computer files.

The use of specialist data-preparation staff is generally associated with batch-processing systems, and is on the decline for a number of reasons. The introduction of more direct methods of data-capture (like the use of bar-code readers at point-of-sale terminals), OMR (see section 3.3.2), and the increasing use of direct entry of data from users' terminals are three factors in this decline.

11.3.3 Data-control clerks

In very large organisations that process massive amounts of data, staff may be needed for data control. The work of the data-control clerk is to maintain a record of all input and output, distribute the large amounts of printed output, and file magnetic disks and tapes.

11.4 Support personnel

The support personnel can provide the user with the advice and help necessary to choose, set up, use efficiently, and keep operational a computer system.

Support personnel are not usually on the full-time staff of organisations that use computers: they are more likely to be employed by computer manufacturers, computer dealers, or computer bureaux, with their services being hired out.

11.4.1 Computer consultants

Computer consultancy may be offered by a computer bureau, a computer manufacturer, a software house, or else by an independent firm of computer consultants. The role of computer consultants is to provide specialist technical advice to computer users. Such advice is necessary because the sheer complexity of computer systems means that few organisations will have sufficient in-house expertise to advise on all aspects of the use of computers. Consultants tend to specialise in specific areas like communications systems, networks, or office automation, and may produce a report for their client recommending a course of action to suit the problem area outlined.

It is always hard for the user to judge the quality of impartiality of the consultant, and work is usually obtained as a result of the reputation obtained from past results.

11.4.2 Hardware and software support

Computer hardware and software can be very complex, especially in the larger mini and mainframe computer systems, and an operator or user must be able to get help when a system does something unexpected. Help is provided by personnel who specialise in either hardware or software support, and who may be employed by a computer manufacturer or a software house. There are very often several types of 'support' available – ranging from 'telephone support', in which advice on the solution of a problem is given over the telephone (also called 'hotline support'), to 'on-site support', in which support staff will go to the user's premises to sort out the problem.

Hardware and software support is particularly important because many organisations depend on the uninterrupted operation of their computer systems to run efficiently. The spread of computer power in the form of micro-computers has increased this need for support, and some large organisations with hundreds of micros in use have set up in-house information centres which both provide this support and also provide training and advice on the operation of micro hardware and software.

'It's user-hostile'

11.4.3 Training

Training is a very important aspect of using a computer within any organisation.

Organisations that develop their own custom software will rely upon the systems analyst to organise the training of staff who are to use the system, as discussed in section 11.2.1.

The users of packaged software are more likely to rely upon the supplier to provide initial training, or may even use one of the many specialist computer-training establishments. These specialist companies will generally offer training in either specific packages or general computer 'awareness', the courses being conducted either at their training centre or else on the user's premises.

Training is likely to be necessary for all computer personnel at one time or other, and courses are available for managers, operators, programmers, analysts, engineers, and end-users.

11.4.4 Service engineers

As with other support personnel, computer service engineers are likely to be employed by dealers, manufacturers, and suppliers and to be hired out to users as they are needed. It is only in companies which use very large computer systems that there will be enough work to occupy a service engineer full time. Some large computer installations will employ hardware maintenance engineers and technicians, especially if a wide range of equipment or a large communications network is used.

11.5 Departmental structures

The use of computer systems to run such business systems as accounts, payroll, and stock control led to the development of the specialist data-processing (DP) department. The size and structure of this department will depend on the amount of data to be processed, and on whether the computer software is being continually updated or is subject to little change.

It is hard to generalise about the size and structure of data-processing departments (if they are indeed called that), but they all need some sort of management structure. At the top of this structure there will usually be a data-processing manager, who may be responsible directly to the board of directors of the company. The larger the department, the greater the number of management or supervisory staff that will be needed to co-ordinate staff activities.

Organisations which use computers only in a very small way - one or two microcomputers, for example - will not have (or need) a specialist department to process information. This section relates only to those companies which make use of mini or mainframe computers maintained by a specialist department to process information. We will look at examples of typical departmental structures and will place the computer personnel discussed above into their operational context.

11.5.1 Unchanging software

In a department in which there is little alteration to the software being used, there will be no need to employ systems analysts or computer programmers.

The two organisation charts in fig. 11.2 illustrate the difference between a small and a large organisation operating largely stable software. As can be seen, the larger department will need additional layers of management in the shape of an operations manager and additional supervisors to deal with the greater number of staff.

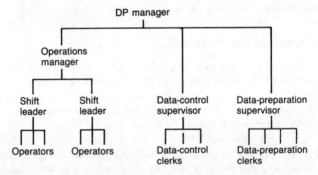

Fig. 11.2 Typical departmental structures in organisations in which software is largely unchanging

11.5.2 Developing software

In a department in which there is continual development of new and existing computer systems, it may be necessary to employ systems analysts and computer programmers. In a small organisation, the roles of systems analysis and programming may be combined, with the staff being called analyst/programmers. Larger organisations involved in the development of new systems will often divide their development staff into teams, with each team working on a particular part of the new system (in the same way as building a house will involve bricklayers, plasterers, etc.). Such organisations will need additional layers of management in the shape of senior systems analysts, who co-ordinate the work of the teams of analysts, and senior programmers, who co-ordinate the efforts of the programming teams. Such large organisations may also have a specialist section devoted to the support and co-ordination of the large number of microcomputer users.

Organisation charts for the data-processing departments in small and large organisations with developing software requirements are shown in fig. 11.3.

11.6 Glossary of terms

Computer user The most important of all computer personnel, for whose benefit the whole system exists.

Systems analyst A specialist whose job is to analyse an activity or system to determine if and how it may be improved using computer systems. Will also be involved in the design, testing, and implementation of the new computer system.

Systems programmer Writes program code for operating systems, languages, and utilities.

Applications programmer Writes program code for applications software like payroll, stock control, etc.

Operator Looks after the routine operation of a computer system.

Data-preparation clerk Converts data into computer-readable form, usually by keying-in.

Data-control clerk Maintains a record of all input and output and controls the distribution of printed output, the reception of data to be processed, and the filing of disks and tapes.

Consultant Provides advice on specialist areas of computing knowledge.

Data-processing (DP) department A specialist department set up to handle data processing in larger organisations that process data centrally using mini or mainframe computers. May also be staffed by analysts and programmers involved in the development of new computer-based systems.

Information centre A department that provides advice and support to users of microcomputer hardware and software within a large organisation.

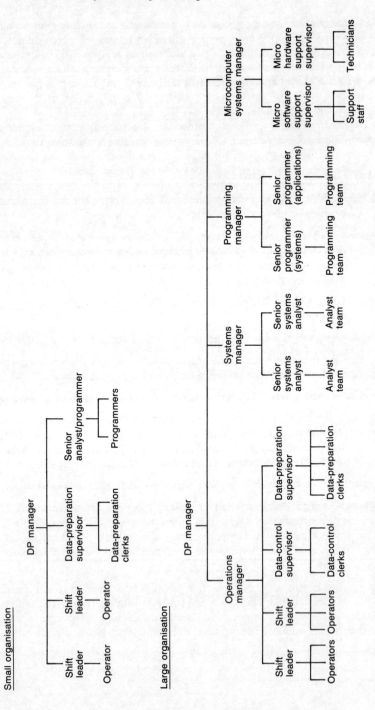

Fig. 11.3 Typical departmental structures in organisations in which software is continually being developed

11.7 Exercises

1 Why are the users the most important of all computer personnel?

2 What are the three categories of specialist computer personnel, and what services do they provide to the user?

3 What are the main parts of a systems analyst's work, and why is it necessary for the analyst to work closely with the user?

4 A centralised payroll and labour-costing system is used by many subsidiaries of a large organisation. All the master data needed to calculate standard payments are held on disk files at the computer centre. Variations, where appropriate, are supplied by the pay section in each subsidiary on specially designed forms, and data preparation is carried out on a key-to-disk system.
Required:

(a) Describe the techniques, both manual and computer, which may be used to ensure that only correct data are processed in the payroll system.
(b) What are the responsibilities of the Data Control section in such a system?   (ACCA, Systems analysis and design)

5 (i) Distinguish between data verification and data validation when applied to batch processing.
(ii) Distinguish between a systems analyst and a computer programmer.
(iii) Explain the terms RAM and ROM.

(ACCA, Numerical analysis and data processing)

6 (a) Distinguish between *software* and *hardware* and indicate the categories of software in common use.
(b) Describe the functions of a typical *operating system.*
(c) Who is generally responsible for maintaining the systems software?

(CBSI, Management services)

7 Draw an organisation chart for a typical DP department structure. Describe the responsibilities of:

(i) Systems Analyst
(ii) Programmer   (CBSI, Management Services)

8 Identify the two main types of programmer and explain the professional relationship between programmers and analysts.

9 List the main types of specialist operational personnel and explain how their work contributes to the operation of a data-processing department.

10 Compare and contrast the role of specialist computer consultants and trainers.

11 Why is there sometimes a need for processing to be undertaken centrally by a specialist data-processing department?

Case-study

You are a systems adviser working for Rutland Computer Consultants. RCC has been approached by a local firm of electrical wholesalers called Rutland Electrical Wholesalers (REW) to assist in the computerisation of its stock-control system.

REW at present runs its stock-control system using a manual method that has been in operation for many years, but it has decided that the time has come for this system to be replaced and for the company to be updated. The present system is inadequate and results in popular lines selling out on the one hand, and overstocking of slow-moving lines on the other. The finance director is also concerned about the length of time taken for credit transactions to be settled. This is due partly to delays in the invoicing department and partly to some customers being given too high a credit limit.

From the results of a feasibility study it has been decided to introduce an on-line integrated order-processing and stock-control system to be operated by a new information-processing department. It is planned that the new system will operate over two shifts. The day shift will be responsible for operating the on-line integrated order-processing and stock-control system. The evening shift will take care of the batch work of producing weekly statements, stock and sales analysis reports, and customer-account reports.

The systems analyst appointed to oversee the introduction of the new system has been involved in a car accident and will not be able to complete the project. You have just been appointed to assist in the development of the new system but arrive to find yourself in charge of the project.

The steering committee, which includes, among others, the accountant, auditor, sales manager, and stores manager, is due to meet in one week's time to discuss the current state of the project. You are required to attend and must have answers to the following questions:

(a) What additional staff are likely to be needed to run the new system? As an illustration, design an organisation chart for the new information-processing department.
(b) How much are the new staff likely to cost the company? (Use newspaper advertisements and information from your local Jobcentre to estimate the likely costs.)
(c) What will each of the new staff do? In order to assist the personnel department, you have been asked to prepare job descriptions and to suggest the requirements to be specified in newspaper advertisements for each of the staff you recommend.

Case-studies in the use of information technology

12.1 Introduction

Information technology is about the combination of computers and communications links to handle information more efficiently than was previously possible. At one time, IT was seen as playing a number of isolated roles within an information system (payroll, accounts, WP). Today IT has become the main integrating element within an information system, with the considered use of IT being an important factor in commercial success. The case-studies below aim to examine the way in which some contrasting but highly successful organisations make use of IT in their operations.

12.2 Benetton – the use of IT in an integrated manufacturing, distribution, and retail system

12.2.1 Introduction

Founded in 1965, Benetton is a highly successful family-controlled firm that manufactures and retails its own range of exclusive clothing through a worldwide chain of shops. Originally a knitwear manufacturer, it was only after some years of operation that Benetton moved into retailing through its chain of shops. One element in the success of Benetton internationally has been its ability to anticipate and respond quickly to changes in fashion. As we shall see, this ability to respond quickly to moves in demand in the fast-moving world of fashion has been made possible by the extensive use of IT in its operation.

12.2.2 The information system

The internal Benetton information system is based on two mainframe computers linked to a network of personal computers. This system is used for general administrative tasks like payroll, stock control, and invoicing, and has links to the other locations involved in the design, manufacturing, warehousing, and retailing of garments. The external information system is based on the use of the GEIS (General Electric Information Services Co.) network that links the Benetton main computer system with the company's agents and factories. To understand the way in which this system operates, we must first look at the way in which Benetton co-ordinates its retail outlets.

Benetton has divided the world into 75 areas, each of which is entrusted to an agent who is responsible for the retail operations in his or her territory. Agents are responsible for showing Benetton's twice-yearly fashion collections to the shop owners, gathering orders, and transmitting them to Benetton's head office in Italy. The agents will usually use a personal computer to link into the GEIS communications network and will transmit orders to an order-handling system. This system collects information from the agent's computers, updates the agent's product and price files, confirms orders, and routes them to the appropriate production centre (the central factories in Italy, or else in Scotland, Spain, or North America – each of which produces goods for a particular market). The GEIS network is also used to transfer orders between factories and for electronic mail between factories, agents, and Benetton head office.

This network provides management with up-to-date information on what is happening in each market, making the tasks of planning and control far easier. The use of this network also reduces the time taken for orders and reorders to reach headquarters, making scheduling of manufacturing easier and resupply more rapid.

We will now look at some other ways in which Benetton uses IT in its operation.

12.2.3 Computer-aided design

Once a jacket or a pair of jeans has been designed, Benetton makes use of CAD systems to produce a template for the range of sizes that the item will be produced in. The CAD system will also automatically calculate the best way to lay the templates on the fabric so as to minimise the wastage of materials used. The use of the CAD system has cut the time taken to produce these templates from around 24 hours, when done by hand, to two hours, thereby minimising the number of specialist staff needed.

The biggest advantage to Benetton of using CAD technology is not in reducing costs but in enabling the company to produce a greater number of garments in various colours and styles. For example, in a typical year Benetton might manufacture over 50 000 000 garments using about 3000 designs and around 200 different colours.

As a further step towards total integration, Benetton is linking up its CAD system with its computer-aided manufacturing (CAM) systems. This is termed CAD/CAM, and will enable designs created on the CAD systems to be transferred directly to computer-controlled knitting machines, increasing the flexibility of the system still further. Figure 12.1 shows these knitting machines in operation.

Fig. 12.1 Computer-controlled knitting machines in one of Benetton's factories

12.2.4 Production and warehousing

Benetton will only manufacture garments in response to orders that have been placed by its shops. These orders are placed into an 'order portfolio' from which production plans (which include the type of packing to be used and personalised store labels) are drawn up. This information is stored in a 'parcels expected' file at the warehouse at Castrette in northern Italy.

When a garment has been manufactured, a bar-coded label will be attached indicating its style, size, and colour, and its price in the currency (one of around 60) of the country in which it will be sold. Garments are then collected into boxes, with each box being labelled with a computer-generated bar-coded label addressing it to the shop that ordered it.

The boxes of garments, which are identified with a customer/store label, enter the warehouse by conveyor belts linked directly to the factories. The flow of goods is controlled by sensors which read the bar-coded labels (as illustrated in fig. 12.2) and identify the boxes that are entering the warehouse, cross-checking them with the 'parcels expected' file. The boxes that are to be delivered are identified by optical readers, and a sorting machine loads the boxes on to chutes ending with telescopic conveyor belts which extend directly into the delivery vehicles. All goods are thus automatically checked out by the computer system and, once the boxes have been loaded and the driver has signed the necessary papers, delivery can begin.

The warehouse is totally automated and requires 16 people to run it, consisting of 8 maintenance personnel, 3 warehouseman, 2 computer operators, 1 general director, 1 director of computer operations, and 1 distribution

Fig. 12.2 Stock movements in Benetton's warehouse are monitored by laser-reading of bar codes on all boxes entering or leaving

director. It is estimated that a similar warehouse organised in the traditional way would need about 300 workers.

12.2.5 Conclusion

The use of its extensive information network enables Benetton to get new products into the shops around six to eight weeks ahead of its competitors, giving a lead that is very important in the world of fashion. This system also means that Benetton can produce and supply goods that have been reordered by domestic and foreign shops very fast, usually within fifteen days. With the use of its sophisticated communications network, Benetton is thus able to respond quickly enough to be able to satisfy the rapid changes of demand in the fashion market.

12.3 J Sainsbury plc – IT in food retailing

12.3.1 Introduction

Sainsbury's is one of the leading food retailers in the UK, serving more than 7 million customers a week in 309 supermarkets that are run by over nearly 80 000 staff. A key factor in Sainsbury's continued growth is its use of IT in the operation of its retail network.

Managing a large and complex organisation calls for accurate and timely information to enable long-term plans and daily operating decisions to be made and their effects to be monitored.

To help meet the information needs of individual managers in all the main parts of the business, extensive use is made of computerised information systems. Most of these are developed in-house within a large DP department, although some ready-made systems (like payroll and accountancy) are used where appropriate.

12.3.2 Overview of information systems

Sainsbury's runs its complex computer operations from two locations, employing over 400 staff. These two DP centres use powerful IBM and Amdahl mainframe computers for a number of internal systems, including management information and accounting systems. Other information systems that are run from these two centres are as follows.

(a) The Central Database system stores information on the major parts of the business and is used by all other systems as the major source of facts about products, depots, suppliers, and branches.
(b) The Purchasing system puts the company buyers in contact with suppliers, and handles ordering, reordering, maintaining delivery schedules, and predicting likely demand for products.
(c) The Warehouse system helps to manage warehouse space and ensure that stock levels are optimised.
(d) The Branch Ordering system enables branches to place orders for goods for delivery the following day. This system makes use of a BT-managed X25 communications network that links the branches with the central computer and the depots.
(e) The Electronic Data Interchange (EDI) system is used to exchange trading information like orders, invoices, and statements with suppliers electronically.
(f) The Payroll system is run centrally and handles the wages for nearly 94 000 staff.

12.3.3 Distribution system

Sainsbury's shops are served daily from four large Sainsbury-owned distribution depots and seventeen other distribution depots operated under contract. The Branch Ordering system is used to enable supermarkets to order goods for delivery the next day. The system works like this:

(a) Orders are transmitted to central computers located at one of the DP centres.
(b) The orders are then allocated between the nearest depots to ensure the most efficient distribution of goods.
(c) Once the orders are received by the depots, the deliveries for each store are assembled and loaded on to delivery vehicles.
(d) The first deliveries leave the depots in time to arrive at all stores by 7.30 a.m. at the latest.

Overall, several hundred minicomputers support ordering and scanning in the stores, each of which is connected to the DP centre. In excess of 60 depots are on-line to the centre and depend upon a 24-hour seven-day processing facility.

12.3.4 In-store systems

Sainsbury's has installed minicomputer systems in all of its retail branches to assist managers in efficient deployment of staff, management of stock levels, and reordering. In all its stores, ICL laser-scanning equipment is in use at the check-outs (fig. 12.3), linked to an in-store minicomputer that assists stock

Fig. 12.3 Laser-scanning equipment in use at a Sainsbury's check-out in Winchester

replenishment and provides management with up-to-date information on sales. In these stores, price changes are controlled from head office, with the price updates being sent over a communications link to update the Item Price File held by the in-store minicomputer. This system is very efficient since price changes are made immediately, avoiding the need to reprice every good on display.

Figure 12.4 shows a hand-set being used to check shelf stock.

12.3.5 Security

In common with many organisations whose operation depends upon their computer systems, there is a corporate policy to ensure that the systems are available for use as required by the business and the impact of failures is

Fig. 12.4 A hand-set being used to check shelf stock in Sainsbury's Taunton branch

minimised by contingency arrangements. Like NatWest (see section 12.4), Sainsbury's operates its computer system over two sites, one of which is in Stevenage and the other in Feltham. These sites are connected by high-speed communications links and use the same types of hardware and software systems to enable each one to act as a back-up to the other in the event of a system failure.

12.4 The National Westminster Bank – the use of IT in banking

12.4.1 Introduction
The NatWest Bank is an example of a very large organisation that makes extensive use of computers, in this case linking together nearly 3000 branches managing around 15 000 000 accounts. NatWest runs its UK operation from three powerful data centres – in London, Leicestershire, and Staffordshire. Most of the bank's branches and special-service departments are linked to its private

high-capacity digital network, via switching centres strategically located around the country.

We will now look in more detail at the component parts of the large NatWest computer system.

12.4.2 The NatWest Digital Integrated Network

NatWest has the largest branch network in the Western world and a large number of specialised departments, and it is essential that staff have both an efficient telephone system and easy access to the data held on the bank's computers. In order to meet these two needs, the Digital Integrated Network (DIN) was created to serve the whole NatWest Group, providing a circuit-switched private telephone network and a private packet-switched data network. All the hardware used is owned and operated by NatWest, but the circuits connecting it are rented from British Telecom and Mercury. There are a total of twenty switching centres connected by 2 Mb circuits, with separate 64 Kb/s lines for the largest users that can also be used as alternative routes. Analogue lines carry most voice and data services from the switching centres to the branches, with 9.6 Kb/s modems for data.

For security reasons, the network does not have any connections to public data services, although the voice network has digital connections to Mercury's public telephone network, enabling cross-country calls from large offices at local rates. The same circuits can be used to provide local numbers for customers to call the centralised departments.

The bank runs its own Network Management Centre that is staffed around the clock in order to monitor all the hardware, co-ordinate repairs and maintenance, and control the connection of new equipment.

The NatWest DIN is illustrated in fig. 12.5.

12.4.3 Network contingency

As in many organisations that rely upon efficient and continuous network operation, contingency is an important part of NatWest's network planning. The following points will give an idea of the nature and complexity of NatWest's contingency planning:

(a) Within the data centres there are reserve CPUs and separate routes via British Telecom and Mercury to at least three DIN centres.

(b) The DIN will route data to alternative data centres if one fails, and will bypass a switching centre if necessary.

(c) Every DIN centre has one or more cable routes, often connecting to different British Telecom exchanges.

(d) Every DIN switching centre has a stand-by generator and battery-backed 'uninterruptable' power supplies, plus automatic fire-extinguishing systems and a comprehensive security system.

(e) Larger branches have connections to two switching centres.

(f) Data circuits to branches have a 'dial-up' connection enabling connection to *any* switching centre.

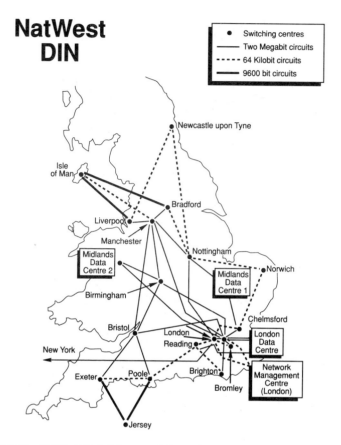

Fig. 12.5 The NatWest Digital Integrated Network

12.4.4 The branch interface equipment

An important device which is integral to the network is the branch interface equipment (BIE). This unit, using specially commissioned software, is an intelligent distributed processor which uses multiple microprocessor technology (32/16 bit) and has its own built-in disk storage.

Within the branches, the BIE forms the two-way interface between the network and the branch equipment – which can include ATMs, keyboard screens, back-office terminals, cashier terminals, printers, etc. – plus the alarm systems. The branch interface is illustrated in fig. 12.6.

12.4.5 Computer systems

The centres are powered by a variety of processors, including hardware from IBM, Amdahl, Tandem and Unisys. Switching units link them to a large number of peripheral devices for data input, storage, transmission, and

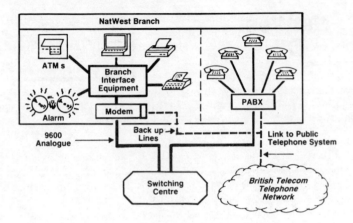

Fig. 12.6 The NatWest branch interface

printing. A large amount of systems development is done in-house, and the computers on which this takes place are configured independently and use separate peripherals from those handling the day-to-day operation of the bank.

Control of each computer complex is exercised from a central control room using VDUs. These control areas are not located physically in the computer room, but computer operators, assisted by a software system known as JES3 (Job Entry System 3), run all operations from them. Each type of peripheral – disk, tape, or printer – is located in a specific area with its own VDU through which the operating staff can initiate and respond to instructions from the main control room. The cheque-clearing system has its own control room, since its operation requires more manual intervention.

12.4.6 Information storage
Information on each of the 15 million accounts, plus the files for all the bank's other systems, is held either on disk or on magnetic-tape cartridge. It is important that the method of storage is able to provide a fast response time and be able to handle the millions of transactions and enquiries received each day. For this reason, the bank makes use of many hundreds of fixed-disk drives, with a capacity of over 4 terabytes (4 000 000 000 000 bytes).

Magnetic tape, although a slow medium for normal processing, is still occasionally used for such things as taking back-up copies of disk storage, or for providing information as input for BACS (Bankers' Automated Clearing Service) and customers' own systems. It is also used as an intermediate medium between disk storage and microfilm.

Both microfilm and microfiche provide a means of storing large amounts of information in a compact form. It is a legal requirement that certain information must be kept by the banks for a number of years, and microfilm provides a convenient medium for this purpose. Microfiche is more easily handled than microfilm and is used for storing information that will need to be referred to more often than that held on microfilm.

Conventional tape units at NatWest are gradually being replaced by large robotic StorageTek tape cartridge units that are able to hold 6000 cartridges with a total storage capacity of 1.2 terabytes.

Data cartridges are another storage medium extensively used by NatWest. These cartridges hold wide magnetic tape (approx. 70 mm) and are used in three main ways:

(a) *Back-up* All the prime records at the data centres are downloaded on to data cartridges, with each centre backing up one of the others' critical files.

(b) *Storage of customer files* All customer statement information for the last eight years is stored on the data cartridges. This information is accessible over the network from any branch.

(c) *Archiving* Files held on magnetic disk that have not been used for a certain time will automatically be archived – i.e. moved from magnetic disks to off-line storage media.

12.4.7 Printed output

Although the bank still uses line printers (operating at 5000 lines per minute), most printed output is produced by IBM laser printers. These printers have a maximum speed of 20000 lines per minute, and they jointly produce some 120000000 customer statements a year.

12.4.8 The software environment

(a) **Operating systems** NatWest mainframes are run with the IBM operating systems MVS/XA, MVS/EXA, and VM. These are connected into three JES3 complexes providing cover for the two live and one development computer centres, all three being controlled from the London centre via the system-control area.

(b) **Programming languages and methods** There are a number of programming languages in use at NatWest, with the majority of existing programs being written in PL1 and ASM (an assembly language). The current strategy within NatWest is to write new programs and systems in COBOL.

Use is made of a number of methodologies in the design and building of programs and systems, with systems analysts using LSDM (Learmonth and Burchett System Design Method). Programmers make use of the JSP (Jackson Structured Programming) method in the production of programs. JSP is a methodology which supports the diagramming of programs into recognisable groups. From this, the programmer is able to check for problems in the logic before the program is written.

(c) **Databases** At present NatWest uses two databases supplied by IBM – IMS (Information Management System) and DB2. IMS is a hierarchical database using inverted-tree data structures, and DB2 is a relational database that stores data in a number of linked tables. DB2 is to be the basis for the redeveloped mainstream banking systems and, when operational, will be able to process 200 transactions per second using databases with up to 15 million records each, across multiple CPUs.

The advantages of using a database rather than a conventional computer file fall into three categories:

(a) by allowing all programs to access the same data, it eliminates the need for the same data to be stored a number of times;
(b) when the data is rearranged, it is no longer necessary to modify every program that uses the data;
(c) back-up and recovery of data is automatically handled by the database system.

12.4.9 Office automation

There are a number of OA systems in use throughout NatWest, and they all offer WP, spreadsheets, graphics, EMail, and an electronic diary system. With an organisation as big as NatWest, a large amount of information is in circulation in the form of memos, information sheets, etc. The OA system makes the production and updating of such circulars much more efficient.

The electronic image is drawn from the OA file and is updated before being printed and used as a master to produce the several thousand copies that may be needed. Each document is out of its file for a fraction of the time that it would be with a manual system, and none is mislaid. Using a document scanner, technical diagrams can be included in the text as required simply by scanning in an existing drawing. Production of technical manuals for staff training is thus greatly simplified.

12.4.10 Business services

(a) Corporate cash management A number of cash-management services are delivered to customers electronically via the bank's Tandem host computers, allowing interaction between the host service and the customers – usually very large companies. The services offered include:

- *Balance and Transaction Reporting Service* (BATRS) This service provides the customer with account balances and details of transactions for both sterling and currency accounts.
- *Money Transfer Service* (MTS) Customers can electronically issue NatWest with payment instructions regarding money transfers they wish the bank to execute on their behalf. The bank will use the most appropriate means, e.g. same-day value in sterling via CHAPS or in foreign currency via SWIFT, or inter-account transfers via NatWest internal systems.
- *The Treasury Data Service* (TDS) This is an in-house service providing subscribers with foreign-exchange and interest rates, which act as a very useful guide for indication and valuation purposes. This service is based on PCs and is electronically updated from the NatWest treasury.

(b) Financial and investment services NatWest offers a range of financial and investment services from over 70 specialist offices around the country. The Trustee computer system, written to support these offices, is able to perform complex capital-gains calculations on disposal of Stock Exchange assets.

The mainframe system is linked to minicomputers in two investment offices where customers' portfolios of securities are regularly reviewed. There are some 55 000 funds containing 1 000 000 active accounts, plus 780 000 holdings spread across 20 000 securities and a further 150 000 other assets.

(c) NatWest Insurance Services NatWest Insurance Services is one of the largest insurance brokers in the UK. It is an independent intermediary, giving customers advice on the best policies available on the market for their needs. The central hardware includes a number of DEC VAX processors which are clustered together, each having access to a large backing store. Software to control the functions required by the various Insurance Services departments enables the processors to be linked to hundreds of DEC colour terminals.

12.4.11 Personnel system

NatWest employs nearly 100 000 personnel of various skills, grades, and categories in the UK, and the records for all of them are held on computer. Details stored include name, birth date, date of entry, present-job starting date, salary (current and historical), qualifications, experience, sex, marital status, grade, future potential, present branch/department, etc.

The system operates to achieve two main functions:

(a) It undertakes the book-keeping of personnel, updating the records when staff join, transfer, or leave. Schedules of amendments to the staff files are produced, and every month the total position and a movement analysis are both listed.
(b) The database is available to the Personnel division to enable it to obtain a variety of analyses and extracts it needs for its planning requirements. There is also ready access to the data for the purpose of staff reviews.

12.4.12 The clearing system

The bank has to be able to process an average of 3 million cheques a day, peaking at around 3.5 million on Tuesdays, and anything up to 5 million at times like Christmas. The cheque-clearing system is controlled by mainframe computers which control IBM cheque-reader sorters (MICR) that are able to read documents at up to 2000 cheques per minute (see fig. 3.9).

In a single year over 2 000 000 000 cheques and credits are moved around the UK banking system, and this figure does not include items paid directly into an account-holder's own branch.

As an E13B MICR reader will not read alphabetical characters, credit vouchers (gas, electricity, telephones, etc.) which are largely printed on line printers and contain alphabetical characters are processed on REL Trace 1 OCR equipment. This system reads credits at 1800 documents per minute.

12.4.13 EFTPOS

The volumes quoted in the previous section are growing each year, and for this reason all banks are looking to capture the financial information where a transaction takes place, and so replace the cumbersome and expensive paper clearing system. A movement towards this is the adoption of electronic funds transfer at point of sale – EFTPOS.

EFTPOS is a system by which goods and services may be paid for by sending details of the transaction over a communication link to the customer's bank and the retailer's bank as the transaction is made. EFTPOS is an electronic clearing system which can accept both credit-card entries and transaction cards (i.e. debit cards, ATM cards, cheque guarantee cards, etc.). Terminals are installed at retail outlets, and magnetically striped cards, with associated personal identification numbers (PINs), are issued to customers. Purchases are made by debiting the cardholder's account and crediting the retailer's bank account, thereby eliminating the costly and time-consuming task of clearing paper.

12.4.14 Electronic data interchange

EDI (see section 10.2.4) covers all forms of paperless trading, and NatWest offers two EDI services:

(a) *BankLine Interchange*   This is an electronic trade payment service that enables corporate customers to send payment instructions to NatWest together with the remittance advice for transmission to the supplier. The linking of financial and trading data in this way enables both parties to carry out a completely automated reconciliation.

(b) *Factornet*   This provides an electronic debt-factoring service for business customers.

NatWest is also looking at EDI technology for other activities, such as the transfer of insurance premiums and claims, collection and settlement of retailer debit-card transactions, and EDI purchasing of NatWest's own stationery requirements.

12.4.15 Power supply

NatWest's London computer centre, being purpose-built, has its own power-generation plant. Electricity is generated by diesel-fuel engines and is the primary source of supply for the computer systems. The London Electricity Board is available as a back-up. The Midlands centres also have power-generation equipment, but in this case it provides only a stand-by facility: fluctuations in the voltage supply of the local electricity board are absorbed by battery sets which, in the event of failure, provide an intermediate supply until the stand-by generators can be brought into use.

At all centres, Johnson Controls computer systems manage the building support systems – power supply, lifts, lighting, air-conditioning, fire protection, security, etc. Instant warning of any particular problem area is given on colour VDUs and printers and preventative or corrective action can be swiftly taken from a central control room.

12.4.16 Conclusion

Originally NatWest automated the branch accountancy and cheque-clearing systems. Today every department/function of the bank from premises to personnel, insurance to investment, international to UK banking relies on the use of IT to help provide the kind of service that customers demand. One special service worth mentioning is the provision of Braille statements for blind customers – a by-product of new technology.

12.5 The University of Brighton – IT in an academic environment

The University of Brighton is a large and rapidly growing organisation with over 2000 staff and more than 10 000 full- and part-time students spread over the four main sites in Brighton and Eastbourne. As in many similar organisations, the use of IT has grown rapidly during the last few years – so much so that every student or lecturer has access to anything from a DEC VAX minicomputer down to a PC.

12.5.1 The Computer Centre

The Computer Centre provides a number of core services to the rest of the university, the most important of which are to operate, develop, and maintain:

(a) the university data communications network,
(b) the central academic computer systems,
(c) the administrative computer systems.

In addition to this, the Computer Centre aims to be an information-provider and contract-negotiator for academic and administrative departments.

As with many academic and commercial computer-services departments, the main role of the Computer Centre has moved from being primarily a provider of central computing power towards being a provider of network facilities. While the centre still runs a considerable central computing facility (see below), the main focus has now moved towards the development of a comprehensive university-wide computer communications network.

12.5.2 Network services

Within the university there are a large number of different types of LAN, including networks of Apple Macintoshes, PC-compatibles, Sun workstations, and even BBC microcomputers. These LANs are spread around the various university departments, and many of them have been linked to the central network services, as shown in fig. 12.7. As can be seen from fig. 12.7, these network services are built around the ACCESS HUB and the STARMASTER system.

The ACCESS HUB (a high-specification modular Ethernet repeater) is used as an entry route for two types of communication: departmental workgroups that are physically close to the Computer Centre, and workgroups that are geographically distant and need to be connected via a communications link.

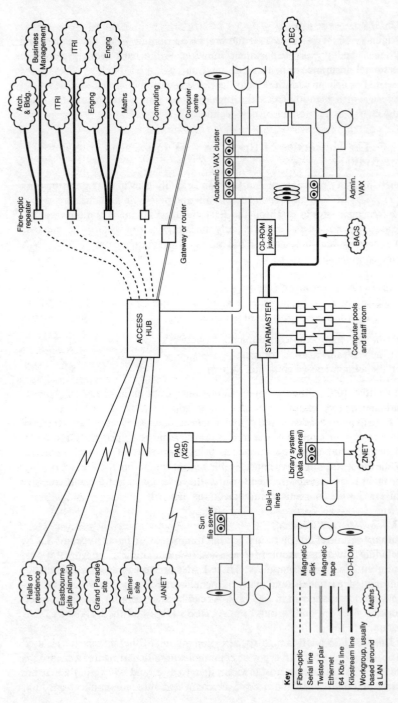

Fig. 12.7 The University of Brighton computer network

The local workgroups are all linked over a variety of media to an Ethernet LAN which acts as a carrier to the individual workgroups, many of which are based around AppleTalk networks. For example, the Computer Centre AppleTalk network is connected to the Ethernet and hence the ACCESS HUB using twisted-pair cable and a gateway. The remote locations, which are up to 50 km away, are linked in via 60 Kb/s channels provided by the PABX and taken from the MegaStream lines that were installed to carry the internal telephone traffic between the many university sites. An interesting feature is that over 100 rooms in the student halls of residence are provided with data points to enable access to the central computer services. JANET (Joint Academic NETwork – see section 8.6.1) can be accessed through the internal X25 packet-switch/PAD and external KiloStream link to the network entry point at the University of London.

The STARMASTER is an intelligent serial switch or PACX (private automatic computer exchange) that acts as the hub of a star network and supports the large academic VAX cluster terminal network, administrative and library catalogue systems, and the Sun 470 server. The academic VAX cluster operates as three closely-coupled processors that have 70 Mb/s parallel links over a cluster controller that enables high-speed disk/tape operations. Although there are over 6000 users registered to use the VAX systems, only 250 concurrent users are able to be logged on to the system at any one time. Of the four VAX computers operated by the Computer Centre, three are used for teaching purposes, with the remaining one being used by the university administration. There is, in total, about 12 Gb of on-line disk storage available across the four systems, and all share a high-speed communications link to DEC (Digital Equipment Corporation) for remote diagnostics in the event of problems occurring with any of the systems.

The administrative system is intentionally kept separate from the academic systems for security purposes and is connected to the STARMASTER over an Ethernet LAN. Linked into this is a connection to BACS (Bankers' Automated Clearing Service) used for payroll purposes.

The library catalogue system is available on-line over some 70 terminals spread across the seven site libraries over the ZNET network, in addition to being accessible from any VAX terminal.

The CD–ROM 'jukebox', shown on the diagram as a separate system, is in fact located within the STARMASTER and is a fourteen-CD system that can provide simultaneous access for up to a dozen users. It is intended that this system will be available over the network to all LAN users within the university.

Finally, there are four monitored and managed dial-in links to STAR-MASTER for the use of staff and students, and these operate at up to 9600 baud.

12.5.3 Library system
The library database is held on a Data General 7800XP minicomputer that has 20 Mb of RAM and 1 Gb of disk storage running the Birmingham Library Services modular library software under the AOS/VS operating system. The

cataloguing and book-ordering modules allow access for library staff to the BLS database of over 10 million records, including *British Books in Print* and HMSO files.

The loans module has around 12 000 registered users and handles routine administrative tasks like loans, returns, renewals, and overdue-reminder notices. The public-access catalogue holds details of some 300 000 titles throughout the university. Other modules provide for checking-in of periodical issues and for request of inter-library loans.

The library has a multi-layer approach to data security that operates as follows:

(a) *Daily*   As books are loaned or returned, in addition to the disk-based master files being updated a record of the transaction is placed on a 12 inch magnetic tape that can be used to restore the files in the event of a disk crash.

(b) *End-of-day*   The borrower, book, and issue datafiles are backed-up on to a 2 Gb cartridge.

(c) *Back-up system*   In the event of a major computer breakdown, all the major library sites are able to use microcomputers to record issues and returns, the data being capable of being uploaded to the main computer when it becomes operational.

12.5.4 Sun system

The Sun 470 server is primarily used to run Unix programs and is connected over the STARMASTER to the university terminal network and via the ACCESS HUB to other Sun workstations in the ITRI (IT Research Institute) and the Engineering department. An interesting feature of this system is that its operations manuals, and some software, are supplied on CD–ROM.

12.5.5 Data security

The Computer Centre is responsible for the security of all programs and data stored in the central computer systems, and programs or data can usually be restored to the user in the event of a loss. The centre has a three-part back-up regime that attempts to take account of most eventualities and works as follows:

(a) *Daily*   At about 7.30 every morning, data is copied on to magnetic tape. These copies are referred to as 'sleep tapes' and they contain a copy of every file that has been altered or created since the last sleep tape. The sleep tape will not, however, make a copy of any file that is in use when the system attempts a copy operation.

(b) *Monthly*   A copy of all data stored in the system is copied to magnetic tape at a time when the number of files open is likely to be at a minimum. For the academic systems – the VAX and Sun computers – this is either done unattended overnight (VAX) or else on a Friday morning (Sun). The administration systems have copies taken on Friday afternoons when the computers have been closed to users. These four-weekly tapes are termed 'hibernate tapes'.

(c) *Every summer* A copy of all data held is made to magnetic tape, and this is kept for three years. The aim is to provide security for students who are on industrial placements or otherwise breaking their studies but who remain members of the university.

In the event of a system or disk crash, these procedures limit possible data loss to only data generated on the most recent working day.

12.5.6 Computer and terminal pools
The majority of computer users within the university use either Apple Macintosh or IBM-compatible personal computers rather than the VAX minicomputer systems. At the time of writing there are over 1200 Macintoshes and more than 500 PCs for use by staff and students, many of which are networked.

Computers for student use are made available in 'pool' rooms containing anything up to 24 machines linked by a LAN. IBM-compatible pool rooms are set up as Novell networks, while Apple Macintosh pool rooms make use of the built-in AppleTalk networking system. Terminal-emulation software is available in some computer pools to enable the VAX systems to be accessed. Although the Terminal pools are still heavily used, dedicated VAX or other terminals will probably be replaced by PC-type workstations.

12.5.7 Future network services
The Computer Centre is currently working towards the integration of all the LANs within the university, using the STARMASTER system as the hub of what will become a very large network. The aim is to facilitate the full integration of the various computer systems so that the VAX system is able to act as a central file server to a high-speed network across which EMail and other services like CD–ROM are available. All new student residences are being wired for computer usage, and the facilities for remote access of systems will be increased as the numbers of students using distance-learning methods grows. The ultimate aim is to create what has been termed the 'electronic campus' – an academic version of an advanced office-automation system.

12.5.8 Computer Centre staffing
Although over 40 staff are employed within the University Computer Centre, most academic departments also employ technical staff part of whose job is to support their departmental computing facilities.

The Computer Centre organisation chart is shown in fig. 12.8.

12.6 The *Guardian* – IT in newspaper production

The *Guardian* is a major national quality newspaper with a circulation of around 250 000 copies per day. First published in 1821 as the *Manchester Guardian*, the name was changed to its present title in 1959, with printing and editorial work moving to London in 1961 and 1964 respectively, thus ending

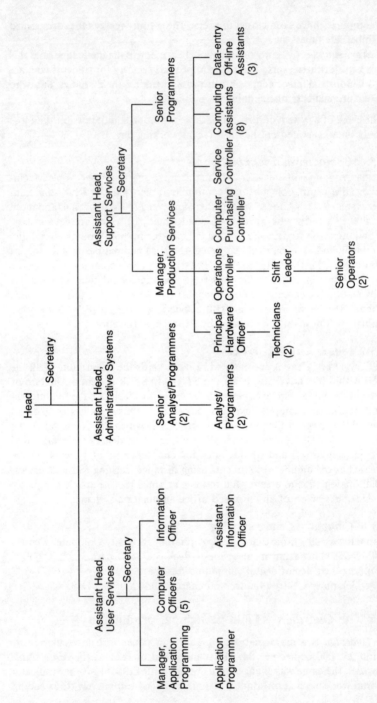

Fig. 12.8 The University of Brighton Computer Centre – organisation chart

the process of changing from a regional to a truly national newspaper. The *Guardian* has a reputation for being innovative and forward-looking as a newspaper, and this is in part reflected in the continuous developments in the use of IT in the way news is gathered, edited, and published.

Producing a daily newspaper like the *Guardian* involves assembling a large number of news stories, photographs, advertisements, listings, cartoons, and general-interest and specialist articles to a predefined format according to a very strict deadline. News stories and photographs have to be received from both home and abroad, edited, and given space and a prominence on the page that has been decided at the daily editorial meeting. Advertising copy will either be received from external advertising agencies or else be generated in-house, with the television, radio, and theatre listings being compiled from information provided. The remainder of the editorial matter in the paper will come from the large number of journalists, both full-time and freelance, employed by the *Guardian*.

The *Guardian* is assembled using a specialist newspaper system produced by Atex, an American subsidiary of Kodak. The Guardian Editorial system is based on some sixteen DEC (Digital Equipment Corporation) PDP-11 minicomputers into which are linked around 280 asynchronous dumb terminals and 160 networked PCs used by the advertising sales department.

The sixteen DEC PDP-11 minicomputers that make up the system work in a co-operative fashion and are linked by a high-speed 16-bit bus. Of these sixteen processors, ten are allocated to editorial, with the remaining six being used for the preparation of advertising copy. Each one of the processors is allocated to the production of a particular section of the newspaper, with Sports and City using processors 5 and 6, Home News using 1–4, Features 7–10, and Foreign News 7 and 8. The processors in the system are 'paired' together so that the operations occurring on any one minicomputer are also noted by its pair. This feature makes the Atex very fault-tolerant, since, if any one minicomputer crashes, its current operations are known and can be shared out between the remaining processors, thereby ensuring that deadlines can be met and the newspaper can be produced.

The whole *Guardian* system is built around a backbone of a twin 10 Mb/s Ethernet LAN, as illustrated in fig. 12.9. A wide variety of hardware is linked to the Ethernet, including the Atex system, the page-layout CAD system, Sun workstations, several Novell LANs made up of IBM-compatible PCs, and several AppleTalk LANs with Apple Macintosh computers. The Ethernet is also linked using a communications bridge and British Telecom MegaStream lines to the print works at Trafford Park in Manchester and the Isle of Dogs in east London, to the *Manchester Evening News* – a sister publication – and to a LAN of nine IBM PS/2s at the House of Commons that is used by parliamentary reporters.

The main purpose of a newspaper like the *Guardian* is to provide the reader with pictures, facts, and analysis on the most newsworthy events at home and abroad. In order to achieve this, a virtually continuous stream of information is received every day in electronic form from sources as diverse as the

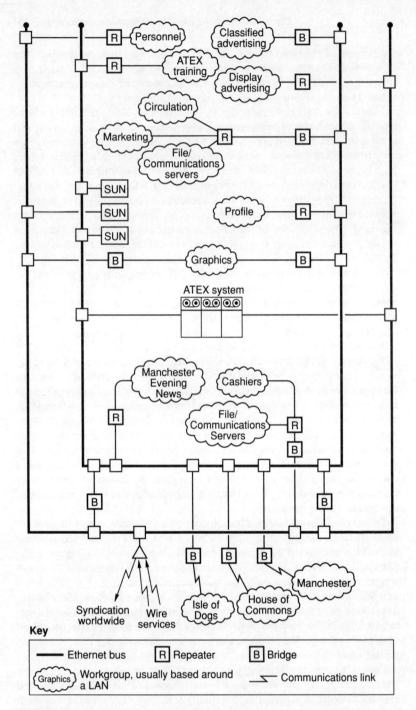

Fig. 12.9 The *Guardian*'s computer network

Key

—— Ethernet bus	R Repeater	B Bridge
Graphics Workgroup, usually based around a LAN		⟨ Communications link

Fig. 12.10 A newsroom at the *Guardian*

Associated Press, Reuters, Extel, the Press Association, the *New York Times*, and the *Washington Post*, in addition to a large number of journalists reporting from anywhere in the world. This information comes in over MegaStream, KiloStream, PSS, satellite, or simply a dial-up-line to the 'wire' room, and is sent over the Ethernet LAN to a Sun SparcStation which inspects the header label of each file, classifies it according to news type (home, foreign, sport, etc.), and sends it back over the Ethernet to the particular Atex minicomputer that handles that type of news. The information is then available for use by in-house journalists and editors (fig. 12.10) and may be used in the next issue of the newspaper. Photographs are also received from sources at home and abroad and may arrive on one of four Associated Press analogue photograph machines located in the 'wire' room.

The layout of each page is created according to a pre-defined format using CAD terminals and specialist Layout page-design software. The output from this sytem – a binary file of each page – is then passed to a Monotype typesetting machine over the Ethernet LAN and a broadsheet-sized camera-ready copy is made. At present photographs and graphics are then pasted on to this page in the traditional way, but this will soon cease and it will be possible to produce complete camera-ready pages that include text, graphics, and pictures.

At the end of this process the pages are faxed over the MegaStream lines from the 'wire' room, using high-resolution 1000 d.p.i. faxes, to printers at the Isle of Dogs, Trafford Park, and Frankfurt in Germany for the international edition of the *Guardian*. Each day's edition is also syndicated to a number of other news agencies and newspapers around the world.

In addition to the daily editions, the *Guardian* is also available on CD–ROM. Each CD–ROM contains one year's editorial matter and is updated quarterly, ASCII text files being sent each day to the company responsible for mastering the disks. In an effort to bring the *Guardian* to people with a visual disability, the editorial matter is also sent over a communications link to the BBC, from where it is transmitted over the television network. People with specially-adapted televisions can then receive the files, pass them to their PC, and then use special voice-synthesis software to read out the text.

12.7 Tasks

1 Research exercise
The nature of IT is such that since these case-studies were written the systems described in them will have been developed and improved. Benetton, Sainsbury's, and NatWest are all 'high-profile' organisations and there are often reports on their progress in newspapers and magazines. To find out what has been happening to each of the companies mentioned above, go to the library and look up the *British Humanities Index* to find what references there are on articles about each of these companies. Make a list of the references about each company, and then ask to see the newspapers or magazines that they are in. You could use this information to update each of the case-studies.

2 Sainsbury's
Of all the large supermarket chains, Sainsbury's currently makes the most use of IT in its operations.

(a) Make a list of the advantages to Sainsbury's of using IT.
(b) Would the same advantages be available to the owner of a small supermarket?

Make a visit to a supermarket that is operated by another company to see how its system compares with Sainsbury's.

3 Retailing
Many retail chains are moving towards the increased use of IT in their operations. The case-study on Sainsbury's above examines the use of IT in food retailing and the benefits that it has brought to that company. Another company that is using IT in a big way is Marks & Spencer, the high-street retail chain. It has, however, made use of different systems to label the goods and to capture the sales data at the point-of-sale terminals. Pay a visit to your local M&S store and make notes on its labelling and data-capture systems. Each check-out is supplied with a hand-held Psion computer – find out what they are used for.

Collect enough information to answer the following questions:

(a) What methods of data-capture are used in the M&S store you visited?
(b) In what way did these methods differ from those used in a typical Sainsbury's store?
(c) What benefits do the data-capture methods used have for M&S?

4 CAD/CAM

The textile industry in the UK makes extensive use of CAD/CAM manufacturing methods. Use the *British Humanities Index* to look up the latest articles that have been published on CAD/CAM in textile manufacturing.

Introduction to systems development

13.1 Introduction

In Unit 1 we looked at a number of information systems that may exist within an organisation, such as those dealing with Sales, Purchases, Finance, and Production/Stores. In this unit we are going to examine the procedure that should be followed when an information system, like one of those mentioned above, is computerised.

Systems development is the process by which a computerised information system is created. A 'system', in this context, refers to a collection of computer programs that will act together to handle information so that the needs of the user are satisfied. For example, a computerised sales-order processing system will automatically handle all the procedures associated with processing a sales order. Similarly, a computerised payroll system will automatically deal with the production of pay-slips, given the necessary information.

The 'traditional' approach to 'computerising' an information system involves seven stages which should be followed to ensure the best chance of success. This approach is widely used but it does, however, have some limitations. This unit will look at each of the stages that go to make up the traditional approach, before going on to examine the alternative approaches that have been developed as a response to its limitations.

13.2 Computerising an information system – overview

The process of computerising all or part of an information system – often called the *systems-development lifecycle* – can be divided into seven stages. Each of these stages, outlined below, plays an important part in ensuring that a systems-development project is successful.

Stage 1   Choosing the information system to be computerised
Which system – Sales, Purchases, Finance, or some other – should be computerised? What are the priorities?

Stage 2 The feasibility study
Once the system has been chosen, which of the solutions proposed will provide the best results? Are the proposed solutions possible and cost-effective?

Stage 3 Full analysis of the system to be computerised
Exactly what will the chosen system need to do?

Stage 4 Designing how the computerised system will work
Using the information gained in the analysis stage, designing exactly how the system will do what is required of it.

Stage 5 Writing the programs
Writing the programs needed to make the system work.

Stage 6 Implementing the new system
Making sure that the computerised system does what it is supposed to do and, once final testing is complete, implementing it.

Stage 7 Maintaining the system
Making the slight adjustments and alterations that will be necessary once the system has been in use for some time.

These seven stages can be illustrated in diagrammatic form as shown in fig. 13.1.

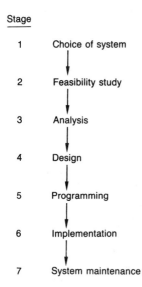

Fig. 13.1 The seven stages of the traditional systems-development lifecycle

The next seven sections will look in detail at the main activities involved in each of these stages.

13.3 Stage 1 – choosing the information system to be computerised

The need to computerise an existing information system, or the wish to develop a new information system, may arise for a number of reasons, some of which are listed below:

(a) Problems with an existing manual information system, such as slowness or inflexibility.
(b) The need to improve the competitiveness of the organisation by offering an improved or different service, such as an improved after-sales service.
(c) A need to reduce costs.
(d) The replacement of old or obsolete hardware.
(e) Dissatisfaction with the existing computerised system.
(f) The wish to add new facilities to an existing system.

In any organisation there may well be several problem areas with the existing information system. The choice of which part of the system to computerise first will be made as a result of balancing priorities.

13.4 Stage 2 – feasibility study

Once it has been accepted that there is a need to develop a new information system, it is wise to conduct a feasibility study. The aim of a feasibility study is to look at alternative solutions to the problem and to examine in greater detail the most promising. Of perhaps five possible ways of producing a new system, it may be that only three are worth looking at in any detail, the others being discarded because they are likely to be too complex or too costly. For the more promising solutions it will be necessary to do sufficient research on each one so that information on the likely benefits, costs, and time needed for introduction is available.

The feasibility study may be done by a working party, composed of experts and possible users of the new system, who will put the results of their investigations into a report to a steering committee made up of senior management. This feasibility report should contain the following information:

(a) *Definition of the system to be computerised* – including inputs, procedures, outputs, and additional features.
(b) *Options considered* – including a statement of the system objectives, alternative solutions, examination of the costs and benefits of each solution, and a recommended solution.
(c) *Recommended computerised system* – including inputs, procedures, outputs, and additional features.

(d) *Changeover procedures* – a statement of the steps to be taken before, during, and after the transfer from the old to the new system.

The feasibility report must be studied carefully by senior management before a final decision is made on the way in which the new system is to be achieved. It may be that the report will not contain enough information for a final decision to be made, in which case it will be handed back to the working party for further work. The final decision to proceed is likely to need the approval of the highest level of management in an organisation, due to the expenditure involved and the effect that a large-scale change may have.

It is possible that the feasibility report will recommend that the most cost-effective solution to the problems facing the company is a redesign of its existing manual information systems, and that computerisation is not necessary.

13.5 Stage 3 – analysis

The analysis stage involves finding out precisely what the information system has to do. This involves a systems analyst in 'fact-finding' and obtaining the answers to a number of simple questions:

- *Where* does the information on a particular form come from, and where does it go to?
- *Who* gets a copy of this information?
- *Why* does this information have to be kept here, or sent there?
- *What* are the general rules of operation, and what happens if there are exceptions to those rules?

In getting answers to these questions, the systems analyst is likely to use the following techniques:

Interviews with managers will provide background information relating to each manager's requirements, while interviews with clerks will provide information on the day-to-day workings of the system. All potential users of the system should, if possible, be interviewed to enable a full picture of the system to emerge.

Questionnaires sent out to all users may collect information on the existing system and obtain helpful suggestions on features that may be included in the new system.

Sampling the progress of individual documents within the existing manual system (if there is one) will provide information on the flow of information, how it is processed, the timings of each activity, and where the documents end up. This will provide the analyst with an insight into how the existing system operates, and highlight its good and bad features.

Document collection is the gathering together of all documents and forms used in the system. This technique, together with sampling, will help the analyst to build up an overall picture of the operation of an existing system.

At the end of the period of analysis, the analyst will be able to build up a model of what the system is required to do. If the new system is to be based on an existing system, much of the analysis work will be concerned with looking at the old system and trying to highlight the best features for incorporation into the new system. If there is no existing system, the analyst will need to find out exactly what is required of the new system from its users, and could also look at the operation of similar systems elsewhere for ideas about the features that could be incorporated into the new system.

The end result of this stage is the preparation of a report to the steering committee that provides the precise details of the requirements and features that the new system should have. The report – sometimes called a *specification of requirements* – will contain information on all aspects of the system and will document every aspect of its operation. It is the information contained in this report that will be used as a basis for designing the new system.

13.6 Stage 4 – design

The process of designing the new system may not have to wait until the end of the analysis stage: it is very likely that many of the features required of the new system will have been specified in broad terms as early as the feasibility study or when choosing the system to computerise. It is preferable, however, that the detailed design of the system is delayed until after the analysis stage, to enable the users to have a greater influence in deciding on the features that the eventual system should possess.

The design stage involves using the specification of requirements as a basis for designing all aspects of the new system. It will be necessary to design the format of the output and input, the processes that must take place, the structure of the files used to store the information, program design, system security, and the business procedures which the new system is to link in with. We will now look at each aspect of this design process.

13.6.1 Output design

In designing the output from the systems, the choice between hard or soft copy will depend upon what the output is used for.

Hard copy   The choice of the type of hard-copy output will depend upon the use for which it is intended. Plain-paper output will generally be for internal summaries and reports, while invoices, pay-slips, and other documents will generally use pre-printed stationery. Direct output on to microfilm or microfiche may be preferred if there is a large volume of output, or if the output is to be used for reference purposes only.

Soft copy   If the information to be output is in response to an enquiry, output to a VDU screen or by means of a voice synthesiser may be adequate. The design of VDU screen displays is an area in which the users of the system can play an active part.

13.6.2 Input design
The choice of input method will be determined by a combination of factors, including the volume of input, the media to be used, and the type of system.

Specialist data entry   It may be appropriate for all data input to be done by specialist data-entry clerks, as in the case of the input of large volumes of similar documents such as time-sheets, expenses claims, or order forms.

Document readers   Optical character readers (see section 3.3.1) are a fast way of entering high volumes of documents containing standardised information, like gas and electricity bills. Optical mark readers (see section 3.3.2) are useful in areas in which there are a limited number of options from which to choose, as on a multiple-choice examination paper or a stock-order form.

On-line data entry   This is the situation in which each user is provided with a terminal which can be used both to enter data and to make enquiries. This is appropriate when the application has a relatively low volume of transactions and requires access to the information held in order to answer enquiries from the public or other users.

Bar-code readers   These provide a useful method of capturing information as a by-product of a process or transaction, as in the case of a supermarket check-out where information on sales is captured as the cost of goods purchased is calculated.

13.6.3 File design
The information that will be used by the system must be stored in special computer files, of which there are two main types (see section 9.1):

(a) *Master files*   These files will be the main source of information on the system, as a payroll master file would contain all the details of each employee's pay records.
(b) *Transaction files*   These contain the input data that will be used to update the master files.

For each file, the analyst will need to specify the names and type of data to be contained, and the way it is to be organised.

13.6.4 Program design
The systems analyst must provide the programmers with a precise specification of the programs required to run the system. The analyst will specify each of the programs required, any links they may have, and their overall logical structure.

13.6.5 Design of business procedures

When a new computerised system is introduced into an organisation, it is highly likely that new manual business procedures will be needed to surround and support it. It may be necessary for the analyst to liaise with management in designing the procedures for handling each document in the system. The responsibilities of each member of staff within the new system and the procedures to be followed in the event of exceptions must also be laid down.

13.6.6 Design of security procedures

It is a wise precaution to incorporate some level of security into any system, to protect against the loss or corruption of data, fraud, and unauthorised access to the information held in the system.

Physical security may involve limiting physical access to the computer room or computer terminals, and the taking of back-up copies of files in case of fire or accident.

Internal system security could include validation and verification checks on input data, authorisation procedures for some types of input data (such as a manager's signature on an overtime claim), the provision of an audit trail of file changes, and the use of control totals. In systems that need a very high level of security, it may be necessary to include such things as encryption (coding) of data held on files, multi-level password systems including the use of magnetic keys, voice-recognition access, and the monitoring of the identity and access time of each user on the system.

At the end of the design process, a detailed system-design report will be produced for the steering committee, containing the designs for each aspect of the new system.

13.7 Stage 5 – writing the programs

Once the 'blueprint' of the detailed system design has been produced, it is passed to one or more programmers who will create the programs needed. Throughout the creation of the programs there will be discussions between the programmers and the systems analyst to clarify any areas of confusion and to make any amendments that have been found to be needed.

At an early stage, the analyst will provide the programmers with a set of test data which they will use to test the operation of each part of the system once it is complete and to test the complete system once it is finished. The test data is designed to test that the system is able to deal with all types of transaction, from the routine to the exceptions to the general rule. Once system testing has been completed to the satisfaction of the analysts, the new system can be handed over to the users for final testing and approval.

13.8 Stage 6 – implementing the new system

Once the detailed system-design document has been completed and given to the programmers, the analyst must then begin the preparations for the system to be installed and handed over to its final users. These preparations and the installation of the new system constitute the *implementation* stage and involve several steps. This section will look at each part of the implementation process.

13.8.1 General preparation

Successful implementation will be based upon the careful planning of each part of the move towards the new system, and the analyst will play a key role in preparing the plan of action. In order for this plan to be a success, the analyst must have the understanding and support of the organisation's management, who must be aware of the tasks and time-scale involved in the implementation.

If the new system will cause staff changes in terms of redundancies or staff increases, the time taken to make such changes will need to be taken into account. The process of losing or employing staff may take many months, and it must be built into the overall plan.

The allocation of duties to staff and an assessment of the training needs of the staff who will use the new system must be carried out in consultation with department heads.

The analyst will also need to make arrangements for setting up the new files to be used in the system, which may involve the keying-in and checking of all data in the existing manual system.

13.8.2 Staff training

The training of staff in the procedures and operation of the new system should be carried out, as far as is possible, before the full introduction of the system. This may be done by using examples of input and output, and time should be allocated to ensure that adequate training is given before staff are required to operate the new system. Training should take place at all levels within the organisation, with managers being given an overview of operations and facilities and operators being trained in operational procedures.

13.8.3 System testing

The initial stage in testing a system is the creation of test data by the analyst that will check all parts of the new system and ensure that it is able to deal with exceptions and errors (see section 13.7). When this first stage of testing has been completed, the system will then be passed over to the user department for final testing.

The user department will then subject the system to a series of further tests using 'real' data, and – if necessary – final adjustments can be made to the system.

13.8.4 File set-up

At some stage it will be necessary to set up the master files that are to be at the heart of the new system. This will involve the collection of the data to be used, some possible adjustments to codes used so that they fit in with the new system, and the keying-in of all the data into the new master files. Once it has all been keyed in, the data must then be checked for correctness (verified), possibly by cross-checking each record with a print-out of the new master file. This is a laborious task but must be done in order to ensure that the data held in the new system is correct and can be trusted.

This part of the implementation stage is perhaps the most laborious, since it may involve a vast amount of data entry at the same time as staff are using the existing system. To reduce the amount of work for staff involved in entering and checking data in addition to running the existing system, it may be wise to use outside staff for the data-input and verification parts of the operation.

13.8.5 System changeover

The changeover to the new system should not take place until each of the following has been finished:

(a) Testing of the new system is complete and the users and analyst are both satisfied with its operation.

(b) Training of staff in the use of the new system is complete, and all staff are aware of the procedures to be followed during the changeover period.

(c) Instruction manuals on how to use the new system have been written and distributed to all users.

(d) The master and transaction files have been created.

(e) New hardware that may have been purchased to run the system has been installed and tested and is operating to specification.

Once these conditions have all been met, it is possible to move over to the new system. There are three ways in which it is possible to change from one system to another: parallel running, immediate changeover, and stepped changeover.

Parallel running   This involves the operation of both the old and the new systems – cross-checking on results – until the new system has proved itself and the old system can be shut down. This is the safest method since if any problems arise with the operation of the new system this can be withdrawn for further work without affecting the operation of the organisation. The big disadvantage of this method is the duplication of effort caused by both systems operating at the same time.

Immediate changeover   This involves closing down the old system at a pre-determined time – say at the end of a working week – and moving to the new system at the start of the next week. This is a simple method of changeover and causes few problems if the new system operates as expected. The risks involved in adopting this method are quite high, however, since it may not be possible to reactivate the old system if the new one is giving problems. For this method to be successful, the preparations for changeover must have been very thorough indeed, and there must be a high level of confidence in the new system.

Stepped changeover   This method is a compromise between the two approaches above, with the users moving over to the new system one stage at a time. In an accounting system, a stepped changeover may take the form of first moving the bought ledger to the new system, and gaining experience and confidence in that area before moving the sales ledger and then each other area in turn. This method of changeover is thus a series of small immediate change-overs. This method can be used only if it is possible to divide the functions of the new system up in a convenient way, say office by office.

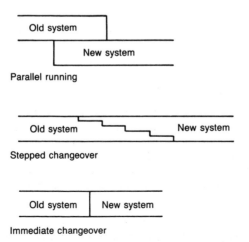

Fig. 13.2 The three methods of changeover from an old to a new system

The advantages of this method are that there is less extra work than with the parallel-running method, and it enables experience of changeover to be gained from the early areas to be converted. This method still carries the risk attached to immediate changeover, however – albeit on a smaller scale – and the stage-by-stage approach may considerably lengthen the overall changeover period.

The three methods are illustrated in fig. 13.2.

Once the changeover has been successfully completed, responsibility for the operation of the new system will then be handed over to the users.

13.9 Stage 7 – system maintenance

Once the new system has been handed over to its eventual users, it will need to be maintained. A large proportion of all programming done in many commercial data-processing departments is concerned with the maintenance of their existing computerised systems. Maintenance of an information system is the adaptation and updating of the system that may be needed for a number of reasons:

(a) *Legislation*   Changes in government legislation, such as an alteration in the level of personal taxation, may require changes to be made in the system.
(b) *Business growth*   The numbers of transactions that need to be put through the system as the business grows may increase and may eventually exceed the original specification and cause alterations to be made to take account of this.
(c) *Changes in business procedures*   Internal reorganisation may need to be reflected by changes in the way the system operates.
(d) *System faults*   Problems or shortcomings that have shown themselves in the system during general use may need to be corrected.

As a system develops and is modified, it is essential that documentation of all changes is made. This will be added to the existing system documentation to form an up-to-date record of the structure of the system to ensure that it is easier to maintain in the future.

13.10 Problems with the traditional approach to systems development

The traditional 'systems-development lifecycle' approach to systems development, as outlined above, has been criticised for a number of reasons:

(a) Users often want the systems faster than they can be delivered, with delays of years being common.
(b) Due to the long development times, the systems delivered may not match the user requirements at the time of delivery.

(c) Programs delivered may have major errors in them.
(d) It is hard for users to specify precise requirements to analysts, leading to errors and omissions in specifying what the system has to do.
(e) Systems may take much longer to develop and cost far more to run than anticipated.

Delays in the development of new systems have led to a situation in which there are probably more systems currently requested and awaiting implementation than have ever been written. The scale of the problem in systems development is enormous, and a number of methods are being tried in order to make the development process more efficient. The main methods that are used will be examined below.

13.10.1 Improving the development process

Traditional systems development is still largely in the 'pre-industrial-revolution' days of hand-built systems and has yet to enter the era of mass-production. Systems have generally been created by small teams of 'craftsmen' analysts and programmers who 'hand-make' each component part, rather than by 'production-line' workers who use standard components.

The United States Department of Defense has created a set of standards for developing new systems, built around the programming language ADA. These standards apply to each stage of the development process, and are designed to produce a system that is faster to create and easier to maintain. The language ADA is also designed so that program code can be reused in other systems, thus speeding up future systems development. This approach has been developed for the creation of military applications, and is best suited to systems that can be precisely specified at the start of the development process – such as systems software and fighter-control software.

13.10.2 The use of packaged software

Many applications like payroll and accounts are well understood, and packaged software is widely available for all types of computer hardware. A limitation of such software is that the organisation will have to adapt to the systems imposed by the software. This may not be a problem for small organisations, but larger, more complex companies may not find such adaptation so easy. It is likely, however, that packaged software of the required quality will simply not be available for some specialist organisations, so that companies must develop software of their own.

13.10.3 The use of systems-development software

This approach uses special software to speed up several stages of the systems-development process.

The work of the analyst is speeded up with the use of programs called *analyst work-benches*, which aim to assist in the definition and linkages of the input, output, and processes of the application being developed.

The work of the programmer is helped with the use of *applications generators* – programs designed to write programs, which will generate much of the programming code needed for an application (see section 7.6). The use of applications generators enables new systems to be 'prototyped' – that is, rough versions of a system are produced. This enables users to see a version of how an actual system will look and run, and allows them to make a meaningful contribution to the final look and function of the system. The prototyping process involves users and development teams in producing successive new versions of the system until a satisfactory system is produced. Once the prototype is refined, it may itself be used or else it may provide the basis for the development of the eventual system using traditional programming techniques.

13.10.4 End-user computing

This is the increased selection by user departments of hardware and software to enable them to become more independent of the traditional data-processing department. The widespread use of microcomputers linked together into local area networks using powerful database, spreadsheet, and applications-generator software is an example of this approach. This approach is often linked with an information centre, set up within the DP department, which co-ordinates and advises user departments and seeks to ensure that the organisation's overall strategy for the use of IT is maintained.

The advantages of this approach are that it transfers the control of the development process back to the user departments for some applications, with the development time for such a system being a few days or weeks, rather than months or years. End-user computing aims to increase the independence of the user department within a consistent overall IT strategy, with the DP department acting in an advisory role.

13.11 Glossary of terms

Systems-development lifecycle   The stages through which an information system is likely to pass during its life, starting with its selection for development and ending with system maintenance.

Feasibility study   The study undertaken at an early stage of the systems-development lifecycle to find out if a proposed system is likely to be possible and cost-effective.

Systems analysis   The process in which an existing or proposed information system is analysed and its operation is documented.

Questionnaire   A technique used during the analysis stage for gathering information from users of an information system.

Document collection   The gathering together of all documents and forms used in an existing system as an aid to analysis.

Sampling   A technique used during the analysis stage for gathering information by tracing what happens to each document used within an information system.

Interviews   A technique used during the analysis stage, in which the systems analyst interviews various users of an information system to obtain information on the operation of an existing system.

Systems design   The stage in which an information system is designed, using the information obtained in the analysis stage.

Implementation   The stage in which users move to the use of the new system, once adequate preparations have been made.

System maintenance   The updating of an information system to ensure its continued usefulness.

Master file   A file in which is stored the master data relating to a particular application. A sales-ledger master file might contain such information as client name, client reference number, account balance, list of transactions over the last six months, credit limit, etc.

Transaction file   A file of information that is used to update the information held on a master file. A sales-ledger transaction file might contain a list of the sales that have been made that day.

File set-up   The process by which information contained in the master files held on the old system is transferred to the new system.

System documentation   Information relating to the development and operation of an information system. May include user manuals, program listing, maintenance log, etc.

Parallel running   The operation of both the old and new systems at the same time during the changeover period, as a means of cross-checking results.

Stepped changeover   The transfer in stages from the old to the new system, with the operation of each new stage being proved before proceeding to the next stage.

Immediate changeover   The complete transfer from the old to the new system at one time.

13.12 Exercises

1 The following are some of the activities which need to be undertaken for software development and operation in a computer system project:

Analysis of requirements
System testing

Detailed specification
Program testing
System design
Maintenance
Program writing
Implementation

You are required to:

(a) *List* the activities in sequence to describe the development process which will take place.
(b) *Describe* 'maintenance' in the software context, giving reasons why the need for it arises.
(c) *State* what can be done both to reduce the requirement for maintenance and to carry out the maintenance efficiently should it be necessary.

(ACCA, Systems analysis and design)

2 (a) Outline the general characteristics of the traditional systems-development lifecycle, reflecting any criticism made of it and mentioning any alternative approaches which answer this criticism.
(b) Briefly consider the objectives of each of the main stages within the traditional development cycle.

(AAT, Analysis and design of information systems)

3 With regard to the implementation of systems, discuss the procedures involved in:

(a) File conversion
(b) Systems changeover

(AAT, Analysis and design of information systems)

4 An important decision to be taken with regard to the implementation of a system is the method of *changeover* to be adopted.
   Describe the different methods of changeover available, and indicate the circumstances in which each would be appropriate.

(ACCA, Systems analysis and design)

5 A stock-control system has been developed to the stage where detailed specifications have been passed from the systems analyst to the chief programmer for program writing to commence.
   Required:

(a) What additional work would the systems analyst have to do after passing specifications to the chief programmer and before the system becomes fully operational?
(b) Describe in detail how the stock master file would be converted for the new system; pay particular attention to the methods that should be used to ensure that the file content is accurate.

(ACCA, Systems analysis and design)

6 There are several manual procedures which are being considered for transfer to a computer in the organisation for which you work. There is, however, a shortage of systems development staff, so only one of the proposed systems can be approved for development at this stage.

Required:

(a) Briefly describe *five* factors which you would use in selecting the one system to be developed.

(b) Identify *five* possible courses of action which may be taken to overcome the shortage of systems development staff and thus permit the more rapid implementation of the systems.

(ACCA, Systems analysis and design)

7 Briefly describe each of the stages in the lifecycle of the development and implementation of an application system, from the production of the initial terms of reference to the post-implementation review.

(IDPM, Data processing II)

8 During the investigation and design of a system to be considered for computerisation the analyst produces the following documents:

(a) a Feasibility Report
(b) a Statement of Requirements
(c) a System Specification

Explain the difference between the documents and define who should receive and consider them. Outline briefly the contents of each report.

(IDPM, Data processing II)

Case-study

Bertz Car Rental is a well established and growing company that specialises in hiring small and medium-sized saloon cars to the public. It currently operates from eleven main sites located near large airports or towns in the southern part of England and has grown by offering an efficient service at very competitive rates. The company runs a fleet of some 250 cars distributed between its eleven branches, and it has a staff of 48.

The services that Bertz Car Rental offers include the usual daily, weekly, and monthly rental facilities; car deliveries to the door; and the facility to leave a hire vehicle at one of the other branches at the end of the hire period. Bertz Car Rental is also working hard to gain a toehold in the large fleet rental market, where cars are leased for one or more years to organisations that do not wish to run their own car fleets.

Flexibility is seen as having been the reason behind the growth of Bertz Car Rental, and top management are keen to make sure that this is not lost as the company gets larger.

As the company has grown, the internal administrative systems have also been developed to cope with the increasing demands of the business. The administrative systems are all manual, however, and it has become obvious that they will cease to be able to cope within a year if the company continues to grow at its present rate.

The management of Bertz Car Rental realise that they are likely to outgrow their existing manual car-rental booking system within the next eighteen months. There is thus a clearly defined need to look at alternative ways of dealing with the booking of rentals, while if possible building in additional flexibility to the system. The decision to change any existing system is not an easy one, since management realise that change will involve disruption, uncertainty, staff resistance, and usually heavy spending. The management of Bertz Car Rental have not taken such a decision easily, and they have waited until the decision has been virtually forced upon them. They are reluctant to change a system that has worked well in the past, but it has been recognised that the future survival of the company may depend upon early action to head off potential problems.

At a special meeting, the board of directors has decided to replace the existing systems within a year, and has set up a working party to find out exactly what the current problems are and to look at alternative solutions to these problems. An important member of this working party will be a professional computer consultant who is to suggest alternative ways in which the existing system could be computerised. The results are to be presented in the form of a report.

(a) What information should be included in the report of the working party?
(b) The decision has been made to employ outside staff on contract for the duration of the project. What staff are likely to be needed for this project?
(c) What techniques is the system analyst likely to use to gather information during the analysis stage?
(d) The project to computerise the car-rental booking system seems likely to take far too long, and the management are concerned that the existing manual system will break down. Suggest ways in which the systems-development process could be speeded up.
(e) The programming of the new system is virtually complete. What tasks remain to be done before the system can be implemented? Make a list and explain the importance of each task.
(f) The management understand that there are several ways of transferring from the old to the new system. Write a report stating the strengths and weaknesses of the methods available. Which method do you feel to be most appropriate to Bertz Car Rental? Explain your reasoning.

Flowcharting and decision tables

14.1 Flowcharting

Flowcharting was developed in the 1940s as an aid to solving problems by computer, by representing the sequence of operations graphically. Although flowcharting was originally designed as a computer programmer's tool, it was soon realised that the technique could be applied to the specification of virtually any procedure. This section will examine the use of the flowchart in the specification of procedures other than computer programs.

14.1.1 Introduction to flowcharting

A flowchart consists of a series of boxes connected by arrows, with each box containing an instruction or question. By following the arrows, and performing each instruction or answering each question as it is encountered, the solution to the problem is found.

Three main types of boxes are used (fig. 14.1):

(a) *Terminator boxes* Every flowchart begins with a terminator box labelled 'START' and ends with a terminator box labelled 'STOP' or 'END'.
(b) *Process box* This box has one arrow entering it and one arrow leaving it and will contain a single instruction to be carried out.
(c) *Decision box* This box has one arrow entering it and two arrows leaving it. One of the arrows leaving it is labelled 'YES' (or 'Y') and the other is labelled 'NO' (or 'N'). The box contains a question answerable in yes/no terms. The appropriate arrow leaving the box is followed according to the answer to the question.

Consider the following procedure:

Before you cross the road you must look right to check that the way is clear. If it is, you must then look left to see if the way is clear. If this is also clear, look right again to ensure that it is still clear before starting to cross the road, looking and listening as you do.

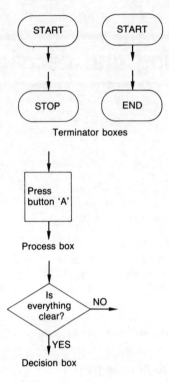

Fig. 14.1 The main types of box used in flowcharts

This procedure has been put into the form of a flowchart and is shown in fig. 14.2. Trace the operation of the flowchart by working through it and following the yes/no branches. Notice that there are three decision boxes and that if approaching cars are detected at any time you must go back to the beginning of the procedure and start again.

There are three points to note about the construction of the flowchart in fig. 14.2 that are common to all flowcharts.

(i) Arrows are joined to other arrows, rather than having several arrows entering a box.

(ii) The flowchart is drawn so that the normal direction of flow is from top to bottom and from left to right.

(iii) When dealing with a particularly complex problem, an outline flowchart can be drawn to show the overall structure of the solution without going into too much detail. Each step in the outline flowchart can then be expanded into more detail by drawing a flowchart just for that step. In this way a large problem can be broken down into smaller sections that can be dealt with separately. This is known as the 'topdown' approach to creating a program.

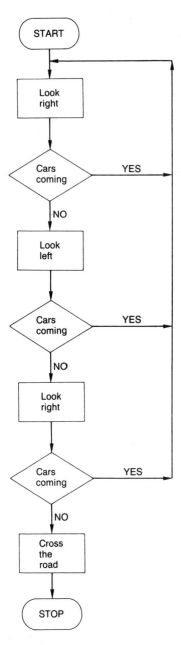

Fig. 14.2 A flowchart showing how to cross the road

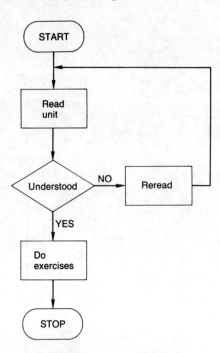

Fig. 14.3 A flowchart showing how to tackle this unit

The flowchart shown in fig. 14.3 illustrates the approach to be adopted when reading this unit.

14.1.2 Worked examples
In the examples that follow, the symbol '<' means 'less than', '≤' means 'less than or equal to', '>' means 'greater than', and '≥' means 'greater than or equal to'.

Example 1 A bus company applies the following rules in deciding what fares will be charged to its passengers:

Passengers under the age of 16 and old-age pensioners are charged half the full fare. All other passengers are charged the full fare, except for bus-pass holders who do not pay a fare.

The procedure to determine which fare to charge, if any, is illustrated in fig. 14.4.

Example 2 The following is a description of the procedure for dealing with delivery charges for goods purchased from Pelham Electronics Ltd:

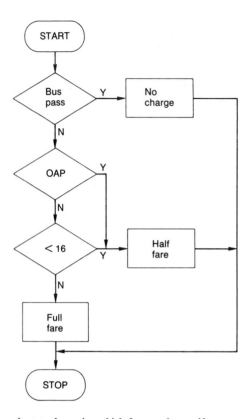

Fig. 14.4 A flowchart to determine which fare to charge, if any

The delivery charge is made according to the distance category of the firm to whom the goods are to be delivered, with all firms being divided between categories 1 and 2.

Category-1 firms are charged £30 for delivery if their invoice total is less than £1000, and £15 for delivery if their invoice total is equal to, or greater than, £1000.

Category-2 firms are charged £40 for delivery if their invoice total is less than £1000, and £20 for delivery if their invoice total is equal to, or greater than, £1000.

A flowchart to determine the delivery charge is illustrated in fig. 14.5.

Example 3 The following discounts are given to customers of Pelham Electonics Ltd:

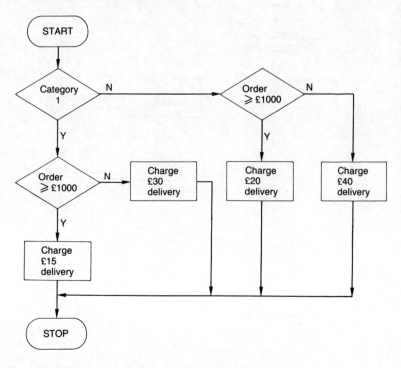

Fig. 14.5 A flowchart to determine delivery charges

Quantity ordered	% discount
1–49	3
50–199	5
200–499	7
500 and over	10

A customer who has been trading with Pelham Electronics for over two years also qualifies for an additional 2% discount, irrespective of order size.

A flowchart to determine the discount is illustrated in fig. 14.6.

14.1.3 Additional flowcharting symbols

The three flowcharting symbols that we have used so far in this unit (see fig. 14.1) may be supplemented when other types of flowchart are drawn. The flowcharts that we have looked at until now have all concerned procedures of various types, but flowcharts may also be used to illustrate the logic of a computer program, when they are termed 'program flowcharts'. The main difference between program flowcharts and those which we have used to illustrate procedures is in the number of symbols used. Figure 14.7 shows two of the additional flowchart symbols.

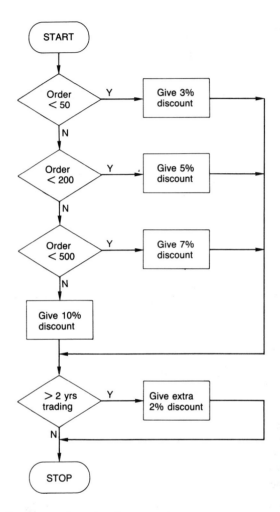

Fig. 14.6 A flowchart to determine discounts

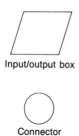

Input/output box

Connector

Fig. 14.7 Additional flowcharting symbols

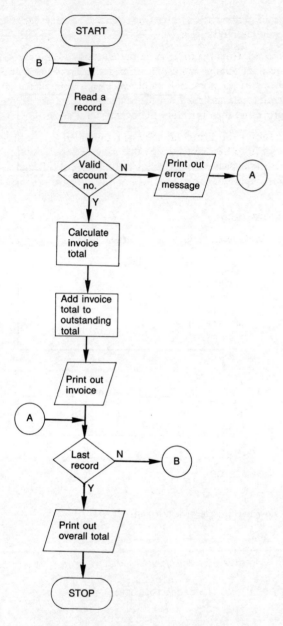

Fig. 14.8 A program flowchart showing how to print out an invoice

To get an idea of how these symbols may be used, consider the following procedure for printing out an invoice:

> Take a record from the file and check that it has a valid account number. If the account number is invalid, print out an error message and get the next record. If the number is valid, calculate the invoice total, add it to the overall total, and print out the invoice. If there are no more records to be processed then print out the overall total and stop.

The program for this procedure may be represented by the program flowchart shown in fig. 14.8. Note the way in which the input/output symbol has been used for the steps involving reading or printing out information and how the connector symbol has been used to simplify the layout of the flowchart.

14.2 Decision tables

A decision table is used in analysing the factors involved in a problem or procedure, so that for any given set of conditions an outcome can be specified.

Decision tables may be used as a means of providing a cross-check on the logic of flowcharts, and may also be used by programmers to analyse complex procedures.

A decision table has the structure shown in fig. 14.9.

Rules
1 2 3 4 5 . . .

Conditions to be tested	Condition stub	Condition entries
Actions to be taken dependent on the combination of conditions	Action stub	Action entries

Fig. 14.9 General structure of a decision table – each rule indicates the action to be taken in response to a particular combination of conditions.

To show how a decision table is built up, consider the following procedure to determine how much discount should be given to customers of ARH Ltd:

> A large-order discount of 5% is given on all orders of over £500. Trade customers receive an additional 25% discount irrespective of order value.

The steps to be taken in drawing up this, or any other, decision table are as follows.

Step 1 – analyse the procedure
The first step in the preparation of a decision table is to analyse this procedure in terms of *conditions* and *actions*. This may be done by reading the procedure carefully and underlining the conditions with a solid line and the actions with a broken line, as shown below:

A large-order discount of 5% is given to all orders of over £500. Trade customers receive an additional 25% discount, irrespective of order value.

Step 2 – calculate the number of rules
Once the number of conditions is known, it is possible to evaluate the number of rules by applying the simple formula:

number of rules $= 2^n$

where $n =$ the number of conditions.

In this procedure we have two conditions, so:

number of rules $= 2^2 = 4$ rules

Step 3 – evaluate the number of outcomes
The number of outcomes is found by analysing the procedure. In this case we are dealing with discounts and it is possible for a customer to receive:

0% if order $<$ £500 and not a trade customer
5% if order $>$ £500 and not a trade customer
25% if order $<$ £500 *and* a trade customer
30% if order $>$ £500 *and* a trade customer

Step 4 – draw up the decision table
The decision table for the above procedure will look as shown in fig. 14.10.

There are points to note about the construction of this decision table that are common to all decision tables:

(a) Four symbols are used:

Y   to indicate that a condition is satisfied,
N   to indicate that a condition is not satisfied,
–   if the outcome of a condition is not relevant to the rule,
X   to show a required action. If there is no action the column is left blank.

(b) The rules are laid out from the bottom line of conditions as alternate Y and N, the next line up being alternate YY and NN, the next line alternate YYYY and NNNN, and the next line alternate YYYYYYYY and NNNNNNNN, and so on until all the rules are complete. (Look out for this in the examples below.)

Conditions	Rules 1	2	3	4
Order > £500	Y	Y	N	N
Trade customer	Y	N	Y	N
Actions				
0% discount				X
5% discount		X		
25% discount			X	
30% discount	X			

Fig. 14.10 A decision table to determine discounts

14.2.1 Worked examples

You will recall some of the following procedures from section 14.1.2.

Example 1 The following is a description of the procedure for dealing with delivery charges for goods purchased from Pelham Electronics Ltd:

The delivery charge is made according to the distance category of the firm to whom the goods are to be delivered, with all firms being divided between categories 1 and 2.

Category-1 firms are charged £30 for delivery if their invoice total is less than £1000, and £15 for delivery if their invoice total is equal to, or greater than, £1000.

Category-2 firms are charged £40 for delivery if their invoice total is less than £1000, and £20 for delivery if their invoice total is equal to, or greater than, £1000.

The decision table for this procedure is shown in fig. 14.11.

	Rules 1	2	3	4
Category 1	Y	Y	N	N
Invoice ⩾ £1000	Y	N	Y	N
Add £15 for delivery	X			
Add £20 for delivery			X	
Add £30 for delivery		X		
Add £40 for delivery				X

Fig. 14.11 A decision table to determine delivery charges

Note There are two conditions which affect the outcome – category and size of invoice. To determine the number of rules, we can apply our formula as follows, where *n* (the number of conditions) = 2:

number of rules = $2^n = 2^2 = 4$

Example 2 A bus company applies the following rules in deciding what fares will be charged to its passengers:

Passengers under the age of 16 and old-age pensioners are charged half the full fare. All other passengers are charged the full fare, except for bus-pass holders who do not pay a fare.

The full decision table for this procedure is shown in fig. 14.12 (three conditions providing $2^3 = 8$ rules). This can be reduced in size, however, since it contains rules that are illogical. Rules 1 and 2 may be eliminated since it is impossible to be both less than 16 and an old-age pensioner. Rules 3, 5, and 7 can be combined since age is not relevant when you hold a bus pass. The reduced decision table is shown in fig. 14.13.

	Rules							
	1	2	3	4	5	6	7	8
Age < 16	Y	Y	Y	Y	N	N	N	N
OAP	Y	Y	N	N	Y	Y	N	N
Bus pass	Y	N	Y	N	Y	N	Y	N
No charge			X		X		X	
Half fare				X		X		
Full fare								X

Fig. 14.12 A decision table to determine which fare to charge, if any

	Rules			
	1	2	3	4
Age < 16	-	Y	N	N
OAP	-	N	Y	N
Bus pass	Y	N	N	N
No charge	X			
Half fare		X	X	
Full fare				X

Fig. 14.13 A reduced version of the decision table in fig. 14.12, eliminating illogical and superfluous rules

Example 3 The following discounts are given to customers of Pelham Electronics Ltd:

Quantity ordered	% discount
1–49	3
50–199	5
200–499	7
500 and over	10

A customer who has been trading with Pelham Electronics for over two years also qualifies for an additional 2% discount, irrespective of order size.

The full decision table for this procedure is shown in fig. 14.14 (four conditions providing $2^4 = 16$ rules). This may be simplified since fig. 14.14 contains a number of rules that are illogical. (It is possible to reduce the number of rules since an order cannot be in more than one quantity range at the same time.) The reduced decision table is shown in fig. 14.15.

	Rules															
	1	2	3	4	5	6	7	8	9	10	11	12	13	14	15	16
Order < 50	Y	Y	Y	Y	Y	Y	Y	Y	N	N	N	N	N	N	N	N
50 ≤ Order < 200	Y	Y	Y	Y	N	N	N	N	Y	Y	Y	Y	N	N	N	N
200 ≤ Order < 500	Y	Y	N	N	Y	Y	N	N	Y	Y	N	N	Y	Y	N	N
Trading > 2 yrs	Y	N	Y	N	Y	N	Y	N	Y	N	Y	N	Y	N	Y	N
Give discount of 3%								X								
Give discount of 5%							X					X				
Give discount of 7%											X			X		
Give discount of 9%													X			
Give discount of 10%																X
Give discount of 12%															X	

Fig. 14.14 A decision table to determine discounts

	Rules							
	1	2	3	4	5	6	7	8
Order < £50	Y	Y	-	-	-	-	N	N
Order < £200	-	-	Y	Y	-	-	N	N
Order < £500	-	-	-	-	Y	Y	N	N
Trading > 2 yrs	Y	N	Y	N	Y	N	Y	N
Give discount of 3%		X						
Give discount of 5%	X			X				
Give discount of 7%			X			X		
Give discount of 9%					X			
Give discount of 10%								X
Give discount of 12%							X	

Fig. 14.15 A reduced version of the decision table shown in fig. 14.14

Example 4   The following is the procedure adopted by a private college in selecting students for an advanced course.

All candidates will be required to attend for interview, provide the college with academic references, and possess at least four acceptable GCSE passes. A place will be offered to candidates who have a satisfactory interview and good references, and possess the qualifications needed. A place, conditional on improvement, will be offered if either the academic references or the qualifications are not up to standard. Candidates who do not have a satisfactory interview or who have unsatisfactory academic references and inadequate qualifications are rejected.

The full decision table is shown in fig. 14.16 (three conditions providing $2^3 = 8$ rules). You will notice that most of the conditions lead to the same action – that of rejecting the candidate. In this situation it is possible to use the ELSE rule, in which all the conditions that lead to the same action are combined under the single heading of 'ELSE'. This is shown in fig. 14.17.

	Rules							
	1	2	3	4	5	6	7	8
Good interview	Y	Y	Y	Y	N	N	N	N
⩾ 4 GCSEs	Y	Y	N	N	Y	Y	N	N
Good references	Y	N	Y	N	Y	N	Y	N
Offer place	X							
Offer conditional place		X	X					
Reject				X	X	X	X	X

Fig. 14.16 A decision table to select students for an advanced course

	Rules			
	1	2	3	ELSE
Good interview	Y	Y	Y	
⩾ 4 GCSEs	Y	Y	N	
Good references	Y	N	Y	
Offer place	X			
Offer conditional place		X	X	
Reject				X

Fig. 14.17 A reduced version of the decision table shown in fig. 14.16

Example 5   The decision tables we have looked at so far have all been *limited entry*, since they have used only the symbols Y, N, – , and X. The *extended-entry* decision table allows other entries to be placed into the lower half of the table.

Consider the following:

> In determining the discount to be given to customers, Kentington Components Ltd gives all customers an initial 5% discount if their invoice value is over £200, and a 2% discount if the customer is an 'esteemed customer'. Esteemed-customer status is given only to a customer who has traded with Kentington Components for over two years. All trade customers receive an additional 30% discount.

An extended-entry decision table for this procedure is shown in fig. 14.18 (three conditions providing $2^3 = 8$ rules).

	Rules							
	1	2	3	4	5	6	7	8
Trade customer	Y	Y	Y	Y	N	N	N	N
Order > £200	Y	Y	N	N	Y	Y	N	N
Esteemed customer	Y	N	Y	N	Y	N	Y	N
Discount allowed %	37	35	32	30	7	5	2	0

Fig. 14.18 An extended-entry decision table to determine discounts

14.3 Worked examples

Example 1 The following procedure is applied by a large firm of accountants when selecting staff for accountancy training:

> Applicants are offered a job as a trainee accountant if they pass the entry test and have the necessary qualifications. If applicants pass the entry test but do not have the necessary qualifications they are accepted if both their interview and their references are good. Applicants who pass the entry test and do not have satisfactory qualifications but who interview well may be offered a clerk's job even if their references are not satisfactory. If they interview badly and do not have the necessary qualifications their application is rejected. Applicants who fail the entry test but do have the necessary qualifications, good references, and a good interview are offered a job as an accounting assistant.

(a) Draw a flowchart of this procedure.
(b) Produce a full limited-entry decision table of this procedure.
(c) Reduce the size of your decision table by using the ELSE rule.

Solution The required flowcharts and decision tables are shown in figs 14.19 to 14.21.

Example 2 Welbeck Motor Factors Ltd offers a number of discounts as an inducement to customers. Discounts are calculated as a percentage reduction of the current price list. All orders worth more than £500 receive a 5% discount. Trade customers receive an additional 15% discount on all orders.

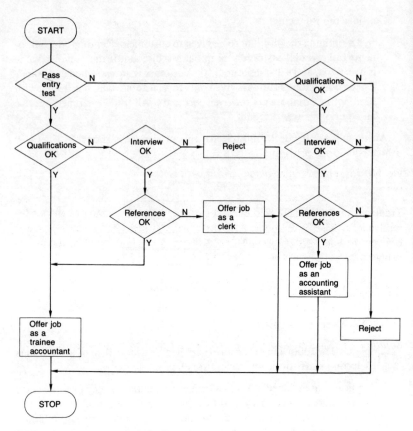

Fig. 14.19 A flowchart to select accountancy staff

	Rules															
	1	2	3	4	5	6	7	8	9	10	11	12	13	14	15	16
Pass entry test	Y	Y	Y	Y	Y	Y	Y	Y	N	N	N	N	N	N	N	N
Qualifications OK	Y	Y	Y	Y	N	N	N	N	Y	Y	Y	Y	N	N	N	N
Good interview	Y	Y	N	N	Y	Y	N	N	Y	Y	N	N	Y	Y	N	N
Good references	Y	N	Y	N	Y	N	Y	N	Y	N	Y	N	Y	N	Y	N
Offer job as tr. acct	X	X	X	X	X											
Offer job as clerk						X										
Offer job as acct asst									X							
Reject							X	X		X	X	X	X	X	X	X

Fig. 14.20 A full decision table for the procedure shown in fig. 14.19. (Note: four conditions provide $2^4 = 16$ rules.)

	Rules				
	1	2	3	4	ELSE
Pass entry test	Y	Y	Y	N	
Qualifications OK	Y	N	N	Y	
Good interview	-	Y	Y	Y	
Good references	-	Y	N	Y	
Offer job as tr. acct	X	X			
Offer job as clerk			X		
Offer job as acct asst				X	
Reject					X

Fig. 14.21 A reduced version of the decision table shown in fig. 14.20, using the ELSE rule

Trade customers who are also members of the Welbeck Group of companies receive a further 5% discount. Any customer who has a bad credit reference is given the appropriate discount but is required to pay cash when the order is placed.

(a) Produce a flowchart of this procedure.
(b) Produce a limited-entry decision table of this procedure.
(c) Reduce the size of your decision table to eliminate redundant and illogical rules.

Solution   The required flowchart and decision tables are shown in figs 14.22 to 14.24.

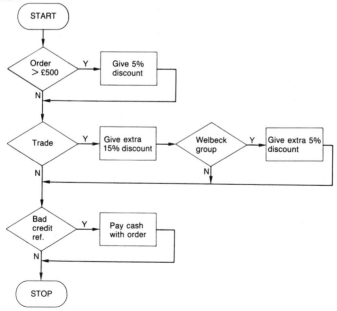

Fig. 14.22 A flowchart to determine discounts and payment method

	Rules				*	*							*	*		
	1	2	3	4	5	6	7	8	9	10	11	12	13	14	15	16
Order > £500	Y	Y	Y	Y	Y	Y	Y	Y	N	N	N	N	N	N	N	N
Trade	Y	Y	Y	Y	N	N	N	N	Y	Y	Y	Y	N	N	N	N
Member of Welbeck Group	Y	Y	N	N	Y	Y	N	N	Y	Y	N	N	Y	Y	N	N
Bad credit reference	Y	N	Y	N	Y	N	Y	N	Y	N	Y	N	Y	N	Y	N
Give discount of 0%															X	X
Give discount of 5%							X	X								
Give discount of 10%																
Give discount of 15%											X	X				
Give discount of 20%			X	X					X	X						
Give discount of 25%	X	X														
Cash with order	X		X			X		X		X			X			

* = illogical rule

Fig. 14.23 A full decision table for the procedure shown in fig. 14.22. (Note: four conditions provide $2^4 = 16$ rules.)

	Rules											
	1	2	3	4	5	6	7	8	9	10	11	12
Order > £500	Y	Y	Y	Y	Y	Y	N	N	N	N	N	N
Trade	Y	Y	Y	Y	N	N	Y	Y	Y	Y	N	N
Member of Welbeck Group	Y	Y	N	N	N	N	Y	Y	N	N	N	N
Bad credit reference	Y	N	Y	N	Y	N	Y	N	Y	N	Y	N
Give discount of 0%											X	X
Give discount of 5%					X	X						
Give discount of 10%												
Give discount of 15%									X	X		
Give discount of 20%			X	X			X	X				
Give discount of 25%	X	X										
Cash with order	X		X		X		X		X		X	

Fig. 14.24 A reduced version of the decision table shown in fig. 14.23

Example 3   Pelham Electronics Ltd pays its sales staff a basic salary plus commission and supplementary payments. The gross pay is calculated according to the procedure below.

Commission due:

Monthly sales (£)	% commission
Up to 1999	4
2000–5000	5
Over 5000	6

The supplementary payments that sales staff may be entitled to are as follows. If sales staff are based in the London office they receive a London weighting of £100 per month. Team leaders receive an additional 10% of their basic salary.

(a) Produce a flowchart of this procedure.
(b) Produce a limited-entry decision table of this procedure.
(c) Reduce the size of your decision table to eliminate redundant and illogical rules.

Solution The required flowchart and decision tables are shown in figs 14.25 to 14.27.

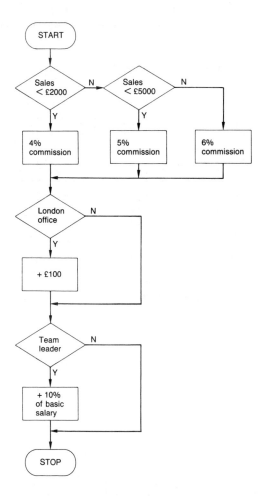

Fig. 14.25 A flowchart to determine gross pay

	Rules				*	*	*	*								
	1	2	3	4	5	6	7	8	9	10	11	12	13	14	15	16
Sales < £2000	Y	Y	Y	Y	Y	Y	Y	Y	N	N	N	N	N	N	N	N
Sales < £5000	Y	Y	Y	Y	N	N	N	N	Y	Y	Y	Y	N	N	N	N
London office	Y	Y	N	N	Y	Y	N	N	Y	Y	N	N	Y	Y	N	N
Team leader	Y	N	Y	N	Y	N	Y	N	Y	N	Y	N	Y	N	Y	N
Basic salary	X	X	X	X					X	X	X	X	X	X	X	X
+ 4% of sales	X	X	X	X												
+ 5% of sales									X	X	X	X				
+ 6% of sales													X	X	X	X
+ £100	X	X							X	X			X	X		
+ 10% of basic salary	X		X						X		X		X		X	

* = illogical rule

Fig. 14.26 A full decision table for the procedure shown in fig. 14.25

	Rules											
	1	2	3	4	5	6	7	8	9	10	11	12
Sales < £2000	Y	Y	Y	Y	-	-	-	-	N	N	N	N
Sales < £5000	-	-	-	-	Y	Y	Y	Y	N	N	N	N
London office	Y	Y	N	N	Y	Y	N	N	Y	Y	N	N
Team leader	Y	N	Y	N	Y	N	Y	N	Y	N	Y	N
Basic salary	X	X	X	X	X	X	X	X	X	X	X	X
+ 4% of sales	X	X	X	X								
+ 5% of sales					X	X	X	X				
+ 6% of sales									X	X	X	X
+ £100	X	X			X	X			X	X		
+ 10% of basic salary	X		X		X		X		X		X	

Fig. 14.27 A reduced version of the decision table shown in fig. 14.26

Note The conditions have been written in such a way that their number is reduced to four, providing $2^4 = 16$ rules. The alternative is to couch the rules as follows:

> Sales less than £2000
> Sales £2000 and over but under £5000
> Sales £5000 and over
> London office?
> Team leader?

This would provide $2^5 = 32$ rules but is unnecessary since the same logic can be obtained with only two conditions for the size of sales, as illustrated in fig. 14.26.

14.4 Glossary of terms

Flowchart The graphical representation of the sequence of logical steps in a procedure, used as an aid to analysis by programmers and others.

Decision table Analytical technique that represents in tabular form the results of possible courses of action or combinations of conditions.

Limited-entry decision table A decision table that limits the symbols used to Y, N, - , and X.

Extended-entry decision table A decision table that allows a wider range of symbols than that used within a limited-entry decision table.

ELSE rule This rule is used to reduce the size of the decision table by combining the action entries when a number of condition entries all give the same result.

14.5 Exercises

1 A market research company has distributed questionnaires to 1000 destinations. They have received replies which have been coded to provide the following card input data:

Type of business:	1 = retail	2 = commerce	3 = manufacturing
Size (employees):	1(<50)	2(51–100)	3(>100)
Turnover:	1($<\frac{1}{2}$m)	2($\frac{1}{2}$–2m)	3(>2m)
Computer budget:	1(<10000)	2(10–50000)	3(>50000)

For example card 1 might contain 2, 1, 3, 1 meaning a commercial business employing less than 50 staff, with a turnover of over £2 millions per annum, spends less than £10000 per year on computers.

The last card type has a type code = 9 to signify the end of data.

It is desired to establish:

(a) The proportion of all companies with a computer budget below £10000.
(b) The number of small (<50 employees) manufacturing companies with a turnover in excess of £0.5 million whose budget exceeds £50000.
(c) The proportion of non-manufacturing companies with a turnover below £2 millions whose budget exceeds £10000.

(AAT, Elements of information systems (pilot paper))

2 You are investigating the stock system of ABC Ltd and you have decided to specify the reordering procedure in a decision table. The narrative description given by the clerk is:

I receive each requisition and consult my stock record to see whether sufficient stock is available to meet each item requested. If there is sufficient I adjust the balance on the stock record and write the quantity to be despatched on the requisition next to the quantity requested before passing it to the despatch clerk. I then check the adjusted balance to see if it has fallen below the reorder level.

If it has and there is no outstanding order on the factory I complete an order for that item. If there is insufficient stock to meet a requisition I write the quantity available on the form and pass it to despatch as normal but take a photocopy and put it in an outstanding requisitions file. I then adjust the balance on my stock record and generate an order if none is outstanding.

If an order is outstanding, I send an urge note to the factory to speed it up.

If there is no stock at all to meet a requisition I file it with outstanding requisitions. If nothing is on order, I generate one and telephone the factory to tell them it is coming. If there is an order I send an urge note as normal and chase it up.

Required: draw a decision table which fully describes this procedure.

(AAT, Elements of information systems)

3 A market research firm has built a file of responses to a questionnaire. Each record in the file includes the following details:

Questionnaire number
Socio-economic group (a, b or c)
Sex (m = male, f = female)
Age
Marital status (m = married, s = single)

Plus 10 questions each comprising:

Question number
Answer (y = yes, n = no)

(a) Draft a flow diagram for a computer program which would read the file for a specific question and analyse the responses as follows:

(i) Proportion of 'yes' answers in the total sample.
(ii) Proportion of 'yes' answers for males.
(iii) Proportion of 'yes' answers for married women in socio-economic group a, with children.
(iv) Proportion of 'yes' answers for females under 30.
(v) Proportion of 'yes' answers for people of 30 or over without children.

(b) If the company has a regular need for such reports suggest alternative methods for obtaining them.

(AAT, Elements of information systems)

4 Draw a flowchart for the following problem:

Read twenty times.
If item is type A print it.
If item is type B print it and write it to tape.

If item is type C print it and store it on disk else store it on error file. At end print totals of A, B, C items and then list the error file.

(IDPM, Data processing I)

5 An organisation uses the following guidelines in its promotion procedures for systems design and computer audit staff:

Only applicants who are over 25 years of age are considered for appointment as Project Leader or Computer Auditor. Furthermore they must have 3 years' relevant experience, management potential, and an appropriate professional qualification. A qualification in computing is required for appointment as Project Leader and in accounting for appointment as Computer Auditor. Unqualified applicants who are otherwise suitable will be offered the position of Senior Analyst. However, an applicant who is over 25 and has three years' experience but who is not qualified and does not have management potential will be appointed as a Systems Designer. If the applicant is qualified but lacks management potential he will be required to attend a course before any decision can be taken regarding promotion. All candidates will be required to satisfy an interview panel.

Required:

(a) Represent the above information using either Flowcharting or Decision Table techniques.
(b) Identify the stages in a system project when Flowcharting or Decision Table techniques will be particularly useful.

(ACCA, Systems analysis and design)

Issues and developments in information technology

This unit will look at some aspects of information technology which are having an impact upon our lives. We will first look at perhaps the single most important development in IT – artificial intelligence (AI) and fifth-generation computers. We will then examine the impact that IT is having upon work in factories and offices, and finally consider the issue of personal privacy.

15.1 Artificial intelligence (AI)

A great deal of work is at present going into the creation of a machine that is 'intelligent'. This is not an easy task for the researchers involved, not least because there is not an accepted definition of what intelligence really is. Alan Turing, the mathematician and early researcher in this area in the 1940s, devised a test for artificial intelligence known as the Turing test. Turing said that if a human being were unable to distinguish between conversation with a person and one with a machine, then it could be said that the machine was intelligent. The conversation would take place over two teletypes, with the judge being able to converse on any subject before making a decision. If the decision was wrong, or if a decision could not be made, then the machine would have passed the test. There is currently no computer system in the world that could even come close to passing such a test, although systems able to converse 'intelligently' on a small domain of knowledge have been developed.

The development of fifth-generation computers (see section 15.2) is a movement towards creating such intelligent machines, since such machines will need to converse, see, reason, and learn. They will also need to possess what may be called 'common sense' – that is, a wide range of apparently trivial knowledge that can be applied to any given problem. Machines currently do not possess any common sense, but, in an attempt to remedy this, researchers in the USA intend to build a computer database that can 'understand' all the knowledge held in an encyclopaedia. If successful, this fifteen-year project may well produce the basis for an 'intelligent' computer, possessing common sense, that could pass the Turing test.

The work done in AI has shown that it is the tasks that humans find hardest – like handling knowledge – that have been the easiest for computers to achieve. Similarly, the things that we find the easiest – like seeing, walking, and talking – are very difficult for computers to achieve. Part of the reason behind this is that the representation and use of knowledge is relatively well understood, whereas seeing, walking, and communication are things that we *do*, but without really *understanding* how we do them. Until these skills are better understood than they are now, the intelligent machine will remain a goal rather than a reality.

We will now look at some of the work that has been done in AI.

15.2 Fifth-generation computers

The development of computers since the Second World War has been dominated by the USA, and this has given it a world lead in computer technology. In 1981 the results of a number of research projects commissioned by the Japanese Ministry for International Trade were announced, unveiling a plan to build what were called 'fifth-generation computers'. The term 'fifth-generation' is based upon the development of computer hardware from valves, transistors, integrated circuits, and large-scale integrated circuits, which form the first four generations. This is illustrated in Table 15.1.

The new generation of machines will be based on very-large-scale integration (VLSI) and be very different from existing computers. It is intended that fifth-generation computers will be able to:

(a) process data in parallel using a series of processors working together (present-day computers process a single instruction at a time – parallel computers will process several instructions simultaneously, assembling the result at the end);
(b) understand spoken instructions in English;
(c) 'see' and react 'intelligently' to the world around them;
(d) act 'intelligently', and be able to learn and make decisions based on incomplete information.

The announcement of Japan's ten-year research programme on fifth-generation computers was followed by the setting-up of similar programmes in the USA and the European Community, and by the Alvey programme in the UK. Many of these programmes have now ended, and, while much useful work has been done in this area, the early hopes have not been fulfilled – the creation of a system that exhibits true artificial intelligence is still in the future.

15.2.1 Expert systems

An expert system is a program that is designed to provide cheap and quick access to the knowledge and experience of a human expert in a particular field. Expert systems are based on the principle that an expert in a particular field is in demand, the expert's time is expensive, and it is the expert's ability to *use*

Table 15.1 The five generations of computers

Generation	Electronic component	Features
First (1940–52)	Vacuum tubes	Very large (several rooms). Generated a lot of heat. Special air-conditioned room needed. Unreliable.
Second (1952–64)	Transistors	Smaller, though still large (a large room). Special air-conditioned room needed. Faster and more reliable.
Third (1964–71)	Integrated circuits	Smaller still. Special rooms still needed. Faster and more reliable.
Fourth (1971–)	Large-scale integrated circuits	Still smaller. Little maintenance required.
Fifth (under development)	Parallel processor?	Low-maintenance chip capable of processing data in parallel? Very fast operation, using exotic chip compounds.

knowledge that makes him or her valuable. The knowledge of the expert is codified and placed into a computer that becomes an expert system capable of taking the place of the human expert.

An expert system will generally be made up of four parts:

(a) the 'knowledge base' – that is, the rules, data, and relationships on a particular area of knowledge that have been obtained from the human experts;

(b) the 'inference engine' – a special program that enables the expert system to be able to handle the knowledge base and arrive at a conclusion;

(c) the 'explanation module' – a program that enables the expert system to explain why it made a certain recommendation or arrived at a certain conclusion;

(d) the 'natural language processor' that allows users to communicate with the expert system in a natural manner.

These four parts are illustrated in fig. 15.1.

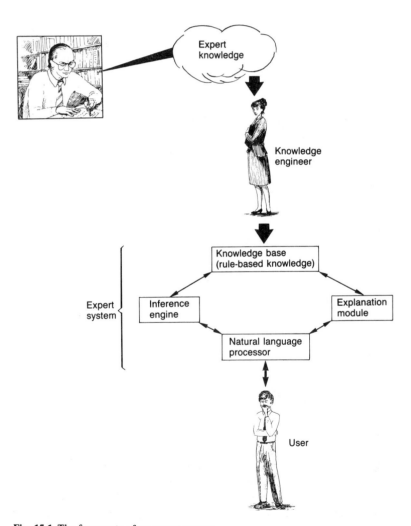

Fig. 15.1 The four parts of an expert system

The theory behind the operation/use of an expert system is that human experts make decisions according to certain rules that they have evolved over years of experience in a particular area of work. These rules can usually be expressed in the form of a series of 'if ... then' statements as shown in the simple example below:

> IF an animal has four legs
>   AND
> IF the animal barks
> THEN it must be a dog.

This 'expert' knowledge depends on two rules upon which to base the conclusion that an animal is a dog (making a poor expert). Expert systems that have been developed commercially may need hundreds or thousands of such rules to structure the knowledge of experts in investment management, commodity broking, or vehicle maintenance.

With the use of the 'natural language processor', the user is able to ask the expert system specific queries about its particular area of expertise and to receive an explanation of how the system reached its conclusion. A dialogue with an expert system that contains the knowledge of a television engineer might go like this:

User: My television does not work when I switch it on
System: Is it plugged in?
User: Yes
System: Is the mains socket switched on?
User: Yes
System: Does another electrical appliance work using the same mains socket?
User: Yes
System: Replace the fuse in the plug attached to the television.
User: Why?
System: Because I am trying to find out if the fuse in the television plug has blown.

Many expert systems at present being constructed make use of an expert-system 'shell'. This is an expert-system program that is empty of any knowledge and must have its knowledge base added before it can be of use. This may be done by the expert or else by a 'knowledge engineer' who, after long observation and discussion with the expert, will draw up the rules by which the expert makes decisions.

The research into expert systems began in the late 1960s, with systems like MYCIN (an expert system which is used for the diagnosis of infectious blood diseases) and PUFF (for lung complaints) being developed on large computer systems. In recent years, however, expert systems have been developed which are intended to be used to give quick advice on specific areas of expertise, so that they are seen more as a management tool like a spreadsheet. Examples are in areas like stock control, share portfolio management, and fault-finding systems.

Expert systems are good for use in areas in which there is already a defined rule-based domain of knowledge – such as the hardware needed for a particular computer configuration, Statutory Sick Pay regulations, or the dismissal regulations in employment law. Expert systems are not so good, however, in areas that involve less easily defined bodies of knowledge.

These systems can be used in two ways: firstly by an expert to obtain a second opinion or confirm a conclusion, and secondly as an instructor – since expert systems are able to explain the reasoning behind the conclusions that have been reached, they can be of great use in passing on expertise to less experienced workers.

There are three respects in which expert systems are limited. Firstly they do not 'think' like a human expert: they only 'know' the rules they have been provided with. They are limited by those rules – they don't know what they don't know; they cannot think about a problem as a human expert can. For this reason, expert systems are very limited in what they can do – they may know all about infectious blood diseases but could not tell if you had the flu. Secondly, in any area of knowledge it is possible to find experts who violently disagree on many subjects. Thirdly, many experts will not be able to express their expertise in making a judgement as a set of rules but will make use of a 'feeling' or 'instinct' that cannot be expressed in rule form. In such a situation it may not be appropriate to use an expert system.

Early expert systems were designed to replace the need for human experts and to be able to act as self-contained experts in their own right – examples include some of the early medical expert systems. Because of the limitations outlined above, however, it was realised that a better view of expert systems is as 'decision support systems' – enabling the user of such a system to make a better decision. The Imperial Cancer Research Fund is developing an expert system that is likely to have something like three million rules when complete but is still designed only to assist the family doctor in making a diagnosis of cancer.

Since the research into expert systems began in the late 1960s, the famous expert systems developed on large computer systems include

MYCIN	An expert system which is used for the diagnosis of infectious blood diseases.
PROSPECTOR	For analysis of rock strata for prospecting purposes.
PUFF	For lung complaints.
INTERNIST-1	For internal medicine.
XCON	Developed by Digital Equipment Co. (DEC) to help in configuring hardware systems.
GASOIL	Developed by BP to assist in the design of the gas/oil separators used in oil-refining.

15.2.2 Voice-recognition systems

Simple voice-recognition systems have been used for some time for applications where it is not possible for the operator to use a keyboard. Such systems work by translating the oral command into a code which the computer can recognise and match against a series of codes that are stored in memory. Before such a system can be used, it must first be taught the set of commands that it will meet, and how it must respond to each of these commands. These systems will usually respond only to a single operator, and must be retaught to be able to cope with different accents/users.

'Good morning, everyone'

The research into continuous-speech recognition is one area that has been identified by a number of fifth-generation research programs as being of special interest. By creating a system that can understand human speech, it will overcome many of the traditional obstacles that people encounter when using computers.

At present, systems for recognising continuous speech analyse what is spoken in two ways at the same time. Firstly, the system tries to match it with a stored version of each word by analysing the sound according to its pitch, harmonics, inflexion, and speed of delivery. Secondly, the system uses grammatical and other rules to attempt to predict what kind of word is most likely to be used in a given context. For example, 'Dear Sir' is far more likely than 'Dear cur', and 'I want to know' more likely than 'I want to no'. The use of such techniques depends upon very fast computers, and may provide the way forward for the development of 'speech-driven' systems.

15.2.3 Image-recognition systems

Image-recognition systems operate along the same principles as voice-recognition systems, with the computer using a camera vision system to 'see'.

It then attempts to match what it 'sees' with a set of images that it has been 'taught' and are already in its memory. Once it has recognised the image, it is then in a position to carry on to the next procedure.

Image-recognition systems are already in use in manufacturing, with car-assembly robots making decisions about which components to use by 'recognising' which car is on the production line. Similar systems are used in quality control to reject components that do not match the image held in the computer memory. These systems are designed for a particular task, however, and they will often need special lighting conditions to operate effectively.

Such systems are limited in their application because they are only able to recognise things that they have been 'taught' exist. To be of greater use, such systems need to be able to operate in the real world where components are not all the same, and where the light will vary as the robot moves around. This will be possible in time, as AI is applied to such systems.

15.3 Privacy

Information has always been held on people by government, employers, and other organisations, but there was no widespread concern about this situation until this information began to be held on computer systems. In this section we will look firstly at what it is about computerised databases that makes them different to manual systems, before going on to discuss some of the fears that have been expressed about the use of computer databases. Finally, we will look at the Data Protection Act 1984.

15.3.1 Features of computer databases
The use of computer database systems to hold and manipulate the information held on us is different from traditional methods of storage in a number of ways:

(a) *Storage capacity and speed of access* Computer databases are able to store virtually unlimited amounts of information that can be retrieved very quickly.
(b) *Accessibility* The use of communications links enables information stored on a computer database to be accessible from virtually anywhere in the country.
(c) *Cross-referencing* Sophisticated programming techniques enable information stored on several different databases to be combined, enabling cross-referencing of all information held on a single person.

15.3.2 Fears about the use of computerised databases
The concerns that are expressed about the increasing use of computerised databases to hold personal information fall into the following categories:

(a) *Unauthorised access* The characteristics of computerised systems linked by a communications network make unauthorised access to personal records far easier.

(b) *Incorrect information*   It is possible that the information held on an individual may be wrong. An incorrect credit rating may, for example, cause someone to be refused a loan or mortgage.

(c) *Information sharing*   The sharing between organisations of information on individuals without their knowledge can lead to problems. The sale of customer lists can lead to unwelcome direct or 'junk' mail.

15.3.3 What information is held?

It is really surprising just how much personal information is held by a wide variety of organisations. Figure 15.2 gives an indication of which organisations hold what information.

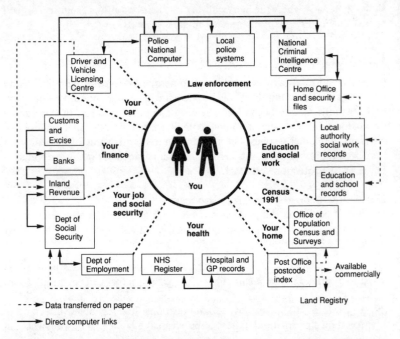

Fig. 15.2 Some of the organisations holding information on individuals in the UK

As can be seen from fig. 15.2 there are a large number of linkages between the different holders of information. The UK government has built a network (called the Government Data Network) to link up government departments, including the DSS, the Inland Revenue, the Home Office, and Customs and Excise. This has made possible the exchange of vast amounts of information presently held in separate systems – something that causes concern to civil-liberties groups, who object to the 'Big Brother' nature of the system and are concerned about State interference in individuals' lives.

Commercial information companies exist that do nothing but collect and provide information on people and organisations. The sale of electoral registers – that is, the lists of all people who are eligible to vote in particular areas – and of information from the official census of all households provides these companies with the basis of databases that hold information on around 43 million people living in the UK. These organisations combine this with information on court judgements and financial status, and then classify each household according to income, location, age, race, and other factors, using the Post Office's post-code system to index the information held. This database can be used to provide lists of people which can be used for direct-mail selling (so-called 'junk' mail) and market research, as well as for specific enquiries about individuals.

15.3.4 The Data Protection Act 1984
The Data Protection Act is the UK government's response to the fears expressed above on the large amount of personal data that is held on computer databases. The Act gives us the right to see the information that is stored on us. We can have it changed if it is wrong, and even claim compensation if the use of incorrect information has adversely affected us. The Act also obliges those who record and use personal data – termed data users – to be open about its use and to follow the 'Data Protection Principles' governing its use. The next few sections will look in more detail at several aspects of the Act.

What the Act covers   The Act covers all data that is either a statement of fact or an opinion about a living individual and is processed by computer. Information held by private individuals or clubs, mailing lists, and payroll information are exempt from the Act and do not have to be registered.

What the Act does not cover   The Act excludes all information that is held on manual records, like card file systems, and information held on organisations – such as businesses – rather than individuals.
'Data' is defined as 'facts or opinions', not 'expressions of intention'. This means that if a computerised personnel record says 'Bob is a lazy and work-shy individual, and I do not intend to promote him', Bob has the right to see the part that says 'Bob is a lazy and work-shy individual' but not the part that says 'I do not intend to promote him.'
Exemptions from subject access include the giving out of information in situations where it may affect the detection or prevention of crimes, the catching or prosecuting of offenders, or the assessment or collection of taxes, and information that is held on computers for less than 40 days.

Individuals' rights under the Act   Since November 1987 we are all entitled, on payment of a fee, to be supplied with a copy of the personal data held on us by anyone who maintains a registered database. If the data held is inaccurate, action can be taken to ensure that the data is either deleted or corrected. If the use of inaccurate data has caused damage, or if damage has been caused by the loss, unauthorised destruction, or disclosure of the personal data, we have a right to seek compensation for that damage.

Register of data users   All data users who fall within the scope of the Act must register with the Data Protection Registrar. The Data Protection Registrar maintains the register of data users, which contains the following information:

(a) the data user's name and address,
(b) details of the personal data held,
(c) what it is to be used for,
(d) the source of the data,
(e) the people to whom the data user may wish to disclose the information,
(f) the overseas countries to which the data user may wish to transfer the personal data.

A copy of the Register should be available for inspection at your local public reference library.

The Data Protection Principles   All data users must comply with the Data Protection Principles, which state that personal data shall

(a) be collected and processed fairly and lawfully,
(b) be held only for the lawful purposes described in the register entry,
(c) be used only for those purposes and only be disclosed to those people described in the register entry,
(d) be adequate, relevant, and not excessive in relation to the purpose for which it is held,
(e) be accurate and, where necessary, kept up to date,
(f) be held no longer than is necessary for the registered purpose,
(g) be surrounded by proper security.

15.4 IT in factories and offices

This section will look at the effects of information technology upon manufacturing and office work. The use of IT in both of these areas has meant that a revolution in working practices has taken place.

15.4.1 IT and manufacturing

The use of computers to automate the production process in factories began in the 1960s and 1970s, with robots replacing humans for such jobs as welding and simple assembly tasks. Many factories producing cars make use of robots for welding and delivering parts to the production line (materials handling). These represent simply the direct replacement of human labour with cheaper automated systems. Current approaches to automation in manufacturing, however, are aiming to increase the flexibility of the production process itself, using the following technologies.

Computer-aided design (CAD) systems are like electronic drawing boards that enable engineers to speed up the time taken to produce drawings. CAD systems can enable companies to generate product designs between two and six times faster than by using manual methods. Chrysler, the American car manufacturer, has a large network of CAD workstations and can generate engineering drawings in 15 minutes that took months to produce in the 1950s. (See also section 12.2.3, which describes an application of CAD in the fashion trade.)

Flexible manufacturing systems (FMS) are groupings of machines that can be easily reset to switch from making one product to making another. An FMS may include machine tools and associated materials-handling devices, like conveyor belts and automatic trolleys, to carry items from one machine to another. These systems can reasily be reprogrammed to produce different items, reducing the amount of setting-up time between the manufacture of different products. The aim of FMS is to make it more profitable for manufacturers to produce smaller production runs.

Computer integrated manufacturing (CIM) is the term given to the linking together of all parts of the manufacturing process, from design, production set-up, and scheduling, to production. The adoption of a standard protocol called Manufacturing Automation Control Protocol (MAP) for all manufacturing computers and machine tools enables the integration of different machinery into a unified manufacturing system. The adoption of a similar protocol called Technical and Office Protocol (TOP) for the design and other office functions will enable the development of unified office systems. MAP and TOP can communicate with each other and should provide the basis for a design and manufacturing system that is fully integrated. These developments are encouraging, but it is likely that such a fully integrated factory will not appear until the late 1990s. When it does, however, it may operate as follows.

The fully-automated factory of the 1990s will be able to produce in hours orders that would presently take weeks to process. Design engineers will use systems which contain the expertise of production engineers and can work out in seconds whether a new product will work and how much it will cost. These systems will, for example, immediately tell the designer whether product designs are strong enough or aerodynamic enough to do their job. They will automatically estimate the cost of manufacture, and list the parts and tools needed for a product's manufacture. The time taken between final design and manufacture will be measured in days rather than the months it takes today.

15.4.2 Telecommuting

The use of computers at work may conjure up the image of a large mainframe computer calculating a payroll in a fraction of the time it once took, or else the office personal computer being used for wordprocessing. The direct replacement of manual or clerical workers by computers or computer-controlled devices has been taking place for some years, with the introduction of the wordprocessor and the database both being part of that revolution.

Another change that is taking place is in the combination of computers with advanced communication systems to form computer networks.

The National Economic Development Organisation has predicted that by 1995 over three million people could be working from home on computer networks, with perhaps five million by the year 2010. This shift towards 'non-office' working is taking place because the nature of the work that many people do is associated with information rather than physical objects. Handling (if that is the right word) information on a computer that is connected to a communications network means that information workers do not need to be located in an office to do their work. It is just as easy to send information to a distant electronic mailbox as it is to send the same information to one located in the same office.

The use of such communications systems to work at home, away from a centralised office, has been called *telecommuting* or *networking*. Some jobs, like programming and journalism, do not need to be done within an office, and companies like ICL have been employing programmers to work from home since as long ago as 1969. The use of the 'electronic office' facilities described in Units 10 and 12 makes it easy for journalists and authors to work at home and send their work to the newspaper or publisher over a telephone line.

A more radical approach to networking was started by Rank Xerox in 1980, by encouraging managerial staff to leave and create a network of small companies that supply Xerox with the same services that the networkers had carried out as employees. These workers were 'information' workers who were able to do their jobs equally well from home or from the office. This move has released an office building and saved Rank Xerox the £330000 a year that it cost to run. The networkers have found that some of them missed the social side of being in an office, and they now make extensive use of electronic mail to keep in contact with each other. Networkers are generally able to be more productive than when they are in an office, and they can often increase their standard of living by doing other work as well.

Telecommuting seems to be on the increase, but it is only 'information' workers that are able to work from home in this way. Service and manual work cannot usually be transferred to the home, so that this revolution is likely to affect only the 'information' sector of the economy.

15.5 Multimedia

'Multimedia' is a global term for the developing computer technology that can combine text, graphics, hi-fi sound, animation, and full-motion video in a single high-resolution display. This has been made possible by the common use of digital recording of text, graphics, sound, and video, coupled with the increased processor speeds required to handle large video files.

The applications of this technology include the following:

(a) *Training* As a cheaper alternative to traditional techniques, many large organisations are using multimedia-based systems for staff induction, training in new procedures, and general management training. Multimedia foreign-language training systems have also been developed for home, school, and office use.

(b) *Architectural visualisations* Using multimedia technology, a building designed on a CAD system can be animated in such a way that a client is able to 'walk through' the building and look at it from a far wider range of views than is possible using CAD.

(c) *Advertising/promotions* Logos, trademarks, and storyboards outlining an advertisement can all be created, animated, and given a soundtrack using multimedia authoring software.

(d) *Home entertainment* Variants of multimedia are systems that plug into a domestic television and use a simple remote-control device. Intended primarily as entertainment/educational systems, the applications available include such things as interactive cartoons, shoot-'em-up games, encyclopaedias, and an interactive multimedia world atlas.

Case-study 1 - British Rail driver training

The simulator is designed to enhance rather than replace existing training and is built around a full-size mock-up of the locomotive controls, using a 37 inch monitor screen for display purposes. The system also has an instructor's console which is used to monitor progress or else change the section of track, signal setting, number of carriages, etc. In addition to video pictures, the system also provides background and running noise, with the sounds changing according to the speed of the train. There are also single sound samples that are used whenever the train goes under a bridge or over points, for example. During the simulation, data on driver performance is recorded for later analysis by the trainee and the instructor.

Case-study 2 - police crowd-control training

Developed by the NCC (National Computer Centre) for the Scottish Police College, Vistrain uses networked interactive video- and computer-based training technology to simulate the situations faced by police before, during, and after a football match. The main benefit of this system is that it moves computer-based training (CBT) from the individual to the group context, with the emphasis being on participative teamwork training.

Multimedia is still a very new technology, and there are a number of differing standards for the hardware components that go to make up a multimedia system. While the components involved will vary slightly, any system capable of effectively running or developing multimedia applications must be built around a fast processor with at least 2 Mb of RAM, a high-capacity hard disk with either a videodisc or a CD–ROM player to hold the large video files, a facility to reproduce hi-fi sound, and a high-resolution monitor.

15.6 Virtual reality

Virtual reality (VR) is a new and developing technology that moves the user from being an observer in front of a computer screen to being a participant within a computer-generated 'virtual' world. VR is built around the use of sophisticated technology including surround-vision helmets, gloves with motion sensors, headphones with full stereo sound, and stereoscopic vision systems. Once wearing this equipment, the user is cut off from the real world and all movements are fed into the virtual world created by the computer. Apart from arcade games, applications for this technology are currently built around training, but the potential uses include:

- education – exploring Tudor England or examining a chemical molecule from the inside;
- retail-space design – retailers could plan their new shops in a virtual supermarket;
- medicine – surgeons could examine the brain without the need for invasive surgery;
- the disabled – users could experience travel to places that would not otherwise be accessible to them.

One current application of VR is in the training of police in high-speed emergency-response driving.

15.7 Glossary of terms

AI Artificial intelligence – the aim of creating an 'intelligent' computer.

Expert system A computer program that contains a human expert's accumulated knowledge and is able to apply the knowledge to the solution of problems.

Fifth-generation computer A computer that possesses artificial intelligence.

Data Protection Act 1984 An Act of Parliament covering the use of computer databases and the access rights of individuals to them.

CAD Computer-aided design – the use of a computer system that enables designers to create design drawings.

CIM Computer integrated manufacturing – a term applied to the linking together of design, production set-up, scheduling, and production process, under computer control.

FMS Flexible manufacturing system – a grouping of machines that can be switched easily between the manufacture of different products.

Telecommuting The use of computers and communications links to work from home.

Networking Another name for telecommuting.

15.8 Exercises

1 'Computers are changing the world, and pretty soon we will all be able to work from home, and offices will be a thing of the past.' State why you agree or disagree with this statement.

2 What is the difference between the following pairs: CAD and CAM; FMS and CIM?

3 (a) Explain the difference between an 'expert system' and an 'expert-system shell'.
  (b) What is the role of a 'knowledge engineer' in the creation of an expert system?
  (c) Make a list of the ways in which your organisation could make use of an expert system.

4 (a) What is a 'fifth-generation computer'?
  (b) List the characteristics that distinguish the five generations of computers.

5 Many people are worried about the use of computer systems that store information about them. What is it about the use of computers to store personal information that concerns many observers?

6 The Data Protection Act 1984 was passed in order to control the use of computerised databanks and to protect the individual from their misuse.

  (a) What information does the Act cover?
  (b) What information is excluded from the Act?
  (c) What rights of access and redress are given to the individual under the Act?

Case-study

Monica Turnbull applied for a job as a cashier to a firm of electrical wholesalers, Flex Components Ltd. Upon being called for interview she was offered the post of cashier 'subject to satisfactory references' being obtained from her previous employer ADC Ltd (which she left to start a family). Ten days after the interview, Flex Components Ltd wrote to Monica to say that it was unable to offer her the post of cashier due to her poor references.

Monica Turnbull was astonished at this news, since she had never received any indication that ADC Ltd might have been dissatisfied with her as an employee, and her manager at ADC Ltd had often referred to her as a key member of the staff.

ADC Ltd is a large company with a centralised computer-based personnel record system. Monica Turnbull has tried to gain access to the information held on her in this system, believing it to be incorrect and the cause of her failure to get the job with Flex Components Ltd. Monica has contacted the personnel section at ADC Ltd a number of times but has been refused access to her personnel records.

(a) What action can Monica Turnbull take to see exactly what information is held on her in the ADC Ltd computerised personnel system?
(b) If the information is incorrect, what can Monica Turnbull do to get it amended?
(c) If it transpires that Monica did in fact fail to get the job at Flex Components Ltd as a result of incorrect information held on ADC's personnel system, what can she do about it?

Research exercises

(a) As you have seen, a vast amount of information is stored about us all on government and commercial computer databases. Make a list of the organisations that might have information about you stored in a computerised database. Of this list, choose the two organisations which are likely to hold the most information about you. Make a visit to your nearest main public reference library and ask to see a copy of the Register of Data Users. Now look up your two chosen organisations and see what information they are legally entitled to hold on you. If you would like to see exactly what information is held on you, ask the librarian how you go about making a request for data access.
(b) The pace of research into artificial intelligence is such that new developments are constantly being reported in newspapers and magazines. To make a check on current developments in this area, go to your local library and use the *British Humanities Index* to see what articles have been published for the last six months. Look under the following headings: computers, artificial intelligence, expert systems, CIM, FMS.

Final assignment

The following assignment involves most of the aspects of information processing discussed in this book.

Burnton Computer Consultants offers a complete consultancy service to local industry and commerce. Since the company was founded in 1979, the range of services offered to the public has increased to include systems analysis, programming, providing computer operators, and customising software – as well as the main business of assisting in the selection, acquisition, operation, and running of business computer systems.

You are a systems consultant for Burnton Computer Consultants and you have been given the job of looking after the Pelham Insurance contract. The following is a brief description of the business and its workings provided by Ms D. Stoker, your manager, who has had some preliminary discussions with the partners of Pelham Insurance.

Pelham Insurance

Pelham Insurance is a well-established insurance brokerage employing eighteen people, with its main office in Burnton and a branch office located in a nearby town. Of the business done by Pelham Insurance, about 45% is in motor insurance, with the remaining 55% being made up of personal, marine, and property insurance.

Pelham Insurance has about 12000 people on its books, with policy renewals being spread more or less evenly throughout the year. All insurance records are at present maintained on a card system at the local office, with one card holding all the insurance details of each policyholder. This card contains details of the name, address, telephone number, insurance policy number(s), type of insurance, renewal date(s), and personal details relating to the type of insurance. For motor insurance the personal details will cover make/ model/engine size of car, driving experience, convictions (if any), size of no-claims bonus, type of risk, and a note of any physical disabilities that may affect the ability to drive. Each type of insurance will have a slightly different set of details, according to whether it is personal, motor, marine, or property insurance.

Most of the business is done on a renewal basis, with a Policy Renewal Note being sent to the policyholder three weeks before the renewal date. If this produces no results, a Renewal Reminder is sent out one week before the renewal date. If no renewal is forthcoming after this, a note is made for the insurance clerk to follow this up and find out why there was no renewal.

The financial side of the business – the receipts from premiums and commissions, payments to insurance companies, payroll, and all other income and expenditure – is handled by a single clerk under the supervision of one of the partners.

As the business has developed, a number of problems have begun to make themselves felt. Firstly there is the problem of manually typing the details on the Policy Renewal Notes, Renewal Reminders, and quotes for new business. This is a very time-consuming job and leaves little time to follow up the non-renewals, and thus means that business is often lost when it need not be. Secondly, the present card system of keeping records means that, in order to ensure that renewal notices are sent out on time, a Policy Renewal Register has to be kept and updated each day, and a manual search has to be done in order to extract the record cards needed. This is not thought to be a very efficient way of doing business. Lastly, the method of recording the financial side of the business does not give the partners the information they need about the state of the partnership's finances. They feel they need to be able to get information faster, so as to enable them to be more accurate in financial planning, and that one way of achieving this would be to speed up the preparation of pay-slips and weekly returns to the insurance companies.

You have been asked by Ms D. Stoker to prepare some proposals, based on the above, relating to each of the questions below:

1 The partners of Pelham Insurance are not yet fully convinced of the need to computerise and have sought out some impartial advice. Explain, in relation to Pelham Insurance, what the major benefits and problems of installing a computer system are likely to be.

2 List the items of software you would recommend to assist Pelham Insurance with the three problem areas mentioned above, and explain of what use each item would be to the business.

3 List the hardware that should be purchased in order to run the software you recommended in 2 above, explaining where, and for what purpose, each item would be used.

4 Using the information relating to the record card and the motor insurance policy as an example, produce a record format that could be used in a new computerised system, specifying the field size and type.

   Assuming 14 000 records, how much computer backing storage would you recommend is purchased, making due allowance for future expansion?

5 Two of the staff at Pelham Insurance are due to retire in a couple of months,

and it has been suggested that they be replaced with a computer operator and a systems analyst. State why you agree or disagree.

6 It has been decided to proceed with the computerisation plans, and the partners wish to know what steps they should take in order to ensure that their computerisation is as successful as possible. Advise the partners of the stages their computerisation project should take, briefly explaining the purpose of each stage.

7 Concern has been expressed about the actual changeover from the present manual system to the computerised system, and the partners are keen to learn how best to go about this. Explain the various methods of changing from one system to another, making your recommendation as to which would be the best for Pelham Insurance, and why.

8 The partners are very worried about possible losses due to:

(a) mistakes and carelessness by staff,
(b) failure of electronic equipment,
(c) unauthorised access to confidential information.

State, and explain, your proposals for each of these problems.

9 Pelham Insurance wishes to streamline its insurance quotes procedure by setting policy rates according to a points system. The rules for awarding points are shown below, the idea being that each type of risk is awarded a points value – the greater the risk, the greater the number of points awarded.

Quotes procedure
The applicant sends in details of his or her age, the make and engine size of car, and the type of policy applied for. From this information a points value is calculated according to the criteria below:

Age	Points	Engine size (litres)	Points
< 18	5	< 1	1
18–25	4	1–1.4	2
26–35	3	1.5–2.4	3
36–50	2	> 2.4	4
> 50	1		

Car	Points	Policy type	Points
British	1	Third party	1
Foreign	3	Comprehensive	4

This means that a 26-year-old driver with a 1.5 litre British car who wants comprehensive insurance will be awarded 11 points, and this will determine the cost of the insurance.

In order to assist the applications programmer, produce an outline flowchart for the above procedure.

Glossary

Words highlighted in **bold** within a glossary entry indicate other entries under which further explanation or information may be found.

1GL First-generation language – **machine code.**

2GL Second-generation language – **assembly language.**

3GL Third-generation language – a **high-level language,** e.g. BASIC, PASCAL, COBOL.

4GL Fourth-generation language – a programming language designed for use by end-users rather than professional programmers. See **applications generator.**

5GL Fifth-generation language – a **non-procedural language** designed for use in artificial-intelligence applications, e.g. PROLOG.

Accounting software Software designed to record financial and other transactions. An accounting system is basically made up of the two main areas of sales and purchases, with each area being composed of a number of sections. Reports and summaries of transactions can be produced from both the sales and purchases ledgers, with the results being combined in a 'nominal ledger'.

Acoustic coupler A device that makes use of a telephone handset as a connection to the telephone system for data-transmission purposes, converting digital to analogue signals and vice versa.

Address The physical location of data stored on a magnetic or optical disk, referred to by disk surface, sector, and track.

AI Artificial intelligence – the aim of creating an 'intelligent' computer, one with which one could hold a conversation indistinguishable from one with a human being.

ALU   Arithmetic and logic unit – the part of the **CPU** in which arithmetic, logic, and related operations are performed.

Analogue signals   Signals representing quantities that can vary continuously throughout a range of values, e.g. the electrical signal representing sound waves transmitted by the UK telephone system. Compare with **digital** signals.

Analyst   See **systems analyst**.

Ancestral files   Files generated from each other for security purposes, to ensure that the information held on master files is not lost. Also known as the 'Grandfather–Father–Son' system.

ANSI   American National Standards Institute.

Applications generator   A program which creates **high-level language** program code given information on the application to be computerised. Also known as a 'fourth-generation language'.

Applications programmer   A computer programmer who specialises in the creation of applications programs like payroll etc. Contrasted with **systems programmer**.

Applications software   Programs that are used for a particular application, e.g. accounts, payroll, games.

Archiving   The process of transferring dormant records on to an off-line storage medium, usually magnetic tape.

Arithmetic and logic unit   See **ALU**.

Artificial intelligence   See **AI**.

ASCII   American Standard Code for Information Interchange.

Assembler   A program that converts a program written in a low-level assembly language into **machine code**.

Assembly language   A low-level language, being a development of machine code in which each instruction has been given an easy-to-remember code. Processor-dependent, it is not **portable** between different types of computer. Also called a 'second-generation language'.

Asynchronous transmission   A method of data transmission in which each character sent is preceded by a start bit and followed by a stop bit.

ATM   Automated teller machine – a device which dispenses cash, answers enquiries on the status of bank accounts, and may also receive deposits.

Audit trail   A method for tracing the transactions affecting the contents of a record.

Automated teller machine   See **ATM**.

Backing store   Another name for **secondary storage**, e.g. magnetic or optical disks, magnetic tape.

Back-up   A copy taken of a disk or file as a security measure in case the original is lost.

BACS   Bankers' Automated Clearing Services – a computerised service for the clearing of cheques and other transactions.

Badge reader   See **card reader**.

Band printer   Similar to a **chain printer**, but with the characters held on steel bands which are exchangeable to provide different character sets.

Bar code   A code of printed parallel lines used for fast data entry into computers, commonly seen on books and groceries but also used in a wide variety of other areas. See also **EAN**.

Barrel printer   See **drum printer**.

BASIC   *B*eginners *A*ll-purpose *S*ymbolic *I*nstruction *C*ode – a **high-level language** originally designed for use in education but now used in a wide variety of areas.

Batch processing   A method of updating a master file which involves a delay during which the transactions are collected, batched, and processed.

Baud rate   The speed of data transmission in **bits** per second. Baud rates are expressed as send/receive values, so that a baud rate of 1200/75 means that data is sent to the user at 1200 baud, and received back at 75 baud.

Binary   A number system based on only two digits (0 and 1).

Bit rate   The rate at which **bits** are transmitted over a communications link, usually referred to as the **baud rate**.

Bits   The digits, 0 and 1, of the binary number system.

Bridge   A device that connects two separate **LAN**s.

Buffer memory   Memory (RAM) in which are accumulated the results from one part of a computer system before processing by another, slower, part of the system, to free the faster one for more work, e.g. the memory found in printers to store the results from the CPU.

Bug   An error in a computer program.

Bus LAN   A **LAN** in which microcomputers, printers, etc. branch off a single strand of cable.

Byte   The basic unit of storage, equivalent to a single **character**.

CAD Computer-aided design – a computer system using a keyboard, **graphics pad**, **light-pen**, and VDU to manipulate designs and generate drawings on a VDU or graph plotter.

CAM Computer-aided manufacture – the use of computerised machine tools and production techniques.

Card reader A device that can read information held in a magnetic stripe on a plastic card.

CD–ROM Compact disk – read only memory, an **optical-disk** reference storage medium based upon the domestic compact disk.

Ceefax 'See facts' – the BBC **teletext** system.

Cell (a) The basic unit on which operations are performed in a **spreadsheet**, formed by the intersection of a row with a column. (b) The area covered by a single transmitter in a **cellular radio** network.

Cellular radio A method of providing a mobile telephone service in which the country is divided into a number of cells, each of which is covered by a transmitter. A computer system automatically establishes and maintains a call by switching between transmitters as the user moves from one cell to another.

Central processing unit See **CPU**.

Chain printer A type of **line printer** in which the characters are held on a continuous chain moving past a series of print hammers.

Character A single letter, number, or symbol – e.g. 'b', '7', or '£'.

Check digit A digit calculated from a code number and placed at the end of it for recalculation as a **verification** technique.

Chip An integrated electronic circuit contained on a wafer of silicon.

CIM Computer integrated manufacturing – the linking together of design, production set-up, scheduling, and production process, under computer control.

COBOL *CO*mmon *B*usiness *O*riented *L*anguage — a **high-level language** designed for use in business systems.

COM Computer output on microform (microfilm or microfiche).

Comms See **datacomms**.

Compiler A **translation program** that creates a new machine-code version of a complete high-level-language program.

Computer An electronic device that can store, retrieve, and process data in accordance with given instructions.

Computer bureau A company that specialises in offering computer-related services, e.g. programming, data entry, etc.

Computer consultant   A computer specialist who provides advice to users on specialist areas of computer knowledge.

Computer network   A linked group of computer systems that is designed to allow the easy exchange of data between the network users. See **LAN** and **WAN**.

Computer operator   A specialist computer worker whose job is to look after the routine operation of a mini or mainframe computer system.

Confravision   The British Telecom public videoconferencing service.

Continuous stationery   A continuous piece of paper on which to print computer output, being perforated at page intervals and having sprocket holes along the edges for automatic feed purposes.

c.p.s.   Characters per second.

CPU   Central processing unit – the main controlling element of a computer, composed of the central memory, the **arithmetic and logic unit**, and the control unit.

Cross-compiler   A **translation program** that generates machine code for a computer other than the one on which it is running.

Cross-field check   A validation check that tests one field given the value in another – e.g. if 'Title' = 'Mr' then 'Sex' must equal 'Male'.

CRT   Cathode-ray tube – a device that converts electrical signals into images on a screen.

CSMA/CD   Carrier sense multiple access/collision detection – a widely used protocol for **bus LAN**s.

Cylinder of information   A file of information stored on the same track on each surface of a stack of hard disks.

Daisy-wheel printer   A **fully-formed-character printer** in which the characters are held on stalks or 'petals' radiating from a central disk.

Data   Facts and figures that have yet to be organised in any way.

Database   A collection of **records** that have been organised to enable the information they contain to be easily retrieved.

Database management system   See **DBMS**.

Data capture   The input of data and its conversion into computer-readable form.

Datacomms   The area of computing which deals with the communication of data between computers over a public or private network.

Data-control clerk   A specialist computer worker who controls the reception of data to be processed, the distribution of printed output, and the filing of disks and tapes.

Data-preparation clerk   A specialist computer worker who converts information into computer-readable form, usually by **keying-in**.

Data Protection Act 1984   An Act of Parliament covering the use of computer databases and the access rights of individuals to them.

DBMS   Database management system – a program that not only systematically organises information but also answers enquiries and will help find particular records in a **database**.

DEC   Digital Equipment Corporation – an American manufacturer of computers.

Decision table   An analytical technique that represents in tabular form the results of possible courses of action or combinations of conditions.

Desk-top publishing   See **DTP**.

Digital   A term used to describe devices that handle digital signals – that is, signals made up of combinations of only two values or states corresponding to the digits 0 and 1 of the binary number system. Compare with **analogue signals**.

Digitiser   A **graphics pad** used to input existing drawings into a computer.

DIP   Document image processing – a system of recording document images in **digital** form, usually on **optical disk**, whose main aim is to eliminate the handling and storage of paper.

Distributed processing   A method of processing in which a number of geographically dispersed computers co-operate in the processing of information.

Document image processing   See **DIP**.

Document reader   An input device that reads information from documents. See **MICR, OCR,** and **OMR**.

DOS   Disk operating system – **systems software** in which the relevant routines are loaded from disk as they are needed.

Dot-matrix printer   A **matrix printer** in which the output is obtained by a series of needles in the print head striking a carbon ribbon against the paper.

Download   To transfer a batch of data from one device to another.

DP department   A specialist department set up to handle data processing in larger organisations that process data centrally using mini or mainframe computers. May also be staffed by analysts and programmers involved in the development of new computer-based systems.

Draft quality   The lowest quality of output from some matrix printers. See **LQ** and **NLQ.**

Drum printer   Similar to a chain printer, but with the characters embossed on to the surface of a drum rotating about a horizontal axis. Also known as a 'barrel printer'.

DTP   Desk-top publishing – the use of a personal computer to produce documents that combine text with pictures and look as if they have been professionally typeset and pasted-up.

Duplex   Simultaneous two-way data transmissions – compare with **half-duplex** and **simplex** transmissions.

EAN   European Article Number – a product-numbering system, using bar codes, that is used in Europe and many other parts of the world.

EDI   Electronic data interchange – the electronic transmission of business information, invoices, orders, etc. between trading partners.

EDS   Exchangeable disk stack – an assembly of six or more hard disks that must be loaded into a special disk drive before the information it contains can be accessed.

EFTPOS   Electronic funds transfer, at point of sale – a type of **electronic funds transfer** in which instructions to transfer funds from the customer's bank account to the retailer's are given electronically as the purchase takes places.

Electronic data interchange   See **EDI.**

Electronic funds transfer   The automated transfer of funds from one account to another by using computers and communications equipment.

Electronic mail   Any form of electronic messaging, although often used to refer solely to **EMail.**

Electronic office   An office in which all information is held on computer systems and is created, managed, and communicated by an integrated database, wordprocessing, and communications system.

EMail   Electronic mail – a messaging service that allocates each user a mailbox into which mail in the form of electronic signals can be placed by other subscribers for subsequent display or printing out. See **Telecom Gold.**

End-user   The computer user – also known as 'liveware'.

EPROM   Erasable programmable read-only memory – a special type of **ROM** that can be reprogrammed.

Ethernet   A type of **bus LAN** developed by the Xerox Corporation.

Expert system   A computer program that contains one or more human expert's accumulated knowledge and is able to apply the knowledge to the solution of problems.

Fan-fold stationery   Another name for **continuous stationery.**

Fax   Facsimile transmission – the transmission of images by using a fax
machine to convert them into digital form for transmission to be
reassembled by another distant fax machine. May be thought of as long-
distance photocopying.

FDDI   Fibre Distributed Data Interface – a high-speed **token-ring LAN**
topology based on a double fibre-optic ring with counter-rotating
tokens.

Feasibility study   The study undertaken at an early stage of the **systems-
development lifecycle** to find out if a proposed computerised system is
likely to be possible and cost-effective.

Fibre-optic   See **optical fibre.**

Field   An area within a **record** that contains a single item of information, like
name, address, or phone number. See also **file.**

Fifth-generation computer   An 'intelligent' computer that is the goal of worldwide research programs in innovative hardware and software developments. See **AI.**

Fifth-generation language   See **5GL.**

File   A collection of individual **records**, as in a personnel file. See also **field.**

File server   A high-volume disk storage unit that is used as a shared resource
over a **LAN.**

File set-up   The process by which information contained in the **master files**
held on an old system is transferred to a new system.

Firmware   Software that has been stored on a **ROM** device.

First-generation computers   Computers manufactured during 1940–52 using
vacuum-tube technology. These early computers tended to be very large,
to generate a lot of heat, and to be unreliable.

First-generation language   See **1GL.**

Fixed-disk storage   Storage on **magnetic disks** that are not removable from the
computer.

Fixed-head disk   A **hard disk** that has a read/write head for every **track**, giving
very fast access times.

Floppy disk   A flexible magnetic disk contained within a protective jacket,
commonly used with microcomputers.

Flowchart   The graphical representation of the sequence of logical steps in a
procedure, used as an aid to analysis by programmers and others.

FMS Flexible manufacturing system – a grouping of machines that can be switched easily between the manufacture of different products.

Font A character set of a given size and style.

Format When applied to disk storage, the combination of tracks and sectors, packing density, etc. used to store information.

FORTRAN *FOR*mula *TRAN*slator – a high-level language designed for use in scientific and engineering applications.

Fourth-generation computers Computers produced since 1971 that use large-scale integrated (LSI) circuits and very-large-scale integrated circuits (VLSI) in their construction.

Fourth-generation language See **4GL**.

Fully-formed-character printer A printer in which the output is created by using a permanent image of each character, e.g. **daisy-wheel printer, line printer.**

Gateway A communications device that enables a terminal on one network to communicate with a terminal or computer on another. Telecom Gold, the British Telecom EMail service, offers gateways to a number of **VANS.**

Gigabyte About 1000 million (1 073 741 824) **bytes.** May be shortened to Gbyte, Gb, GB, or G.

Grandfather–Father–Son system See **ancestral files.**

Graphical user interface See **GUI.**

Graphics pad A device that enables drawings to be plotted or traced into a computer or freehand drawings to be input.

Graph plotter A specialist device used to output high-quality graphs, diagrams, or copies of drawings.

GUI Graphical user interface – a **mouse**-driven method of using software that involves screen-based **windows** and **icons** to operate the software.

Hacker A computer enthusiast who delights in exploring and experimenting with computer systems (usually those belonging to other people).

Half-duplex Two-way data transmissions that can only receive or transmit at any one time. Compare with **duplex** and **simplex** transmissions.

Hard copy Output in a permanent or printed form.

Hard disk A rigid **magnetic disk** used for the storage of information. See **EDS** and **Winchester disk.**

Hardware The physical components of a computer system.

Hash total   A **verification** technique that involves the calculation of a value that has no intrinsic meaning, such as the total of all the invoice numbers in a batch to check that all invoices have been processed.

Header label   Information located at the start of a reel tape that includes the file name, the creation date, etc.

High-level language   A problem-oriented language, designed for use in a specific application area, that uses English-like instructions, each of which is equivalent to a number of machine-code instructions. Also termed a 'third-generation language'.

IBM   International Business Machines – the world's largest computer manufacturer.

ICL   International Computers Limited.

Icon   A visual prompt for an option available in a **menu** of computer facilities.

Image scanner   A device that captures an existing picture or drawing by converting it into digital form.

Immediate changeover   The complete transfer from an old to a new information-processing system at one time.

Impact printer   A printer which prints by the physical impact of a device upon the paper, e.g. **daisy-wheel printer, dot-matrix printer, line printer**.

Implementation   The stage of the **systems-development lifecycle** in which users move to the use of a new information-processing system, once adequate preparations have been made.

Information   Organised facts and figures relating to a specific area.

Information centre   A department that provides advice and support to users of microcomputer hardware and software within a large organisation.

Information processing   A general term that describes the use of computers to process data and information.

Information technology   A general term that covers the application of computers and telecommunications to the collection, processing, storage, and dissemination of voice, graphics, text, and numerical information.

Ink-jet printer   A non-impact **matrix printer** that forms characters by projecting ink droplets on to paper at high speed.

Input device   Hardware designed to enable data to be captured and changed into a form that can be understood by a computer.

Integrated package   Applications software that is made up of several general-purpose programs, usually **wordprocessing, database**, and **spreadsheet**. Provides for easy data transfer between areas.

Interpreter A **translation program** that converts a single line of a high-level program into machine code and executes it before returning for the next line of the program.

IPSS International Packet Switching Service – the international **packet-switching** service run by British Telecom, providing access to packet-switched networks in over thirty countries.

ISDN Integrated Services Digital Network – a term given to a proposed future network that will be able to provide a number of services (including fax and EMail) along a single digital communications link.

JANET Joint Academic NETwork – a **WAN** linking academic and research institutions in the UK (and some elsewhere).

Keying-in Entering data into a computer system by means of a qwerty or other keyboard.

Kilobyte About 1 thousand (1024) **bytes**. May be shortened to Kbyte, Kb, KB, or K.

KiloStream A digital data-communications service operated by British Telecom.

LAN Local area network – computers and peripheral devices linked together within a single building or group of buildings to enable the sharing of information and other resources. See also **WAN** and **VANS**.

Laser disk See **optical disk**.

Laser printer A **matrix printer** in which a laser beam carrying the output signal is scanned across a print drum that picks up printing ink that transfers the image to paper. Uses similar printing technology to photocopiers. Also called a 'page printer'.

LCD Liquid-crystal display – a device (similar to those used in some digital watches) producing an image by means of crystals sensitive to electrical signals.

Letter-quality See **LQ**.

Light-pen (a) A device, used in conjunction with special hardware and software, that shines light on to a VDU screen to indicate a choice from a **menu** or to input a location in graphics work. (b) An input device used to capture data held in **bar codes**, e.g. in library-book issuing.

Limit check A **validation** technique that checks to see if a value exceeds a preset limit.

Line printer A high-speed fully-formed-character impact printer that appears to print an entire line at a time, e.g. chain printer, drum printer.

Liquid-crystal display See **LCD**.

Liveware   The end-user.

Local area network   See **LAN**.

l.p.m.   Lines per minute.

LQ   Letter-quality – a term applied to the highest-quality hard-copy output. See also **NLQ** and **draft quality**.

Machine code   The lowest level of computer language, in which each instruction is a code instructing a processor to perform a specific operation. Machine code is a processor-dependent language and is not **portable**. Also called a 'first-generation language'.

Magnetic disk   A flat disk with a surface on which data can be stored by magnetic recording. See **EDS, floppy disk, hard disk, Winchester disk**.

Magnetic-ink character recognition   See **MICR**.

Magnetic tape   A plastic tape coated with particles on which data can be stored by magnetic recording.

Magneto-optical disk   A reusable **optical disk** – sometimes referred to as an 'MO disk'.

Mail merge   The combining of a list of names and addresses with a standard document, enabling otherwise-identical letters to be personalised. See **wordprocessing.**

Mainframe computer   A computer that can support a very large number of users using a number of different programs. Will usually need to be installed in a special air-conditioned room.

Management information system   See **MIS**.

Master file   The file in which is stored the master data relating to a particular application. A sales-ledger master file might contain such information as client name, client reference number, account balance, list of transactions over the last six months, credit limit, etc.

Matrix printer   A printer in which the characters of the output are composed of a large number of individual dots, e.g. **dot-matrix printer, ink-jet printer, laser printer,** and **thermal printer.**

MAU   Multi-station access unit – a device used to connect a number of PCs, printers, etc. to a **token-ring LAN**.

Megabit   About 1 million (1 048 576) **bits.**

Megabyte   About 1 million (1 048 576) **bytes.** May be shortened to Mbyte, Mb, MB, or M.

MegaStream   A very-high-speed digital data-communications service offered by British Telecom.

Menu   A display of options available in a computer system from which a user may select an appropriate one.

Menu-driven   A term applied to software that relies upon the extensive use of **menu**s in its operation.

MICR   Magnetic-ink character recognition – a data-capture technique of reading characters printed in magnetic ink.

Microcomputer   A small desk-top computer that can support a single user using one or more programs.

Microfiche   A microform medium on which is stored printed output that has been photographically reduced by up to 48 times. Data is stored on a grid pattern on a sheet of film that is commonly 148 mm × 105 mm.

Microfilm   A roll of film that contains photographically reduced images of printed output arranged sequentially along its length.

Microform   The general term given to media, like microfilm and microfiche, that contain micro-images.

Minicomputer   A computer that is designed to support fewer users than a mainframe computer but which may be able to handle a large number of users using different programs. May not need to be installed in a special room.

MIS   Management information system – an internal system by which an organisation provides each layer of management with the information necessary to make decisions. The information may be produced either manually or by a computer.

Modem   *Mo*dulator/*dem*odulator – a device to convert **digital** computer signals into **analogue signals** to enable transmission by the telephone system, or to convert the transmitted analogue signal back into digital form.

Monitor   A **CRT** used with a computer.

Mouse   A hand-held device which, with its associated software, enables the user to move the cursor around a VDU screen.

MS–DOS   *Mi*cro*S*oft *D*isk *O*perating *S*ystem – a widely used single-user, single-tasking operating system used on microcomputers that was produced by the software house MicroSoft.

Multimedia   A global term for technology that can combine text, graphics, hi-fi sound, animation, and full-motion video in a single high-resolution display.

Multiplexer   A device that allows the sharing of a single communications link between a number of users by sending sections of each user's transmission in turn.

Multi-tasking   A term applied to hardware or systems software that enables the processor to deal with a number of tasks – commonly associated with **time-sharing.**

Multi-user   A term applied to hardware or systems software that enables the processor to deal with a number of users – commonly associated with **time-sharing.**

Mux   Shortened form of **multiplexer.**

Natural language   The language with which we communicate – English.

Near letter-quality   See **NLQ.**

Networking   Another name for **telecommuting.**

Network topology   The way in which a network is laid out, e.g. star, ring, or bus configuration.

NLQ   Near letter-quality – a term applied to the second highest quality of printed output. See **draft quality** and **LQ.**

Non-impact printer   A printer that does not use physical impact of a print element to print, e.g. **laser printer, ink-jet printer,** and **thermal printer.**

Non-procedural language   A method of programming in which it is not necessary to define the steps in a solution, the solution instead being achieved by a precise definition of the rules, relationships, and variables that apply to a problem. Also called a 'fifth-generation language'.

OA   Office automation.

Object code   A translated machine-code version of a program.

OCR   Optical character recognition – the technique of optically reading special typefaces, conventional type, or even handwritten information and converting it into computer-usable form.

Off-line   Not connected to a computer or network.

OMR   Optical mark recognition – a system for reading options indicated by marks made in predetermined positions on specially printed documents.

On-line   Connected to a computer or network.

On-line processing   A method of processing in which the master file is updated as soon as the transaction data is entered.

Open Systems Interconnection   See **OSI.**

Operating system   Another name for **systems software.**

Optical character recognition   See **OCR.**

Optical disk   A disk on which information is stored as a series of etched pits on the surface and read by a laser beam. See **CD–ROM** and **WORM disk.**

Optical fibre   A fine strand of extremely pure glass that is used for data transmission by light-signals.

Optical mark recognition   See **OMR.**

Oracle   *O*ptional *R*eception of *A*nnouncements of *C*oded *L*ine *E*lectronics – a **teletext** service operated by the IBA.

OS/2   A single-user, multi-tasking operating system that is intended to replace MS–DOS as the standard microcomputer operating system.

OSI   Open Systems Interconnection – a set of standards that define communications **protocols.**

Output device   Hardware designed to output the results of processing on paper or microform (hard copy) or aurally or visually (soft copy).

PABX   Private automatic branch exchange – a digital exchange that can handle computer communications and provide **gateways** into mainframe computers via the **PDN.**

PACX   Private automatic computer exchange – an intelligent switch that can form the hub of a **star LAN.**

Packing density   The density with which data is stored on a disk or tape.

PAD   Packet assembler/disassembler – the computer which divides signals into 'packets' and vice versa in a **packet switching** network.

Packet switching   A method of data transmission in which each complete message is divided into one or more 'packets' that can be sent along a communications network, to be reassembled by the receiving computer.

Packet SwitchStream   See **PSS.**

Page printer   Another name for **laser printer.**

Parallel running   The operation of both old and new systems at the same time during the changeover period from one to the other, as a means of cross-checking results.

PDN   Public Data Network – a digital data network operated by British Telecom.

PDQ   A proprietary **card reader** used to capture customer data as part of an **EFTPOS** system.

PIN   Personal identification number – a number that must be entered by a user before a terminal can be used to access information or complete a transaction.

Pitch   In printed output, the number of characters per inch.

Pixel   Picture element – one of the small dots that go to make up a screen display.

Portable   With reference to a computer language, able to be used with more than one type of processor or machine.

Prestel   A **viewdata** service operated by British Telecom.

Primary storage   The **RAM** within the **CPU**.

Printer server   A disk storage unit that may be a subsystem of a **file server**, available over a **LAN** and used for **spooling** print jobs.

Private automatic branch exchange   See **PABX**.

Private automatic computer exchange   See **PACX**.

Program   A set of instructions that determines what a computer is to do.

Programmer   A person who writes computer programs. See **applications programmer** and **systems programmer.**

PROLOG   *PRO*gramming in *LOG*ic – a **non-procedural language** ('fifth-generation language') used in expert systems and artificial-intelligence applications.

Protocol   In data communications, a set of conventions governing the format of data transmissions between two communicating computers.

Prototyping   The use of an **applications generator** or a similar piece of software ('fourth-generation language') to produce a draft version of an applications program. This prototype may be used as a basis for producing a final version of the application using traditional programming techniques.

PSS   Packet SwitchStream – the UK **packet-switching** service operated by British Telecom.

Public Data Network   See **PDN.**

QWERTY keyboard   The standard English-language keyboard layout that has the letters QWERTY on the top row of alphabetical keys.

RAM   Random access memory – a **volatile** form of computer memory that is used to hold programs and data.

Random access   A method of access to information in which each record can be accessed directly. Associated with magnetic-disk and optical-disk storage.

Range check   A **validation** technique that checks to see if a value falls within a pre-set range of values.

Real-time   Now!

Reasonableness check   Another name for **validation.**

Record   A component of a file, containing a number of **fields.**

Reel tape Magnetic tape, 0.5 inch wide, that is used to store information.

Repeater A device used to extend the size of a **LAN** by joining two lengths of cable and repeating the signal.

Resolution A term relating to the clarity of an output image – the higher the resolution, the more **pixels** per area of the screen or dots in a print matrix and the sharper the image produced.

Ring LAN A LAN in which PCs, printers, etc. are each connected to a common loop around which signals circulate.

ROM Read only memory – a non-**volatile** form of computer memory that is used to store programs that will be used frequently and will not need to be altered.

SatStream A digital data-communications service offered by British Telecom which provides satellite communications links.

Search criterion A requirement that enables a **DBMS** to retrieve desired record(s) from a database.

Secondary storage Storage exterior to the **CPU**, e.g. on **magnetic disk, magnetic tape,** or **optical disk.**

Second-generation computers Computers produced during 1952–64 that used transistors in their construction. These computers were an advance on first-generation computers in their reduced size and increased power and speed.

Second-generation language See **2GL.**

Sequential access See **serial access.**

Serial access A method of access in which it is necessary to work from the start of the file when searching for a particular record. Usually associated with magnetic tape. Also called 'sequential access'.

Silicon chip See **chip.**

Simplex Data transmissions that can go in only one direction. Compare with **duplex** and **half-duplex** transmissions.

Single-user A term applied to hardware or systems software that is designed to enable the processor to handle only one user at a time.

Smart card A credit-card-sized computer system that contains a microprocessor and a memory.

Soft copy Video or audio output.

Software The instructions, or computer programs, that tell a computer what it is to do. See **applications software** and **systems software.**

Software house A computer bureau that specialises in writing programs.

Software package   A set of programs designed for a specific purpose, e.g. a spreadsheet software package.

Source code   Programs in their original form, before translation into machine code.

Spelling checker   A facility often found on wordprocessing packages that checks and queries the often appalling spelling of words in word-processed text.

Spooling   The technique of sending output to disk or tape to be printed later, rather than outputting it directly.

Spreadsheet   A general-purpose calculation program in which data and labels are entered in cells, with all operations being performed on the contents of the cells. Spreadsheets may be used to perform virtually any calculation.

Star LAN   A LAN in which PCs, printers, etc. radiate from a central hub or network controller.

Stepped changeover   The transfer in stages from an old to a new system, with the operation of each new stage being proved before proceeding to the next stage.

Storage device   Hardware that stores information in a form that can be readily accessed by a computer system. See **magnetic disk, optical disk, magnetic tape.**

Supercomputer   A very powerful computer that has been designed to process data at very high speed and which is used for calculation-intensive applications like weather forecasting and graphics simulations.

SWIFT   Society for Worldwide Interbank Financial Telecommunications – a private communications network linking some 1500 member banks and financial institutions worldwide.

Synchronous transmission   A method of data transmission in which the sending and receiving modems transmit bits according to an agreed time sequence. Contrast with **asynchronous transmission.**

Systems analysis   The stage in the **systems-development lifecycle** in which an existing or proposed information system is analysed and its operation is documented.

Systems analyst   A computer specialist whose job is to analyse an activity or system to determine if and how it may be improved using computer systems. Will also be involved in the design, testing, and implementation of any new computer system.

Systems design   The stage in the **systems-development lifecycle** in which an information system is designed using the information obtained in the **systems-analysis** stage.

Systems-development lifecycle The stages through which an information system is likely to pass during its life, starting with its selection for development and ending with systems maintenance.

Systems maintenance The updating of an information system to ensure its continued usefulness.

Systems programmer A computer programmer who specialises in writing program code for **systems software** and **utility programs**.

Systems software The name given to programs that control the operation of computer hardware. Systems software is usually made up of programs written for a particular processor to relieve the applications software of routine hardware-control tasks and to provide operators with a number of systems-management utilities.

Tape streamer A tape cartridge that is used to take **back-up** copies of the data held on hard disk.

Telecom Gold An **EMail** service offered by British Telecom.

Telecommuting The use of computers and communications links to work from home.

Teletext A broadcast television-based **videotex** service.

Telex A national or international messaging service that operates over the existing telephone network.

Thermal printer A non-impact **matrix printer** that forms characters by using heat to transfer ink from a print ribbon to paper.

Third-generation computers Computers produced during 1964–71 that used integrated circuits instead of transistors in their construction.

Third-generation language See **3GL**.

Time-sharing A systems-software feature enabling the processor to handle a number of users and peripherals by allocating very short periods of processor time to each task or peripheral in turn – a prerequisite of large business information-processing systems.

Token-ring LAN A **ring LAN** that makes use of a circulating token to control data traffic.

Touchscreen An input device for use with menu-driven software, the user indicating a particular choice by touching the appropriate **icon** or other reference displayed on a screen.

Track One of the concentric bands of storage area on a magnetic disk.

Trailer label Information located at the end of a reel tape that is used as a cross-check once processing is complete.

Transaction file   A file of information that is used to update the information held on a master file. A sales-ledger transaction-file might contain a list of the sales that have been made that day.

Translation program   A program that converts a **high-level language** program into **machine code**. See **compiler** and **interpreter**.

Typeface   See **font**.

Unix   The name of a multi-user multi-tasking operating system that will run on microcomputers and minicomputers.

Utility program   Systems software designed to assist the operator to perform routine tasks like copying files and making back-up copies of disks.

Validation   The checking of input data to ensure that it meets pre-set criteria. Also called a 'reasonableness check'.

Value-added network services   See **VANS**.

VANS   Value-added network services – the information, EMail, and other services offered to computer users and available over the telecommunications network.

VDU   Visual display unit – a device that enables a user to input information to a computer by using a keyboard, a **light-pen**, or **touchscreen** facilities.

Verification   The checking of input data to ensure that it is correct.

Videoconferencing   The use of sound and vision links to connect and enable a conference to take place between individuals in different locations.

Video scanner   A device that can be used to capture in digital form the image of either an existing two-dimensional picture or of a three-dimensional object.

Videotex   A **menu-driven** service which provides access to a large central database of information that is divided into pages. A term used to describe both **teletext** and **viewdata**.

Viewdata   A telephone-based **videotex** service, e.g. Prestel.

Virtual reality   Technology built around the use of stereoscopic surround-vision helmets, gloves with motion sensors, and stereo headphones to create a computer-generated virtual world with which the user can interact.

Visual display unit   See **VDU**.

Volatile   A term used to describe computer memory whose contents will be lost when the electricity supply is turned off, e.g. RAM.

WAN   Wide area network – describes the linking together of computers and peripherals over a region, country, or number of countries.

Wide area network See **WAN.**

Winchester disk A **hard disk** assembly enclosed in a sealed unit.

Window A portion of a screen within which a software application may be used. Most systems are able to have more than one window on the screen at one one time, but usually only one window will be 'open', i.e. active for immediate use.

Wordprocessing The application of computer technology to the creation and output of documents. Wordprocessing enables documents to be stored and reused, enabling changes to be made to the text without having to retype the entire document. It may also provide features like an on-line dictionary, a spelling-checker, a thesaurus, and **mail-merge** facilities.

WORM disk Write-once read-many disk – an optical disk that may be written to once but, once full, is not reusable. Designed for applications which require permanent records to be kept.

WP See **wordprocessing.**

Unit 14, question 1 (*opposite*)

Total = Total replies

A =   Companies with computer budget < £10 000

B =   Manufacturing companies with < 50 employees, turnover > £0.5m, computer budget > £10 000

C =   Non-manufacturing companies with turnover < £2m, computer budget > £10 000

Answers to flowchart and decision-table exercises

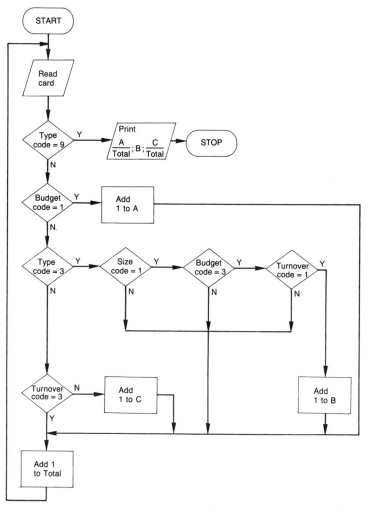

Unit 14, question 1 (*see opposite*)

	Rules						
	1	2	3	4	5	6	7
Stock > requisition	Y	Y	Y	N	N	N	N
Stock > zero	–	–	–	Y	Y	N	N
Stock ≥ reorder level	Y	N	N	–	–	–	–
Stock = zero	–	–	–	–	–	Y	Y
Outstanding order?	–	N	Y	Y	N	Y	N
After balance	X	X	X	X	X		
Send to Despatch	X	X	X	X	X		
Photocopy				X	X		
Put in outstanding reqn file				X	X	X	X
Place order		X			X		X
Send urge note			X	X		X	
Telephone factory							X

Unit 14, question 2

Unit 14, question 3(a) (*opposite*)

Total = Total answers

Yestotal = Total of 'Yes' answers (i)

A =   'Yes' answers from males (ii)

B =   'Yes' answers from married women in socio-economic group a, with children (iii)

C =   'Yes' answers for females under 30 (iv)

D =   'Yes' answers from people of 30 or over without children (v)

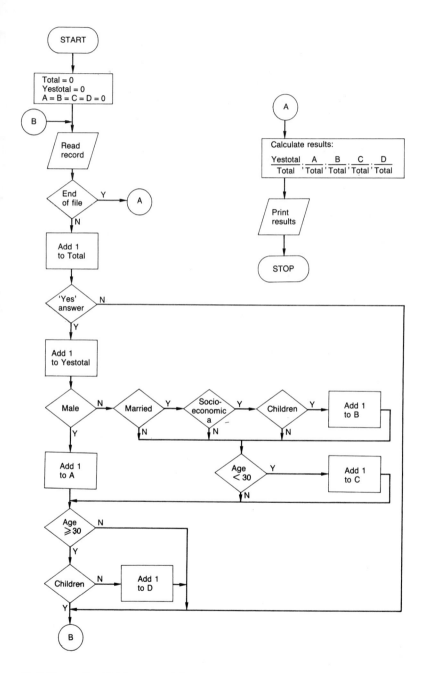

Unit 14, question 3(a) (*see opposite*)

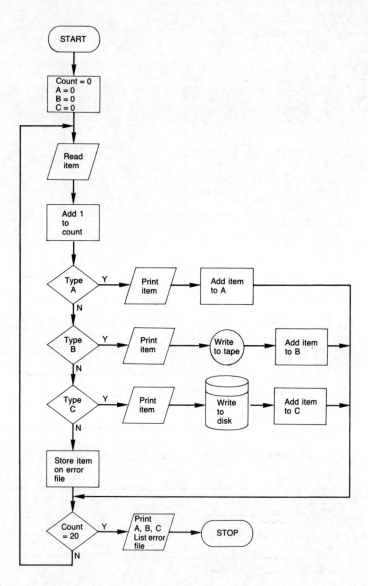

Unit 14, question 4

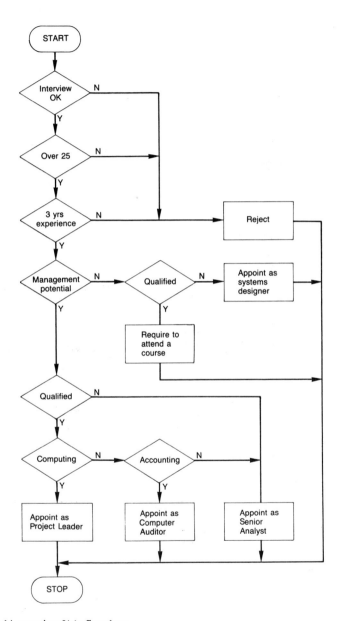

Unit 14, question 5(a): flowchart

	Rules					
	1	2	3	4	5	ELSE
Satisfactory interview	Y	Y	Y	Y	Y	
Over 25 years old	Y	Y	Y	Y	Y	
3 years' relevant experience	Y	Y	Y	Y	Y	
Management potential	Y	Y	Y	N	N	
Qualification?	Comp	Acc.	N	N	Y	
Appoint as Project Leader	X					
Appoint as Computer Auditor		X				
Appoint as Senior Analyst			X			
Appoint as Systems Designer				X		
Require to attend a course					X	
Reject						X

Unit 14, question 5(a): decision table

Index

Index

Page numbers in *italics* refer to definitions given in the Glossary.